Swift & Bold

DAVY

Swift & Bold
The 60th Rifles During the Peninsula War

Gibbes Rigaud

LEONAUR

Swift & Bold: the 60th Rifles During the Peninsula War
by Gibbes Rigaud

originally published in 1879 under the title
Celer Et Audax: a Sketch of the Services of the Fifth Battalion
Sixtieth Regiment (Rifles) During the Twenty Years of Their Existence

Published by Leonaur Ltd

Text in this form and material original to this edition
copyright © 2008 Leonaur Ltd

ISBN: 978-1-84677-526-0 (hardcover)
ISBN: 978-1-84677-525-3 (softcover)

http://www.leonaur.com

Publisher's Notes

The opinions expressed in this book are those of the author
and are not necessarily those of the publisher.

Contents

What beauties doth Lisbon first unfold!
Her image floating on that noble tide,
Which poets vainly pave with sands of gold,
But now whereon a thousand keels did ride
Of mighty strength, since Albion was allied,
And to the Lusians did her aid afford:
A nation swoln with ignorance and pride,
Who lick yet loathe the hand that waves the sword
To save them, from the wrath of Gaul's unsparing lord.

Childe Harold, Canto 1, Stanza 16

Respice—Adspice—Prospice

I dedicate these pages to the 'Riflemen of Hereafter,' trusting I may in some measure lead them to emulate the actions of their predecessors;

To the 'Riflemen of the Present,' now serving, or with whom I served for thirty-two years, trusting they will do all they can to gather materials for a complete 'Record of the Services of the Sixtieth;'

And to the memory of the 'Riflemen of the Past,' who fought and won for us, their successors, the honours of which we are so justly proud.

The knights' bones are dust,
Their good swords rust,
Their souls are with the saints, I Trust.

Gibbes Rigaud
Oxford
December, 1879

Preface

The history of the 60th Regiment covers a period of one hundred and twenty years. It is seventy years, a long life, since the battle of 'Talavera' was fought; but there are fifty years before that—*viz.* from 1757 to 1809—during all of which the first four battalions of the 60th were at work making history, but no one has attempted to write it.

It was not until Captain Wallace of the 1st battalion 60th Rifles set to work, that even the statistics of the corps, (dull to many readers but most valuable in themselves) were, with great labour by him, collected and published under the title of *A Regimental Chronicle.*

At the end of his preface Captain Wallace 'earnestly asked all who were interested in the subject to help him to make as complete as possible the volume which he hopes to publish at some future time, containing the historical records of the 60th King's Royal Rifles.'

Being one of those who take great 'interest in the subject,' and feeling that he alone, who had gleaned the matter for the history of the earlier battalions, could arrange it properly, I turned my thoughts to the 5th battalion.

The 5th battalion existed for twenty years, during which time it went through the whole of the Peninsular War from Roleia to Toulouse, and gained those honours of which the corps is so justly proud. The narrative of its services is therefore a complete episode in the regimental history, and with its disintegration ends what may be called the existence of the 'old sixtieth,' and that of the 1st and 2nd battalions King's Royal Rifles commences.

I had been entrusted by the Reverend Charles Raikes Davy with all the papers which his father had left, who as Major Davy took the 5th battalion 60th out to Portugal in 1808, and died in command of the 1st battalion 60th Royal Rifles as a general in the army. These letters and papers gave an interesting connection with the battalion up to 1810-11, and I asked Captain Wallace to send me what he might have got together regarding the 5th 60th, saying 'I would try and help him with his coming records.'

He sent me accordingly all his gleanings, arranged from year to year in a way which greatly assisted the task I had set myself to perform. There was also, with his memoranda, much which had been kindly given to him by Captain Boyle of the Rifle Brigade, who also made me acquainted with two books of reference (previously unknown to me, but of which I was fortunately able to obtain copies), namely, the *Royal Military Chronicles* and the *Royal Military Calendar*.

To trace the history of the 60th in Spain was very difficult, detached as they were from first to last, and this has forced perhaps more of the Peninsular History to be compiled than if I had had to follow an unbroken battalion with its brigade.

I may well use the word 'compiled,' for if plagiarism be a sin, then am I in a state of condemnation. I could not write a new history, so I have taken all that I thought useful to my purpose from others, and have freely copied whole passages from Napier and Gleig, the *Wellington Despatches* and Sir E. Cust's *Annals*, the *Annual Register*, or Robinson's *Life Of Picton*. Nor are these all the books I have drawn upon. Little beyond the arrangement can be called original, and it is because the whole is so woven from the threads of others that I found it impossible to be always using inverted commas, or give more than general references at the foot of the pages as to my sources of information.

I often found however that the clearest and best accounts of any action are those written by 'the Duke' himself, and freely have I copied his clear and nervous English.

I knew not till now how difficult it was to write even such a narrative as this, or the care and labour that must be bestowed at times on clearing up a small point; and, if so with me, how much more must it have been the case in a great work like Napier's? Is it strange that he should *sometimes* be in error? It would be far stranger if he were *always* right.

That a Napier should make a wilful misstatement I hold to be impossible, but that the great Sir William at times fell into error, and at times was prejudiced, I cannot doubt, and, rash as it may seem, I have more than once ventured to impugn his accuracy, as in the instance of his stating that the 5th battalion 60th was principally composed of Frenchmen, and that Picton refused to give assistance on the Coa, and in the details of what the third division did at Busaco.

Napier's prejudice against Picton is much to be lamented, because it is very hard to remove a reproach which has been once made and accepted, and even now the memory of Picton suffers from the unjust aspersions which a sentence of Napier's can cast upon it, accepted as his words are by myriads of readers who never perhaps see the defence or contradiction.

Whilst these pages have been in preparation, a most excellent book has been given to the public in Clinton's *War in the Peninsula*, &c, printed for the Chandos Library; yet here again the charge against Picton at the Coa is made and dwelt upon; and again (at p. 387) Wellington is said on the field of 'Quatre Bras' to have 'ordered Picton, with whom at the time he was barely on speaking terms, to throw forward his line.'

A small amount of research would have proved the error of these statements. The diary of Sir John Burgoyne, parts of which are given in the life of him written by his son-in-law

Lieutenant-Colonel the Hon. George Wrottesley, and Robinson's *Life of Picton* would have set the matter at rest one would have thought; and from the latter work I cannot help extracting a letter which 'the Duke' himself addressed to the author.

To H. B. Robinson, Esq.
London
August 28, 1835
Dear Sir,
I have received your letter, and I have the greatest satisfaction in giving you the assurance, that, not only I was not on bad terms with the late Sir Thomas Picton, but that in the whole course of the period during which I was in relation with him, I do not recollect even a difference of opinion, much less anything of the nature of a quarrel.

My first acquaintance with Sir Thomas Picton was when he joined the army in the Peninsula as a general officer on the staff. I had solicited his appointment, because I entertained a high opinion of his talents and qualities, from the report which I had received of both from the late General Miranda, who had known him in the West Indies. I never had any reason to regret, on the contrary, I had numberless reasons to rejoice, that I had solicited his appointment. It was made at a moment at which an unmerited prejudice existed against Sir Thomas Picton, the recollection of which was effaced by his services.

I afterwards solicited his appointment to the staff of the army in Flanders; than which I cannot give a stronger proof, not only of my sense of his merits and former services, but likewise that I never was otherwise than on the best terms with him. The country was deprived of his valuable services on a glorious field of battle, in a short time after he joined the army; and there was no individual in that army or in England who lamented his loss more sincerely than I did.

I have the honour to be, dear Sir,
Your most obedient humble servant,
Wellington

The reproaches against Picton should not be repeated. I in my turn however, in spite of much painstaking, have probably made mistakes. I alone am responsible for them, and shall feel obliged to those who will point them out. This is but an instalment I hope, and, when Captain Wallace has completed his work, I should like to give him this for incorporation in it free from all errors.

Moreover, I trust that my putting this narrative into the hands of old Sixtieth men will materially aid his efforts, by showing them how difficult it is after the lapse of years to recover past facts, and stimulating all those who are still alive to write down, and send to him, all that they can gather or remember of the present 1st and 2nd battalions.

Thanks are due to Colonel de Rottenburg also for furnishing some particulars about his father, who raised the 5th battalion 60th and was its first Lieutenant-Colonel, and to Colonel Gerald Graham, R.E., who kindly obtained for me most of the embarkation returns which will be found in the Appendix.

CHAPTER 1

Beginnings: 1797-1807

The Act 38 Geo. III, cap. 13 was passed as an amendment, to the Act 29 Geo. II, cap. 5, under which the first four battalions of the 60th Regiment had been raised, and it empowered the King to 'Augment His Majesty's Sixtieth Regiment of Infantry, now consisting of four battalions of one thousand men each, by the addition of a fifth battalion, to consist in like manner of one thousand men;' and the Act would appear to have limited the services of this battalion (as the other Acts did with regard to other battalions) to America; and it was not until 1813, when another short Act of two clauses was passed to authorize the raising of 8th, 9th, and 10th battalions, that power was given 'to employ such regiment, or any part thereof, in any country or place out of Great Britain.'

This restriction does not appear to have prevented the 5th battalion, when raised, from being employed wherever its services were required, and any difficulty that might have occurred, was probably obviated by the fact that the men forming the battalion were not enlisted under that particular Act, but had been already attested for 'general service.'

The Act speaks of the 'present juncture of affairs rendering it expedient to facilitate the speedy raising of the battalion;' and when one thinks of the disturbed state of Europe and America in 1796, one cannot be surprised that the 5th battalion was completed speedily by turning over to it *en bloc* a number of ready-made foreign soldiers and officers who had taken service under His Britannic Majesty.

Among other foreign troops serving England at that period there were Lowenstein's Fusiliers and Chasseurs, and Hompesch's Hussars, and other foreign corps, which had served in St. Domingo in 1795 and returned to England in 1796, when Hompesch's 'Mounted Riflemen' and Hompesch's 'Fusiliers' were placed on the establishment.

Count Hompesch, afterwards a Lieutenant-General, who raised the 'Mounted Riflemen,' had entered the English service at the same time with Francis Baron de Rottenburg, and when Count Hompesch's brother raised the regiment called 'Hompesch's Fusiliers,' De Rottenburg became first major and afterwards lieutenant-colonel of it.

De Rottenburg had already gained experience and had practice in organization. He began his military life in the French army, in the 77th regiment of the Line, of which Prince Auguste D'Orenberg, Count de la Marche, was the colonel proprietaire. He was some years in, and served one campaign with it, and when he left it on the breaking out of the French Revolution a flattering address was presented to him by the officers of the corps.

De Rottenburg then served as lieutenant-colonel and *aide-de-camp* to General Count de Salis Marcelins, Inspecting General of the Neapolitan army, who was re-organizing the forces of the King of Naples and Two Sicilies, and when that duty was performed left with his general.

He next commanded a regiment of infantry, and served through the wars between the Poles and Russians, and was present and was wounded at the great battle fought before Warsaw, which lasted three days.

In 1797, when a fifth battalion was to be raised for the 60th Regiment, the task was entrusted to De Rottenburg, and he was appointed the lieutenant-colonel of it.

The men in Hompesch's corps were of all nations, except

English and French, and four hundred of the 'Mounted Rifle-men' formed the nucleus of the new battalion, but they were chiefly Germans, and in Germany De Rottenburg placed recruiting officers for the purpose of raising men.

It was at Christmas time, 1797, that the battalion was first formed in the Isle of Wight, but the stay there was short, for the men were ready-made soldiers who had seen service, and though not altogether homogeneous, the elements proved to combine excellently well.

The battalion thus formed was the original of those battalions now so well known, and so distinguished in every sense of the word, as 'Riflemen.' The men were dressed and equipped as Jägers. They were armed with rifles, and carried what were called 'rifle-bags' made of leather, instead of knapsacks; they grew the moustache, and they were dressed in green. In this particular they claim priority, in time, to all other battalions in the British army; in other respects, they and their successors leave their position to be decided for them, only averring their unwillingness to accept anything but equality, as regards devotion, with the most devoted servants of their Sovereign and country.

There was another foreign corps at this time also, known as Lowenstein's 'Chasseurs.' This regiment had been raised for the Dutch service by the Prince of Lowenstein Wertheim, about the year 1793; it was first stationed at Maestricht and Venloo, and a portion of it took part, from October to December 1794, in the defence of Grave. At the evacuation of Holland, the Prince of Lowenstein's regiment entered the British service and embarked for England at Winsen. In 1795 it went to the West Indies, with the expedition under Sir Ralph Abercromby, was present at the reduction of St. Lucia and St. Vincent, in the expedition against Porto Rico in 1796 and 1797, and had a detachment also stationed in Trinidad, when Colonel Thomas Picton was Governor there.

Portions of both Hompesch's and Lowenstein's corps, both

mounted and dismounted, served under Sir Ralph and General Hutchinson in Egypt, during the rebellion in Ireland in 1798, and were disbanded at Portsmouth in 1802.

From Lowenstein's corps the 5th battalion 60th received about 500 men, but not until they were serving in the West Indies, two years after their first formation.

De Rottenburg organized his new battalion entirely for the special duties of 'Riflemen.' They were to be 'the eyes of the army.' He instituted a perfect system of light drill for riflemen, and out-post duties; this system he printed in a book, which was afterwards embodied in the book of *Field Exercise and Involutions of the Army,* with a complimentary order by the Duke of York, then commander-in-chief.

A good organiser, drill, and disciplinarian, De Rottenburg was also a genial, kind-hearted man. He used to say that he 'never flogged his men when in command of the 5th battalion 60th, but governed them in a patriarchal manner, more as a father would his children, than as commanding officers used to do in those days.' But he could be stern, if necessary; and in writing to Portugal to Major Davy in after years, he says, 'I always told you you might depend on the bravery of my disciples, but I have been concerned to learn that three rascals deserted, were retaken, and have not been shot—ill-judged mercy to the guilty is injustice to the faithful soldier.' So good indeed was the system and teaching of this lieutenant-colonel, that ten years later he was employed as a brigadier-general at a camp on the Curragh, and at Ashford in Kent, and he was the father of the Light Infantry of the British army, and such fine regiments as the 68th, 71st, and 85th, all of which, with others, passed through his hands, are the best witnesses to the assertion that the 5th battalion 60th could not have had a better instructor in its first start in life.

That life was a short one; its whole term was only twenty years, but it had much that was eventful compressed into its short existence.

Formed at Cowes at the end of December 1797, the battalion was moved to Ireland in about three months afterwards, arriving there in April 1798.

The date and place of their destination will at once bring to mind the condition of that unhappy country at the period spoken of; and it is no object at this minute to trace its political or social entanglements, but to remind ourselves of what awaited the soldier on his arrival in the sister-island, and place on record his connection with any special military event.

In this year then we find them taking part in the operations carried on by General Moore in Wicklow and Wexford. On the 10th June 1798, Lieutenant-General Sir James Stewart, who was at that time in command of the southern division, received orders from General Lake to send the Light Brigade under Major-General John Moore (consisting of about 1800 men with a proportion of artillery) from Bandon into the county of Wexford.

Here was a first piece of early training for their future campaigns. They marched the same evening; and on the 18th, after a march of seven days, in which they accomplished 130 miles, they arrived at Ross. On the 20th they engaged the enemy at Goff's Bridge. On the 21st they took possession of the town of Wexford, before the arrival of troops from any other quarter, and again on the 24th of June they had another affair with the rebels.

On this day a part only of the 60th, with five companies of Light Infantry and the 29th Regiment, were employed by General Moore, but a portion, or the whole, were, during the rebellion of 1798, in constant activity, and fought at Vinegar Hill and Enniscorthy, besides their engagements at Goff's Bridge and Wexford, and minor affairs in Wicklow.

In December they went into winter quarters at Clonmel. But not long was their rest in that place; in January 1799 the battalion was marched to Cork, where it embarked in the summer for Surinam, in the reduction of which place 400 of the 5th battalion 60th were employed under lieutenant-general Trigge.

Surinam, now better known perhaps as Dutch Guiana, was then in possession of Holland. The Dutch were the first European settlers in Guiana, having organised trading stations on the coast as early as the year 1580. The English had settlements there in 1657, but they were conquered by, and ceded to, the Dutch after a short time, and from that period until 1790, when Demerara and Essequibo fell into the hands of the English, they (the Dutch) retained possession of most of that country. But now in 1799 a considerable and valuable portion of this their possession was to be wrested from Holland, and to pass into the colonial property of the English.

On the 31st of July a body of troops sailed from Port Royal for the attack on Surinam. This body had been collected from Grenada, St. Lucia, and Martinique, and the 5th battalion 60th from Ireland under the command of De Rottenburg was added to the force. The troops were convoyed by a squadron of two sail-of-the-line, five frigates and some smaller vessels.

On the 16th of August the squadron anchored. The river Surinam is the most considerable of the rivers flowing from Guiana into the Atlantic. It is navigable for 300 miles, but large ships cannot pass many miles above Paramaribo, the capital town, which is built on the western bank of the river at about ten miles from its mouth.

The Dutch made no fight for their possession. Very shortly after coming to an anchor a summons was sent to the Governor to surrender the colony. On receiving the summons he sent off a committee, composed of some military officers and influential individuals, to arrange terms for a capitulation.

On the 19th the admiral and general with the frigates and smaller vessels proceeded two miles up the river and landed a detachment of the 5th 60th, which took possession of the redoubts and batteries at Braam's Point. These had been abandoned by the Dutch on the approach of the troops, and on the following day (August 20th) the capitulation was ratified. Under the arrangements thus made all the ships of war, artillery, provisions and stores, were delivered up to his Britannic Majesty; and on the next day (the 21st) 400 men of the 5th 60th were accordingly landed and took possession of Fort Amsterdam; the garrison, consisting of 250 Dutch troops and 500 Walloon guards, were permitted to march out with all the honours of war, all the other forts being surrendered at the same time.

Glad doubtless were the Dutch soldiers to be relieved from the duties of these garrisons. De Rottenburg with his battalion, which now received its additional 500 men from Lowenstein's Chasseurs, which formed a part of the forces employed, was left in charge; and doubtless no longer felt surprise that no opposition had been encountered. He used to describe the position of the fort they had to occupy as being surrounded by jungle infested with tigers; and so miserable were his men that they were seized with a regular attack of nostalgia, and suicides became so frequent that it was only by the use of very energetic measures that he succeeded in putting a stop to the practice.

Weary must have appeared the years passed here from 1799 to 1803, but in that latter year they were moved from garrisoning Surinam to the pleasanter quarter of Halifax, where they remained throughout the year 1804 and part of 1805. The change was good for the battalion, and the battalion was popular among their new friends. A street was named after the lieutenant-colonel, and an address presented on leaving, when in November 1805 they were once more moved, from the American Continent to England. They arrived there and

Note.—The military history and the horrors of the Irish rebellion in '98 would not be easy to trace in a manner suitable for this narrative; but as the affair at 'Goff's Bridge' has been mentioned as the first service of the 5th 60th, and was considered of some importance at the time, the following account of it given in the Appendix (No. 21. 2) at the end of Musgrave's *Memoirs of the different Rebellions in Ireland*, will not be without some interest for the present members of the corps.

were quartered in Portsmouth in 1806, whence in 1807 they were again moved to Ireland and quartered in Cork.

Dublin Castle
23rd June, 1798
This day the following letter was received from Lieutenant-General Lake by Lord Castlereagh.

Wexford
22nd June, 1798
My Lord,
Yesterday afternoon I had the honour to dispatch a letter to your lordship from Enniscorthy, with the transactions of the day, for His Excellency the Lord Lieutenant's information; and the enclosed copy of a letter from Brigadier-General Moore to Major-General Johnson, will account for my having entered this place without opposition. General Moore, with his usual enterprise and activity, pushed on to this town, and entered it so opportunely as to prevent it from being laid in ashes, and the massacre of the remaining prisoners, which the rebels declared their intention of carrying into execution the very next day; and there can be little doubt it would have taken place, for the day before they murdered above seventy prisoners and threw their bodies over the bridge.
I have, &c,
G. Lake
Lord Viscount Castlereagh

From enquiry the numbers killed yesterday were very great indeed.

(Enclosure)
Camp above Wexford
22nd June, 1798

Dear General,

Agreeable to your order, I took post on the evening of the nineteenth, near Foulkes's-mill, in the park of Mr. Sutton. Next day I sent a strong detachment under Lieutenant-Colonel Wilkinson, to patrol towards Tintern and Clonmines, with a view to scour the country, and communicate with the troops you directed to join me from Duncannon. The lieutenant-colonel found the country deserted, and got no tidings of the troops. I waited for them until three o'clock in the afternoon, when, despairing of their arrival, I began to march to Taghmon. We had not marched above half a mile, when a considerable body of the rebels was perceived marching towards us. I sent my advanced guard, consisting of the two rifle companies of the 60th, to skirmish with them, whilst a howitzer and a six-pounder were advanced to a cross road above Goff's-bridge, and some companies of Light Infantry formed on each side of them under Lieutenant-Colonel Wilkinson. The rebels attempted to attack these, but were instantly repulsed and driven beyond the bridge. A large body was perceived at the same time moving towards my left. Major Aylmer, and afterwards Major Daniel, with five companies of Light Infantry and a six-pounder, were detached against them. The 60th regiment, finding no further opposition in front, had, of themselves, inclined to their left to engage the body which was attempting to turn us. The action here was for a short time pretty sharp. The rebels were in great numbers, and armed with both muskets and pikes. They were, however, forced to give way, and driven, though they repeatedly attempted to form, behind the ditches. They at last dispersed, flying towards Enniscorthy and Wexford. Their killed could not be ascertained, as they lay scattered in the fields over a considerable extent; but they seemed to be numerous. I enclose a list of ours. The troops behaved with great spirit. The artillery and Hompesch's Cavalry were active, and seemed only to regret that the country did not admit of their rendering more effectual service. Major Daniel is the only officer whose wound is bad: it is through the knee, but not dangerous.

The business, which began between three and four, was not over till near eight; it was then too late to proceed to Taghmon. I took post for the night on the ground where the action had commenced. As the rebels gave way I was informed of the approach of the 2nd and 29th regiments under Lord Dalhousie. In the morning of the twenty-first we were proceeding to Taghmon, when I was met by an officer of the North Cork from Wexford with the inclosed letters. I gave, of course, no answer to the proposal made by the inhabitants of Wexford, but I thought it my duty immediately to proceed here, and to the post above the town, by which means I have, perhaps, saved the town from fire, as well as the lives of many loyal subjects who were prisoners in the hands of the rebels. The rebels fled upon my approach, over the bridge of Wexford and towards the barony of Forth. I shall wait here your further orders. Lord Kingsborough has informed me of different engagements he had entered into with respect to the inhabitants; I have declined entering into the subject, but have referred his lordship to you or General Lake.

I received your pencilled note during the action

of the 20th; it was impossible for me then to detach the troops you asked for, but I hear you have perfectly succeeded at Enniscorthy with those you had. Mr. Roche, who commands the rebels, is encamped, I hear, about five miles off; he sent Lord Kingsborough to surrender on terms. Your presence speedily is upon every account extremely necessary.

I have the honour to be, &c. &c,

John Moore

CHAPTER 2

Ireland: 1808

We have now arrived at that period when the most stirring events in European history took place, and in contemplating which we are lost in doubt as to whether we should most admire the gallant bravery, the endurance and constancy of courage of the soldiers, or the brilliant genius and wonderful self-reliance of the greatest captain of this or perhaps of any age, which inspired those soldiers with that confidence in himself and themselves which is so requisite to an army both in difficulties and success.

To write again the story of the Peninsular war is not the object in hand, but to trace as far as we can the connection of the 60th with its principal events; and, in doing this, one must repeat in some measure the story of each battle as it arrives, for there was hardly an affair of importance in which the 60th had not their part. Unluckily, one must use the term 'as far as one can'; for, divided as the battalion was, and distributed by single companies to different brigades, it would be impossible to follow their steps in the same way as can be done with regiments which served together; and seventy years have now elapsed since Sir Arthur Wellesley landed at Mondego Bay, and of those who landed with him none now remain.

It is therefore much to be lamented that none of the actors in those scenes described the special part played by their comrades and themselves, nor have any of their successors in the corps gleaned from them, as we might have done thirty-five years ago, many facts and anecdotes now irrecoverably lost.

The search, the inquiry, now is laborious, and the gleanings a handful instead of a full sheaf. In one direction alone has success attended inquiry, and that has been in obtaining from his son, the Reverend Charles Raikes Davy, the papers of Sir William Gabriel Davy, who as Major Davy went out in command of the 60th from Cork, with Sir Arthur Wellesley's expedition; but, interesting and valuable as these papers are to us, they are limited to the period between Cork and the year 1811.

Of the origin of the war we shall say no more than that: Napoleon having seized the greater part of Spain had in 1806 placed his brother Joseph on the throne; Europe was surprised, Spain indignant at the usurpation. The Royal family of Portugal fled. Spain was betrayed by her chief minister, her king was made captive, and the British Government resolved to help Spain and Portugal. Having determined to send out powerful military aid to the Peninsula, the Government of England entrusted the command in the first instance to Sir Arthur Wellesley, already gloriously known by his Indian achievements as the victor of Assaye, and more recently by the easier overthrow of the Danish militia; and 10,000 men were placed under his orders, who had been assembled at Cork for an expedition to South America. Sir John Moore, then in Sweden with 12,000 men, was also recalled for the same purpose, and two smaller divisions set sail from Ramsgate and Margate.[1]

The 5th battalion 60th had been moved over to Ireland. Its strength had been augmented in December, 1806, to an effective strength of 44 officers, 22 sergeants, and 800 rank-and-file. It embarked at Ramsgate, and sailed August 31st. It landed at Monk's Town, and the leading division marched into Cork

1. See *Epitome of Alison's History*, pp. 306-7.

on the 16th of September, 1807. The battalion was 900 strong, but not complete in officers, as will presently be shown by a letter of Major Davy's. Francis Baron de Rottenburg was still the lieutenant-colonel of the battalion, and remained in the 'Army List' as belonging to the 60th until 1812; but his close connection with the corps was just about to cease. In the spring of 1808, just before the expedition sailed for Portugal, De Rottenburg was appointed a brigadier-general of the forces serving in North America; and his place as commanding officer was at once taken by Major William Gabriel Davy, who had been in the regiment as captain from 1802, and had been promoted Major on the 5th of February, 1807.

If the influence of a great general is felt in every part of an army, not less in those units, the sum of which compose that army, is the force of character and high military qualities of the officer commanding the mainspring of their machinery. No regiment, it may be said, that has great traditions, but what points to some lieutenant-colonel, who, as it is said, 'introduced our system,' whose name is still held in respectful memory, and who still exerts a certain subtle influence even from his grave. The materials which De Rottenburg had to work with were good, but he too was a skilled workman; and under him, and with the service that they had seen in Ireland and South America, in Nova Scotia, and at home, the battalion had become one of excellent experience. Their dress as Jägers, too, was sure to give a distinction which would tend to *esprit*: and De Rottenburg, and Davy after him, always enforced on the attention of their soldiers the fact that they were 'riflemen'; that their responsibilities were greater than those of others; and as trust was placed in them, unflagging must be the endeavours of each officer and rifleman to maintain the reputation which the battalion had obtained during its ten years' existence.

At a most important moment, then, a few weeks only before embarkation, Major Davy succeeded to the command; and a superior soldier himself, acquainted with all the most minute regimental details, he began his preparations for the coming war. Davy was the eldest son of Major Davy, H.E.I.C.S., who was Persian Secretary to Warren Hastings. He was born at King's Holm near Gloucester, and was educated at Eton. When he left that College he had a commission in the 61st Regiment, and served at the Cape of Good Hope and in Canada, and, as has been already stated, came into the 60th as a captain in 1802.

The knowledge of detail, and the care he took in instructing those under his command, is well illustrated in the book containing his own regimental orders, which has been preserved; and in which he has first, in early June, laid down most excellent rules for the guidance of officers and men on board ship, supplementary of course to 'His Majesty's Regulations for troops embarked on board transports,' and then continued the regimental orders given from time to time.

The Duke of York (then colonel-in-chief of the 60th), who commanded his Majesty's army, had done much at that period to improve the internal economy of regiments, and add to the comforts of the soldier; and Davy gave full directions for all duties—day and night watches, stowing of arms, cleanliness, cooking and parades, exercising the men with arms, and especially in knowledge of bugle sounds.

Even as the orders to be observed on the line of march given to the Light Brigade by General Robert Crawfurd cannot be improved upon by the present generation, so the regimental orders of the battalion for duties on board ship were quite exhaustive; though at the present day, when inculcating the necessity of cleanliness, we should not add to the words, 'The men are to put on clean linen twice a week;' those which follow here, 'the hair must be well combed and tied every day—without putting any grease in it.'

We smile at these expressions now, but British soldiers and sailors gained as many victories even with 'pigtails on' as they have since they were cut off.

We must not occupy too much space with copies of these orders, interesting as they are, but one or two extracts may be made:

Regimental Orders
Cork
June 14th, 1808
The battalion is to be under arms in complete marching order tomorrow morning at eight o'clock to march to Monkstown, there to embark in the transports allotted for its reception.

The embarkation is made, and the 5th battalion leaves the shores of these islands for six long years, and we must trace their course from Monkstown in 1808 until they shall return from France in 1814, and be again landed at Cork, whence they are now taking their departure.

But they did not sail at once. They were put on board the *Juliana*, *Atlas*, and *Malabar* transports, and from this date the orders issued at regimental headquarters are dated from the latter ship: and having given his final instructions to those on board the *Juliana* and *Atlas*, Davy led the minds of his 'riflemen' to thoughts of what was before them.

Regimental Orders
Cork Harbour
On board the *Malabar*
June 27th, 1808
As there is every reason to imagine that the battalion will shortly be honoured with an opportunity of distinguishing itself in the field, the commanding officer feels it his duty to recall the attention of the younger part of the officers to the absolute necessity of making themselves acquainted with the several duties of the outposts, that they may be enabled to lead and instruct the men entrusted to their care. He also expects they will seri-

ously consider that any neglect on their part before the enemy may cause the most fatal consequences, (from the particular service allotted to the battalion,) not only to themselves, but to the whole army.

He doubts not their own good sense will point out to them the necessity of impressing upon their minds that vigilance and activity are the first duties required from an officer on an outpost, and hopes they will not lose the opportunity of profiting by the advice which may be given to them by such of their brother officers who have had the advantage of acquiring experience upon actual service.

The men are to understand that by the maintenance of order and discipline we can alone look forward to a successful opposition to the designs of an enemy; they must on every occasion conform with alacrity to the orders of their officers, and as great fatigue is often connected with the duties of Light troops, they must cheerfully submit, and bear like men the hardships attending a soldier's life. He feels convinced of their bravery, and is satisfied that they will never yield in that respect to any troops in his Majesty's service.

The true "Rifleman" will never fire without being sure of his man, he should if possible make use of forced balls, and only load with cartridges in case of necessity, as when a brisk fire is to be kept up. And he will recollect that a few well-directed shots, that tell, will occasion greater confusion than thousands fired at random and without effect, which will only make the enemy despise our fire, and inspire him with confidence in proportion as he finds us deficient in skill and enterprise.

It is particularly recommended to the men, and will be strictly enforced, to behave with humanity to the people in an enemy's country, and not to plunder or destroy their houses, or attempt their lives, without the most urgent necessity, or an order to that effect. Interest and humanity both require the maintenance of a strict discipline, as the only way to conciliate the minds of the people, and to make them our friends. A contrary conduct, besides all other disadvantages attending, will certainly reflect strongly on the credit of the corps.

It is the duty of every officer carefully to provide for the wants of his men. This, he may be assured, will give him their confidence and esteem, and on some particular occasion the maxim may be adopted that, "necessity knows no laws;" but it must never be forgotten, that the "laws" are again in force the moment that necessity ceases, and the officers will recollect that the wants of their men are not to be provided for by allowing individuals to plunder or maraud.

The officers should endeavour to learn the capacities and characters of their men that they may employ them to the best advantage; this may be easily done by conversing with them, and hearing their opinion and sentiments on different subjects.

The commanding officer will feel sincere pleasure in recommending and rewarding all such non-commissioned officers and men as may distinguish themselves by their good conduct in the field; but if, on the contrary, any man should be guilty of cowardice, desertion, or any other such infamous crime as may reflect on the credit of the corps, he will show no mercy to such an offender, but use every exertion to bring him to the punishment he deserves.

Such were the sensible and excellent principles which Davy gave his battalion to reflect on during the voyage, and having said thus much he left it to have its effect, and only issued one other order of general interest before sailing.

We all know that the best drilled and disciplined battalions cannot manoeuvre in active service, and on broken ground, as they can in the barrack square; but relatively the best trained soldiers during peace will manoeuvre best in the field in spite of obstacles. Some of the aids however to nice accuracy in home drill can never be usefully tried in the field, and there are some things which must be discarded. Davy saw this, and his last order to his riflemen is as follows:

Regimental Orders
On board the *Malabar*
Cove of Cork
July 2nd, 1808
As it is not practicable in the field, when firing in advancing, for the serjeants to run out and mark the line on which the skirmishers are to form previously to their firing, the men must be instructed that, on the signal to fire being sounded, the rank which is to go forward moves twelve paces in front, each man counting his steps, and will then wait for the signal to fire being given by the whistle. No time ought to be lost in scrupulous attention to dressing. Eight or more men of the flank files of the line must be kept back a little so that the whole may form a semicircle, by which the flanks will be better covered. It is a matter of course that the men will profit by any advantage which the ground will offer for their protection, and place themselves behind hedges, trees, fences, ditches, &c, and consequently the distance which one line of skirmishers has to pass through another when firing in advancing must be entirely regulated by these circumstances, and it, must be clearly understood that it is only in open ground which affords no cover, (if ever riflemen should be employed to act in such,) that the distance of twelve paces is to be observed.
The fire in retreating is to be executed on the same principles as that in advancing.

Davy's next orders are dated 'On board the *Malabar*, 28th July, 1808. Off Mondego Bay.'

These orders are simple but of great value, the principles laid down will be endorsed by all 'riflemen, and have been held as sound, and always to be inculcated, from that day to this.

There are however some expressions such as 'forced balls' and 'powder horns' which may require a word of comment in these days of 'breech-loaders of precision.' The workmen of today may be as good as those of seventy years ago, but assuredly they would 'quarrel with their tools' were they asked to make war with the weapons of that period.

The battalion was clothed in green jackets with scarlet facings, and blue pantaloons. They were armed (as also were the 95th Regiment, now the 'Rifle Brigade') with a rifle known by the name of 'Baker's Rifle,' which weighed 9½ lbs. The barrel of this rifle was 2½ feet in length, it had seven grooves, making a quarter-turn in the length of the barrel, and its calibre was a twenty bore. It was loaded with considerable difficulty, and Major Davy wrote the following letter to obtain mallets for 'forcing the balls home.'

New Barracks
Cork
June 11th, 1808
Sir,
The 5th battalion, 60th Regiment, never having been provided with small wooden mallets for the purpose of driving the forced rifle-balls into the barrel, and this instrument being absolutely necessary in the field, I feel it my duty to represent that one mallet for every two men should, if possible, be furnished. They should be made of hard wood with a handle about six inches long, pierced with a hole at the extremity of the handle for fastening a string to it.

I annex a requisition for the same, and have the honour
to be,
Etc., etc.
(Signed) *W. G. Davy*
To the Assistant Adjutant-General
Cork

When the 2nd battalion 60th Rifles, were engaged in the
Kaffir war in 1851, 2, 3, they were armed with the 'Brunswick
rifle,' having two deep grooves and a belted ball. The loading
of this arm was at times so difficult that it was found necessary to furnish each rifleman with a packet of ten rounds of
plain musket ammunition, to be used on sudden emergencies,
when easy and rapid loading was essential; a thing difficult by
day or night with the Brunswick rifle.

The mallets were in use only a short time, and then withdrawn. The powder was carried separately in powder-horns,
which were also liable to be lost; and among the regimental
orders preserved are some for Boards and Courts of Enquiry
on the loss of these flasks in action, and a copy of a letter on
the subject which Major Davy wrote the following year, ask-
ing to be furnished with flasks of a better description.

Guarda D'Abrantes
June 14th, 1809
Sir,
I beg leave to state to you, for the information of his
Royal Highness the commander-in-chief, that the powder-horns with which the 5th battalion 60th Regiment
is supplied, have, by experience, been found to be ill-
adapted to the service, and by their construction have
not only occasioned much loss of powder, and subjected
the colonel to great expenses in repairs, but have proved
after all to be entirely useless, being too large and having
no measure fitted to them.
They have been furnished by Messrs. Beseley and Re-

ise of Parliament Street, London, after patterns delivered to them, but experience having now shown their inutility, I beg leave to suggest the propriety of providing the battalion with powder-flasks of the same description as those in possession of the 95th Regiment, large enough to contain forty rounds of fine-grain powder at five drachms each round, including the priming with proper measures adapted to them for different distances.

To the Adjutant-General of Forces
Horse Guards
London

The equipment and clothing of his battalion had much of Davy's attention. He preserved a 'sealed pattern' of the so-called 'linen' for the soldiers shirts: it is a loosely and coarsely-made fabric of a whitey-brown colour, and more worthy to be called 'canvas' than anything else; but there was 'shoddy' even in those 'good old times,' and contractors fattened on the poor soldier whose wants they did not supply.

Unremitting, however, was Davy's attention to the needs of his battalion, and the comfort of all dependent on him. A strict disciplinarian, he also fulfilled the promise made in his 'orders' to do his best for those whom it was in his power to reward.

His own letters recommending men for promotion, and the letters written to him in Spain, and from Spain after his return home on promotion, plainly betoken the affectionate esteem in which all his officers held him.

That he was not esteemed a hard man is shown by the accompanying note which he received during the few weeks he was in Cork, and which must have amused him sufficiently to make him preserve it among those letters which he has left.

From the date, the soldiers alluded to must presumably have had 'leave ashore on pass' from the *Malabar*.

(Copy)
Major Davy
Cork
July 6th, 1808
My dear Sir,
I know you will be glad of an opportunity to pardon. Two of my friends have over-staid their pass, and will present you this note. They had leave at twelve o'clock yesterday. They walked far—the day was hot—the liquor strong. I beg you will, for all these good reasons, suffer these good old soldiers to escape with admonition only.
I have the honour to be, My dear Major,
Yours sincerely and obediently,
J. Floyd

Kindly-hearted Floyd was doubtless listened to. Another important point to be looked to was his complement of officers. There were four other battalions and a frequent interchange of officers. Some officers of a regiment (and generally the smartest) are away on staff or detached duties—and Davy, like many another commanding officer, could but try to gather all his chickens together as the following letter, written soon after he had taken over the command, will show.

New Barracks
Cork
June 7th, 1808
Sir,
As the 5th battalion 60th Foot is under orders for embarkation, I feel it my duty to enclose to you a state of the absent officers, and vacant commissions, by which you will perceive that at the present moment there are two captains, three lieutenants, and one ensign, employed upon the staff and recruiting service; and that eight lieutenants are wanting to complete the battalion to its proper establishment.

I must also beg leave to represent that of the subalterns doing duty with this regiment at least four (from youth and inexperience in the profession) are unfit to be trusted with the command of detachments, should the service require them to be made, and which from the nature of that for which this regiment is particularly appointed there is every reason to suppose may be the case. 'Under these circumstances I trust I may be allowed to request, that, should H.R.H. be pleased to make any further appointments to this battalion, the officers to whom they may apply may be ordered without delay to follow the regiment to the place of its destination.

I have the honour,

Etc., etc.

(Signed) *W. G. Davy*

To the Military Secretary to

His Royal Highness the Commander-in-Chief

It is well to consider all these points, for, as has been said above, what the army owes to its general the battalion owes to its lieutenant-colonel, and what the 5th battalion was in the Peninsula, ay! what the 60th Rifles is now, is to be traced back to the formation of the 5th battalion by De Rottenburg, and the great pains with which his major, loyally following in his footsteps, got it ready for the great struggle which was coming. It was not an idle boast on his part, when, in writing home the following year from Lisbon to the Military Secretary at the Horse Guards, he said:

I can with truth assert that no commanding officer in his Majesty's army has had more difficulties to encounter than fell to my share from the constitution and organisation of the battalion, the class and character of the men composing it, the nature of the service they had to discharge, and other circumstances which it would be unbecoming in me to express, &c.

He seems to have felt the necessity of exerting every energy, to come up to what was expected of him. He says in another letter, of about the same date as that quoted above, to the Horse Guards:

It was a maxim of the late Sir John Moore, and which he several times repeated to me, that "one 'rifleman' should be deemed an equivalent, when posted, to three sentries of the Line."

Proud then of his position, and only fearing lest another should supersede him, he was refreshed a little later by the following letter from De Rottenburg, showing how he recognised that the building was erected on his own foundations, and that he who had aided in its erection was to be allowed to look after the structure uninterfered with by a superior officer.

Goldsgreen
Near Hayes
Middlesex
August 15th, 1808
My dear Davy,
I left Ireland a month ago, and on my arrival in this country waited upon the commander-in-chief and assured him that I had left the battalion in very good hands, and that there was no necessity whatsoever to post a lieutenant-colonel to the same, with which report his Royal Highness was very well pleased, and promised me you should continue in command. It is not decided yet if I am to go to Halifax or Canada; but as the season is far advanced I shall, in all probability, not be able to start before next spring.
Captain McMahon will set off next week to join you. I shall endeavour to procure you some more subalterns. Salaberry is not appointed yet, should I not succeed he must of course join you again.

I hope ere this you have laid hold of *Maistre* Junot, and that you are enjoying the pleasures of Lisbon.

I dined with General Bowyer ten days ago, Picton and Caruthers were of the party, and we drank your health and success to you, etc., etc.

Let me soon hear from you, and believe me,

Most sincerely yours,

Frs. De Rottenburg

To Major Davy

Commanding 5th Batt. 60th Regt.

Portugal

The postmark on this letter is August 17th, the day of Wellesley's first battle, 'Roleia;' but there must have been some strange delay in its reaching him for whom it was written, as the second post-mark is on April 3, 1809.

CHAPTER 3

Roleia & Vimeiro: 1808

The British expedition, intended to aid the patriotic exertions of the nations of the Peninsula, having been collected at
Cork, to the extent of 9000 soldiers, set sail from that port on
the 12th of July, and Lieutenant-General Sir Arthur Wellesley
leaving the transports to plough their way slowly through the
Bay of Biscay, sailed ahead in the *Crocodile*, anticipating his
forces in order to learn the state of affairs in the Peninsula,
and in conjunction with the naval authorities to fix on the
best spot for landing.

He arrived on July the 28th at Corunna, but his interviews
with the Galician Junta were far from satisfactory, and finding what were the tone and complexion of thought in Spain,
Wellesley left that people to their own devices, and took
his course to Oporto; here he found that the army of the
Portuguese, though little more than 10,000 or 12,000 badly
equipped and undisciplined peasants, were concentrated in
the valley of the Mondego, and he proceeded by sea to the
mouth of the Tagus, where he consulted with Admiral Sir
Charles Cotton, in command of the British fleet off that port.
Sir Arthur (finding that General Junot, then in military possession of Portugal, was in so strong a position in the neighbourhood of Lisbon, as to render a landing in that quarter impracticable) resolved to return in the *Crocodile*, meet the fleet
of transports and disembark them, midway between Oporto

and Lisbon, at Mondego Bay. The fort of Figueras had already been taken possession of by the partisan Zagalo, and was now occupied by a detachment of British marines.

The fleet of transports arrived on July 30th, and commenced landing there on August 1st. The last brigades disembarked on the 3rd, on which day, most opportunely, General (afterwards Sir Brent) Spencer arrived with his troops from Cadiz, and this reinforcement raised the force of the expedition to about 13,000 men[1].

To write a new history of the war is not our object, nor is there room for another by the side of Napier and Alison; but if the part taken by the 5th battalion 60th is to be traced, and intelligibly told, frequent reference must be made to those two great authors and the *Wellington Despatches*, and the sketches of military operations will be freely copied from the *Annals of the Wars*, by Sir E. Cust, and Mr. Carter's admirable volume of *Medals of the British Army, and how they were Won*. With all these assistances there is still, in the case of the 60th, a difficulty (at times insuperable) in tracing their special action. This arises from the fact that single companies of the 5th battalion were detached to different brigades and divisions, and, whilst the brigade and division may have the well-earned praise of Napier, the poor little company attached is generally left out of the account. But there is a consequence which is not unpleasant to the recollection of those connected with the regiment, and that is that the 60th, at least some portion of it, was everywhere where action was proceeding, and they can claim a more wide-spread interest and influence in every operation than can some other regiments, however fine their traditions, which operated in their entirety.

On August the 1st and 2nd the disembarkation was rapidly proceeding. The strength of the battalion, as embarked, was two field officers, seven captains, eleven lieutenants, seven en-

---

1. See *The Annals of the Wars,* by Hon. Sir E. Cust. *Epitome of Alison*, and Napier's *Battles and Sieges in Spain.*

signs, six staff, fifty-two sergeants, fifty corporals, twenty-one buglers, and 886 riflemen. There had been one case of desertion at Cork, and one man discharged on board the *Malabar* before sailing. The grand total of those embarked amounted to 1152, but among these were sixty women and fifty children! One can but ask, "*Que faites vous dans cette galere?*"

The following is the nominal roll of the officers who sailed in each transport:

LIST OF OFFICERS WHO EMBARKED WITH
5TH BATTALION 60TH, ON JUNE 15TH, 1808

On board the *Malabar*

Major W G Davy	Ensign Wm Wynne
Alex CapAndrews	Paymaster George Gilbert
Captain James Holmes Schoëdde	Adjutant F de Gilse
Lieutenant Wm Linston	Surgeon M E Parker
Lieutenant F Eberstein	Quarter-Master J A Kemmeter
Ensign J R Darcy	

On board the *Juliana*

Major Wm Woodgate	Lieutenant M du Chastelet
Captain Thomas Hames	Ensign John Joyce
Captain John Wolff	Ensign John Sprecher
Lieutenant Charles Koch	Ensign J L Barbaz
Lieutenant G H Zulke	Ensign Charles Debree
Lieutenant F Steitz	Assistant Surgeon Chas Wehsarg

On board the *Atlas*

Brevet-Major John Galiffe	Lieutenant Francis Holmes
Captain Michael Wend	Lieutenant Charles Sawatzky
Captain P Blassiere	Lieutenant Muller
Lieutenant Alex McKenzie	Ensign Julius von Boeck
Lieutenant Lewis Ritter	Assistant Surgeon J A du Moulin

There were at the time of embarkation, as has been represented, some officers away: of these Captain de Salaberry had remained as brigade major to Baron de Rottenburg, and Captain Prevost was on foreign service as *aide-de-camp* to General Sir G. Prevost, who was colonel commandant of the 5th battalion; but the latter rejoined later. Lieutenant H. Hoffman was on the recruiting service in Germany, the battalion not being up to its proper strength of fifty-five sergeants, fifty-one corporals, twenty-one buglers, and 950 riflemen.

On landing in Portugal, the first week in August, the 5th battalion 60th were placed in a Light Brigade, together with 2nd battalion 95th, fifty dragoons of 20th Light Dragoons, and a detachment of artillery, under the command of Brigadier-General Fane; but a redistribution took place on 18th of August. Five companies with head-quarters were left in the Light brigade with the 58th Regiment and five companies of the 2nd 95th, and one company was attached to each of the 1st, 2nd, 3rd, 4th, and 5th Brigades.

Subsequently one company was transferred from Light brigade to 7th brigade, and another company to the 8th Brigade, so that only three companies remained with head-quarters in the former.

Such an arrangement, naturally, was somewhat embarrassing to the commanding officer, and after a little time (in May, 1809) Major Davy having waited on Sir Arthur and represented his difficulties, Sir Arthur approved of his suggestion, and gave an order to that effect, *viz.*

. . . . that Major Davy might at any time place himself with any detachment or portion of his regiment which he might consider would put him in the position to be of most use to his battalion and the public service.

Sir Arthur Wellesley lost no time in advancing to attack Junot. The French troops were scattered, but General Laborde had been detached with a division to cover their concentration, and watch the English movements. This led to the first fight between the French and English in the Peninsula.

With the troops of General Spencer from Cadiz Sir Arthur had 12,300 men and eighteen guns, and to these were joined some 1600 Portuguese under General Freire, of which 260 were cavalry.

The advance was commenced on August 8th, and on the 9th his advanced guard entered Leyria, to prevent if possible the junction of Loison and Laborde. His movement was successful. On the 11th he reached Leyria with his whole force, and Loison, finding him there before himself, fell back on Santarem; while Laborde, not knowing where Loison was, advanced to Batalha, then fell back to Obidos, and on the 16th was at Roleia.

On the 15th the British arrived at Caldas, while the enemy was at Roleia, ten miles distant, occupying Obidos (only three miles off) as an advanced post. As possession of the latter village was important to the contemplated operations, Sir A. Wellesley resolved to occupy it, and as soon as the British infantry arrived upon the ground in the evening, sent out in four companies of Riflemen (two each from the 5th battalion 60th and 2nd battalion 95th) for this purpose.

The French picquets, consisting of a small detachment of infantry and a few cavalry, were, after a trifling resistance, driven out of the windmill of Brilos and retired, without loss to the British; but, on a portion of the latter pursuing to a distance of three miles from Obidos, they were attacked in their turn by a superior body of the enemy, who tried to cut them off; the main body of the detachment advanced to their support, when two bodies of French troops of superior strength appeared on both flanks, so that Major-General Spencer, who had gone out to Obidos on hearing that the Riflemen had gone in pursuit, had some difficulty in effecting a retreat thither. The French then retired entirely from the neighbourhood and the British remained in possession of the village.

'In this skirmish,' wrote the general, 'occasioned solely by the eagerness of the troops in pursuit of the enemy,' the 95th had one captain killed, one lieutenant wounded slightly, and four riflemen missing; the 5th battalion 60th had one rifleman killed, five wounded, and seventeen missing.

This was the first occasion on which the rival armies came to blows.

Laborde was now posted at Roleia, and Loison, who was in the field with a body of about 5000 men who had gone to relieve Elvas (besieged by the Portuguese), was now hastening to join him, and it was in anticipation of his arrival that Laborde maintained his position at Roleia after the British arrived at Caldas on the 15th. Roleia was situated on an eminence, having a plain in its front, at the end of a valley commencing at Caldas and closed to the southward by mountains which united with the hills forming the valley to the westward. The main body of the French were on the heights in front of the village, their right resting on the hills, their left upon an eminence, on which was a windmill, and with advanced posts both in the hills on each side of the valley and in the plain beneath, the whole covering four or five passes into the mountains in rear.

To dislodge the French from this position, the British army broke up from Caldas on the morning of the 17th of August and advanced in three columns to the attack. The right column, consisting of 1200 Portuguese infantry, and fifty cavalry, moved to turn their left and get into the mountains in their rear. The left, consisting of Major-General Ferguson's 2nd brigade (36th, 40th, and 71st) and Brigadier-General Bowes' 4th brigade (6th and 32nd), three companies of the 60th Rifles, a brigade of light artillery, and twenty British and twenty Portuguese cavalry, was destined under the command of Major-General Ferguson to ascend the hills at Obidos, and turn all the enemy's posts on the left of the valley, as well as the right of his post at Roleia. This force was also to watch for

Loison, who had been heard of the night before as advancing from Rio Mayor towards the French right.

The centre column, consisting of 1st brigade (General Hill), 3rd brigade (General Nightingale), 5th brigade (General Crawfurd), 6th or Light brigade (under Brigadier-General Fane), 60th and 95th, except three companies 60th detached with Ferguson, 400 Portuguese light infantry, the British and Portuguese cavalry, a brigade of 9-pounders and another of 6-pounders, was destined to attack the French position in front.

Directly the advance commenced the riflemen were detached into the hills on the left of the valley to keep up the communication between the centre and left columns, and to protect the march of the former along the valley. The enemy's advanced posts were successively driven in, and the 60th and 95th were soon in the hills on the right of the enemy, while General Hill's brigade and Brigadier-General Nightingale's advanced directly against their position, that of Brigadier-General Crawfurd remaining as a support and reserve. The Portuguese gained a village on the left, and General Ferguson's column commenced to descend from the heights into the plain. From this dangerous situation, however, the French extricated themselves by a precipitate, though orderly, retreat into the mountain passes in their rear; and although the British infantry pursued rapidly, the want of a sufficient force of cavalry prevented any considerable loss being inflicted on them during the movement.

It now became necessary for the British General to make fresh dispositions to attack the formidable position which Laborde took up on the heights of Zanbugeira or Columbeira, being still in hopes of being joined by Loison; and, as the Rifles were already in the mountains on his right, no time was to be lost in attacking the different passes, both to support them as well as to dislodge the enemy.

The Portuguese infantry were directed up a pass to the

right of the whole; the light companies of Hill's brigade and the 5th Regiment moved up a pass next on the right; the 39th supported by the 1st battalion 9th Regiment under Brigadier-General Nightingale a third pass; and the 45th and 82nd passes on the left. These passes were difficult, and some were well defended. The 9th and 29th gained the summit of the heights before the others, just as Laborde was concentrating his left wing on the centre; and the 29th, taken in flank and assailed in front, lost heavily. Their leading companies however rallied on their left wing, and they were promptly reinforced by the 9th, when they soon regained the summit, and there maintained themselves until further reinforcements came up on their right: the Rifles under Fane had also appeared at a distance on the left, and the skirmishers which covered the other attacks began to emerge from the thickly-wooded descent. Laborde had therefore no choice but to retreat, since his flanks were turned, his communication with Loison cut, and the position forced. This he succeeded in effecting in good order, owing principally to the weakness of the British General in cavalry, and the difficulty in bringing troops and artillery up the mountain passes to support those who had first ascended. Laborde tried to make a last stand near the village of Zanbugeira, but was forced to take refuge in the higher mountains, having lost three guns and 600 men killed and wounded. The British loss was nearly 500 in all; the loss of the 60th being eight riflemen killed, Lieutenants Steitz and Darcy, and Adjutant de Gilse, with five serjeants and thirty-four riflemen wounded, and sixteen missing.

Sir Arthur, unable to pursue, and having to remain near his shipping for expected reinforcements and supplies, resolved however on moving down near the sea by his right in an endeavour to gain Torres Vedras, command the great road to Lisbon, and get between that city and the divisions both of Laborde and Loison. In the night however came information that the reinforcements had arrived, and to cover their landing the army marched instead on the 18th to Lourinha, and on the 19th to Vimeiro, a village near the sea, but nine miles short of Torres Vedras. On the 19th a brigade under General Anstruther was landed with great difficulty and some loss; the next night another brigade under General Acland was landed, and by these accessions the strength of the army was raised to 16,000 men with eighteen guns, exclusive of the Portuguese.

Meanwhile, between the 18th and 20th the different French corps had assembled at and about Torres Vedras, Marshal Junot, Duke of Abrantes, having also brought up with him from Lisbon a reserve of 2000 infantry, 600 cavalry, and ten guns, which formed their advanced guard in a strong position in front of the town; the divisions of Laborde and Loison occupied another strong position behind it, and the French cavalry patrolled right up to the British position on the 19th and 20th, thus debarring Sir Arthur from obtaining any detailed information as to their own position.

Nevertheless he resolved by a forced march on the 21st to turn the position of Torres Vedras and gain the heights of Mafra with a strong advanced guard, while the main body should halt four or five miles short of that place so as to intercept the French should they try to regain the capital by the route of Montechique. For this purpose the army (with its reinforcements) was redistributed during the 20th and formed into eight brigades, and the alteration alluded to above took place in the distribution of the 60th. One company each had been attached to 1st, 2nd, 3rd, 4th, and 5th brigades respectively, the other five companies and head-quarters being attached to the 6th (or light) brigade; but Sir Arthur thinking that the new brigades were not complete without a company of riflemen, took two companies from the 6th and attached one each to the 7th and 8th brigades, the 7th being placed under Brigadier-General Anstruther, and the 8th under Major-General Acland; three companies and head-quarters still remaining with Fane and the 6th brigade.

Such were Sir A. Wellesley's plans, but Sir Harry Burrard not approving of the bold advance, Sir Arthur had to refrain, and it was left to the French to take the offensive; and while his cavalry concealed his movements, Marshal Junot decided to march on the night of the 20th and fall on the British at daylight on the 21st. The British position at Vimeiro may be shortly described thus. The village stands in a valley, through which runs the river Maceira; it is shut in at the back and to the westward and northward by a mountain, the western point of which touches the sea, while the eastern is separated by a deep ravine from the heights over which passes the road leading to Vimeiro from Lourinha and the northward. The greater part of the infantry under Hill, Ferguson, Nightingale, Bowes, Crawfurd, and Acland were posted on this mountain with eight guns, Hill being on the right and Ferguson on the left. The heights, separated from the mountain to the east by the valley of the Maceira, trend in a north-easterly direction. There being no water here, only the 40th regiment and some picquets occupied the spot.

Immediately in front of the village to the east and south, and blocking the interval between the two heights, was a rugged isolated hill with a flat top, commanded itself on its right by the mountain to the westward of the town, but commanding all the ground to the south and east for a considerable distance. Upon this hill was posted Brigadier Fane with his riflemen, three companies 60th, one company 1st 95th, and four companies 2nd 95th, and the 50th Foot on the right overhanging the descent to the river Maceira; the 2nd battalion 52nd and 97th of Fane's brigade occupied the centre; Anstruther's brigade was on the left, the 2nd battalion 9th being held in reserve; and the 2nd battalion 43rd occupied a churchyard, and guarded a road leading over the extremity of the heights to the village: with these troops were three 6-pounders and three 9-pounders. The cavalry, Portuguese, and reserve artillery were in the valley between the hills on which the infantry stood and close to the village, so as both to flank and support Brigadier-General Fane's advanced guard.

The first indication of the approach of the French army was given about eight in the morning, when large bodies of their cavalry appeared in front of the British left upon the heights on the road to Lourinha. They were followed by masses of infantry, and it became evident that the left of the position was their object. Ferguson's brigade with three guns was therefore moved at once across the ravine to the heights on the road to Lourinha. These were followed by Nightingale's brigade with three guns, and Adams' and Bowes' brigades. The Portuguese were moved up to support Crawfurd, and the 4th and 8th brigades formed a third line in column, in rear of the 2nd and 3rd.

For the defence of the hill in front of Vimeiro the troops already there under Fane and Anstruther were considered sufficient, having the support of the cavalry in rear of their right, while the 1st brigade (Hill's) was moved to the centre of the mountain, on which the mass of infantry had been posted, as a support to them and a reserve to the whole army.

The attack commenced about ten o'clock. Two columns under Generals Laborde and Brennier advanced; the first against the flat hill before Vimeiro, the second against the British left. Two more brigades under Loison followed in the same order at a short distance, and Kellermann with a body of grenadiers succeeded Loison. The cavalry, 1300 in number, under Margaron, were divided, part on the right of Brennier, part in rear of the reserve.

The artillery (twenty-three small pieces) was distributed among the columns, and opened its fire wherever the ground was favourable.

The attack[2] on the English centre by Laborde and his column of 6000 men had no sooner reached the summit of the hill than the British artillery and shrapnel shells—then used

---

2. See Alison's *History*, and Napier's *Battles and Sieges*, &c.

for the first time—spread havoc through their ranks, and a charge with the bayonet by the 50th completed their repulse. A second attempt was not more successful; and the French right, under Solignac, after a severe contest with Ferguson's brigade, was at last driven headlong down the steep by so tremendous a rush with the bayonet, that the whole front line of one French regiment, above 300 men, went down like grass before the scythe. An attempt to retrieve the day with Brennier's division and the reserve under Kellermann, though at first partially successful, also terminated in entire discomfiture.

The charge of the 50th completed the crushing repulse which Fane had given to the principal attack of Loison and Laborde. This attack, says Napier:

> . . . . was well led and covered with skirmishers. It forced its way up with great vehemence and power, but with great loss also; for General Fane had called up the reserve artillery under Colonel Robe to reinforce the six guns already on the platform; and while they smote the column in front, another battery, belonging to one of the brigades then ascending the left-hand ridge, smote it in the right flank; and it was under this conjoint fire of artillery and a wasting musketry that they reached the summit, there to sustain a murderous volley, to be charged by the 50th overturned, and driven down again.

We dwell upon this point in the first of 'the Duke's' great battles (the affair at Roleia being generally called 'a combat'), not only because it is of the greatest interest, but because with Fane was the principal detachment and head-quarters of the 60th Rifles.

Brennier had been taken prisoner, and eagerly enquired of other prisoners 'if the reserve had attacked?' The answer was in the affirmative; and Sir Arthur, with his marvellous power of appreciating the value of any information, and drawing rapid but clear conclusions, overheard it. Judging therefore the French power exhausted, and the moment come for rendering victory decisive, with the genius of a great captain he resolved to make it not only decisive on the field, but of the fate of Portugal. He designed to push his own right wing and centre under Hill on Torres Vedras, to which they were two miles nearer than any part of the French army; that stroke was sure, and Junot would have been cut off from Lisbon. Meanwhile Sir Arthur meant in person vigorously to drive him across the Baragueda mountain on to the Tagus, by which he would lose his remaining artillery, and have, with disorganised and dispirited troops, to seek refuge under the guns of one of the frontier fortresses.

This great project was stifled as soon as conceived.

The Government had sent Sir Harry Burrard out to Portugal, an officer senior to Sir Arthur.

Sir Harry had not landed, but he had not approved of Sir Arthur's bold plan of marching on Lisbon, and had obliged him to alter his arrangements before the 20th. Sir Harry had not been present at the beginning of the battle; but before the end he arrived on the ground and assumed the command. Wellesley's proposed manoeuvres were too enterprising for Sir Harry, a cautious veteran of the old school; and the French, to the infinite chagrin of Sir Arthur, were suffered to regain by a long circuit the important defile.

General Burrard 'could not comprehend such a stroke of war, and not only stopped the execution, but ordered Ferguson to halt[3].' He issued his orders to the army to halt and pile arms, that they might remain in position for the momentarily expected arrival of Sir John Moore. Sir Arthur could not restrain the bitterness of his disappointment at this order, and turning to the officers of his staff said, 'Gentlemen, nothing now remains to be done but to go and shoot red-legged partridges.'

---

3. See Sir E. Cust's *Annals of the Wars* &c.

The battle of Vimeiro may be cited as the first instance in which the French became acquainted with the peculiar character and organisation of the British army in battle.

The stolid firmness and resolute thrust of the infantry, and the wonderful skill and precision of the artillery, were not at all like the bearing of other opponents over whom they had obtained such easy victories, and the knowledge here obtained had considerable influence on the whole war.

If 'Vimeiro' taught the French to respect their then present enemies, it gave confidence and self-reliance to the British soldier and his general. Sir Arthur before leaving England had, in conversation with Lord Castlereagh, said that others 'were, or seemed to be, afraid of Napoleon and the French, but that he was not so;' and now his short experience had taught him a feeling which he expressed to Anstruther, who towards the end of the day asked if he should bring up his brigade to reinforce him, in the words, 'No, Sir, I am not pressed and I want no assistance. I am beating the French, and am able to beat them wherever I may find them.'

On the morning of the 22nd Sir Harry Burrard was himself superseded by Sir Hew Dalrymple, so that within thirty hours there had been three successive commanders-in-chief. And now at length an advance on Torres Vedras was agreed upon; but on the 23rd Kellermann arrived at the outposts with a proposal from Junot for a suspension of arms. On this day the convention called 'the Convention of Cintra,' but really signed thirty miles from that place, was executed for the evacuation of Portugal, and the fortresses of Elvas and Almeida were given up, and between the 15th and end of September the whole French army, to the number of 32,000, sailed from the Tagus and were safely disembarked in France.

But notwithstanding these great and substantial results of 'one month with Sir Arthur,' there was some real indignation expressed, and much idle clamour in England; and the generals were ordered home for enquiry into and explanation of their conduct of affairs. The importance was better appreciated by Napoleon, who said, 'I was about to send Junot to a council of war, but the English got the start of me by sending their generals to one.'

The praise of Sir Arthur Wellesley, more valuable than a medal, was freely given to the troops in his reports home. With regard to Roleia he writes, in his despatch to Viscount Castlereagh:

> I cannot sufficiently applaud the conduct of the troops through this action. The enemy's positions were formidable, and he took them up with remarkable ability and celerity, and defended them most gallantly; but I must observe that though we had such a superiority of numbers employed in the operation of the day, the troops actually engaged in the heat of the action were, from unavoidable circumstances, the 5th, 9th, and 29th Regiments, and the riflemen of the 95th and 60th, a number by no means equal to the enemy. Their conduct therefore deserves the highest praise, &c, &c.

And again, in his despatch addressed to Sir Harry Burrard from Vimeiro (August 21st) he says:

> The valour and discipline of His Majesty's troops have been conspicuous on this occasion, as you, who witnessed the greater part of the action, must have observed, but it is a justice to the following corps to draw your notice to them in a particular manner.

Among those then enumerated stands, '5th battalion 60th, commanded by Major Davy.'

When Sir Harry Burrard received from Lord Castlereagh the acknowledgement of these despatches he forwarded it to Sir Arthur, with a gracefully worded letter which was published in orders, and it is fair to remember (as he is much blamed by many for stopping the onward movement of the British troops) that Sir William Napier makes the following apology for his doing so: he says:

> Burrard's decision, with exception of the unaccountable order to arrest Ferguson's career, was not without a military justification, admitted to be of weight by Sir Arthur, but it was that of an ordinary general in opposition to a great captain.

The following copy of Lord Castlereagh's despatch after Obidos, and the letter from Brigadier-General Fane to Major Davy, covering the one alluded to above from Sir H. Burrard to Sir Arthur, with that which Lord Castlereagh wrote after 'Vimeiro,' were published in regimental orders, and have been preserved amongst the Davy papers.

> General Orders
> Headquarters
> Lourinha
> August 18th, 1808
> The lieutenant-general was perfectly satisfied with the conduct of the troops in the action of yesterday; particularly with the gallantry displayed by the 5th, 9th, 29th, 5th battalion 60th Regiment, and 95th Regiment, to whose lot it principally fell to engage with the enemy. From the specimen afforded yesterday of their behaviour in action the lieutenant-general feels confident that the troops will distinguish themselves whenever the enemy may give them another occasion; and it is only necessary for him to recommend to them a steady attention to the preservation of order, and regularity, and strict obedience to the commands the officers may give.

> General Orders
> Headquarters

Vimeiro
August 21st, 1808
Lieutenant-General Sir Arthur Wellesley congratulates the troops on the signal victory they have obtained this day over the enemy, and returns them his warmest thanks for their resolute and heroic conduct, and experienced the sincerest pleasure at witnessing various instances of gallantry of the corps, and has in particular to notice the distinguished behaviour of the Royal Artillery, 20th Light Dragoons, 36th, 6th, 43rd, 50th, 52nd, 5th battalion 60th, 71st, 82nd, 95th and 97th Regiments. It will afford the lieutenant-general the greatest pleasure to report to the commander-in-chief the bravery displayed by all the troops, and the high sense he entertains of their meritorious and excellent conduct throughout the day.

Downing Street
Sept. 4th, 1808
Sir,
I received by your *aide-de-camp* Captain Campbell your despatches of the 15th and 16th August, the first containing the account of the affair at Obidos which obliged the enemy to retire his advanced posts; the other of the 17th containing the account of your attack, with the troops under your command, on the advanced corps of the enemy in their formidable position near Obidos and of their entire defeat.

These despatches having been laid before his Majesty, I have to convey to you his Majesty's entire satisfaction in the able, spirited, and decisive conduct you have displayed, by which so much credit has been reflected upon his Majesty's arms, and the progress of the army towards the complete reduction of the enemy was so greatly facilitated.

His Majesty has also signified his royal pleasure that his most gracious approbation should be signified by you, to Major-General Spencer, and to the generals and other officers under your command, for the skill, valour, and perseverance they exhibited, and to the troops in general, for the courage, coolness and determination which appears to have marked their conduct.

I have the honour to be, Sir,

Your most obedient humble servant,

(Signed) *Castlereagh*

To Lieutenant-General Sir A. Wellesley, K.B.

Near Quilus

Sept. 21st, 1808

Dear Sir,

By direction of Lieutenant-General Sir A. Wellesley, I do myself the honour to enclose to you copies of two letters, the one from the Right Hon. Lord Castlereagh, principal Secretary of State for Foreign Affairs, and the other from Lieutenant-General Sir H. Burrard; both of which you will be good enough to communicate to the regiment under your command.

I am very happy in being afforded this opportunity of congratulating you, and my friends the 60th, upon the flattering approbation our services have met with from our Sovereign.

Believe me. dear Sir, with much esteem,

Your most obedient servant,

(Signed) *H. Fane*

Brigdadier-General

To Major Davy

Commanding 5th Battalion 60th Regiment

Ocyras

Sept. 15th, 1808

Dear Sir Arthur,

I enclose you a copy of a letter just received from Viscount Castlereagh (inserted in the General Orders of the 16th inst.), and I request you will do me the honour and justice to believe, and to impress on the minds of your corps, that if I could have found words that would have more strongly conveyed to his Majesty's Ministers my thorough conviction of the conduct and bravery displayed by yourself, and the troops under your command, on the 31st of August, I should have been happy and proud to do it.

I shall ever consider it as one of the most fortunate circumstances, that an opportunity was afforded me of witnessing what an able general can accomplish with a well-disciplined British army.

I have the honour to be,
With great respect and esteem,
My dear Sir Arthur,
Your very faithful, humble servant,
(Signed) *Harry Burrard*
Lieutenant-General.
The Right Hon. Lieutenant-General Sir A. Wellesley, K.B.

De Rottenburg also sent his congratulations in a friendly letter from home, an extract from which runs as follows:

Ashford
Kent
Oct. 12th, 1808
My Dear Davy,
You may easily conceive how highly I have been gratified on reading in the papers of your distinguished conduct in the field. The Duke of York spoke to me in high terms of the battalion, and I most sincerely congratulate you on the honour and glory you have acquired. I always told you that you might depend upon the bravery of my disciples.

My compliments to Majors Woodgate, Galiffe, and all
our gentlemen.

Believe me, yours most faithfully,

(Signed) *Francis De Rottenburg*

To Major W. Davy

Commanding 5th Battalion 60th Regiment

Portugal

The loss of the battalion in the battle of Vimeiro was fourteen riflemen killed, Lieutenants Koch and Ritter, one sergeant, and twenty-one riflemen wounded, and ten missing.

CHAPTER 4

Corruna: 1808-1809

At the end of September, 1808, Portugal being freed from the French and the fortresses of Elvas and Almeida given up, and the three generals having been recalled to England, there was a temporary lull in active operations.

Reinforcements had arrived after Vimeiro. Sir John Moore had brought a force of 11,324, which was lauded at Maceira August 29, after having been delayed and refused permission to land at Corunna by the Portuguese. 1023, commanded by General Beresford, embarked at Madeira August 17th, landed at the Tagus in September. 11,069, commanded by Sir D. Baird, embarked at Falmouth, sailed October 9th, arrived at Corunna October 13th, and landed 29th ditto. 2021, under Lord Paget, embarked at Portsmouth and landed at Corunna October 30th.

These, with some smaller reinforcements and the troops of Sir A. Wellesley's expedition, brought up the grand total of troops embarked for Portugal and Spain in 1808 to 48,341.

On the 6th of October a despatch arrived in Lisbon containing the first determinate plan of a campaign in Spain, and Sir John Moore appointed to command the whole; and he was ordered to take the field immediately, and to fix upon some place, either in Gallicia or on the borders of Leon, for concentrating his own forces with those of Baird and the rest of the army.

His own force was organised in three columns, two of which were directed upon Almeida by the routes of Coimbra and Guarda, while the third, comprising the artillery, the cavalry, and the regiments quartered in the Alemtejo, was destined to move by Alcantara upon Ciudad Rodrigo.

Now, was the 5th battalion 60th Rifles in this expedition, and at Corunna?

If it were so we should be desirous of tracing its doings, but there was no mention of it in any despatch, and there has never been any tradition in the regiment that they had any share in Moore's brave stand in January 1809. Of late some have said, 'They were there, but in reserve;' and Mr. Carter, in his *Medals of the British Army and how they were won*, has amongst the large number of regiments mentioned as having been at Corunna included the '60th 2nd battalion, Lieutenant-Colonel Codd, and 60th 5th battalion, Major Davy.'

Does Napier say they were there? or what does he say, for he speaks what he does know, and is for the most part an accurate man?

Sir John Moore, he has said, was ordered off in October. In December, 1808, Sir John Cradock was sent out to take charge of affairs in Portugal, 'and though fully sensible of his own difficulties, with a very disinterested zeal, resolved on making the reinforcing Sir John Moore's army his first care;' and then pointing out how small was the force he had to draw upon, says, 'There was also a battalion of the 60th Regiment, composed principally of Frenchmen recruited from the prison ships, but it had been sent back from Spain, as the soldiers could not be trusted near their countrymen.'[1]

To settle these doubts it might be difficult to prove the negative proposition that 'they were not there,' but for the affirmative statement of Sir William Napier, that 'they were in Portugal,' and therefore could not have retreated to Corunna with Moore.

1. Napier's *History of Peninsular War*, bk. 6. chap. 1. vol. 2. p. 115

Sir William is (in the main) right. And it may be asserted that the whole of the 5th 60th marched with Moore's expedition; but the statement that the battalion was 'principally composed of Frenchmen recruited from the prison ships' is certainly beyond the facts of the case.

Let us proceed to the argument of dates, and first give a short analysis of Moore's movements.

On the 8th of November, 1808, Sir John Moore was at Almeida. On the 11th he crossed the frontier of Spain and marched to Ciudad Rodrigo. On the 13th of November the head of the British columns entered Salamanca. On 11th of December Moore commenced his forward movement. On the 20th, depending on the Spaniards to hold the capital, he advanced and formed his junction with Sir D. Baird at Mayorga. On the 21st took place Lord Paget's brilliant cavalry affair with the 10th and 15th Light Dragoons at Sahagun.

Soult called in his detachments. Napoleon ordered a suspension of operations in the south, and put himself at the head of 50,000 best troops, including Ney's corps and the Guards, and threw himself on the line of the British retreat, whilst Soult attacked in front.

Two days were passed in crossing the gorges of the Guadarama mountains in a hurricane of wind and snow. On the 26th Ney had interposed himself between the British and the Portuguese frontier, luckily not reaching Benavente first; Moore destroyed the bridge (over the Esla) at Castrogonzalo, and the French were detained two days. On the 28th the British dragoons defeated the cavalry of the Guard, and Lefebre Desnouettes was made prisoner.

1809, January 1st, the French effected their passage and concentrated their columns at Astorga, having in ten days advanced 200 miles from Madrid.

Napoleon left the army for Paris.

January 5th, the skirmish at Villa Franca took place. 6th to 8th, Moore halted at Lugo, but Soult declined the combat.

11th, Moore arrived at Corunna; and on the 14th the transports arrived from Vigo.

The French allowed the embarkation to proceed quietly for two days, but on January 16th, when Moore's force was reduced to 14,000, Soult attacked with 20,000, but was repulsed.

The next question is, can anyone say for certain where the 5th 60th was from the battle of Vimeiro in January 16, 1809?

Luckily the answer has been preserved in Davy's own order book, which, with his letter book and a duplicate copy of the muster roll of the battalion of December 1809 (after Talavera), is among the papers he so fortunately preserved. The regimental orders after Vimeiro are dated thus:

August 25, from Ramalied.
August 26 and 27, from Emaliel.
September 10, from St. Anthonio.
September 18, from Lameah.
September 20 to October 9, from camp near Quilus.

And in General Orders, October 8, five companies were attached to the brigade of Lord William Bentinck, and five to that of General Beresford.

October 16 and 17, from Rio Mayor.
October 19, from Leria.
October 23 to 26, from Coimbra.

And the whole of these orders at Coimbra refer to careful but urgent preparations for immediately taking the field, repairs, arms, ammunition, chargers, mules, bat-men, Portuguese servants, great-coats, &c, &c.

November 4 and 5, from Trangosa.
November 13, from Villa de Pedro Alonzo.
November 16 to 29, from Salamanca.
December 24, from Lamego.
February 3, 1809, to 14, from Oporto.
March 7, from Belem.

The orders dated at Coimbra appear to have been addressed to the whole battalion; but in marching from Coimbra to Salamanca, it is known to have been again divided into two detachments by General Order, October 8, 1808. And not only the words in the regimental order book imply this, but we are told by Napier that:

> . . . . want of transport and supplies had obliged the British to march in small and successive divisions, it was therefore the 23rd of November before the centre, consisting of 12,000 infantry and a battery of six guns, was concentrated at Salamanca.

On the 9th of November, 1808, there appeared the following regimental order:

> The Major, as yet, has had much reason to be satisfied with the behaviour of the men on the march, and only regrets that the misconduct of a few individuals should have reflected on the character of the whole; he strongly recommends a continuance of that, meritorious conduct which has procured them the good wishes of the inhabitants of the towns in Portugal through which they have passed, and doubts not that they will, together with himself, see the necessity of more particularly conciliating the good-will of the Spanish nation, into whose territory the battalion is about to march.

On the 13th of November, the very next order in the book, which is dated from 'Villa de Pedro Alonzo,' is as follows:

> It is with deep concern that the major discharges a most painful part of his duty, that of announcing to the battalion that in consequence of the misbehaviour of the five companies detached they have been sent back to Lisbon; under these distressing circumstances the major calls upon every individual of the regiment to use his utmost efforts to vindicate and maintain the well-mer-

ited reputation which the battalion has acquired in the field; and doubts not that with the cordial co-operation of the whole they will be able to do away that disgrace which must otherwise for ever reflect upon the character of the battalion.

This order to be read in German.

These orders speak for themselves; irregularities of some sort had condemned the separate wing to return. Davy himself saw hopes of removing the slur which he felt cast upon his wing by misconduct on the part of some not with him. However, he had the still greater annoyance of returning to Portugal himself. Three days later the general, considering that it would be of more advantage that the whole battalion should be together under Davy's own eye, sent him back also; and the very next order in the book is as follows:

Regimental Orders
Salamanca
Nov. 16th, 1808
The battalion must be prepared to march on the shortest notice.

The last order from Salamanca was dated November 29. The next order in the book is dated from 'Lamego' on the 24th of December, 1808. Now Lamego is only forty-six miles from Oporto. Let Napier say what the army in Spain was doing:

The 24th (December), General Hope with two divisions had gone back by the road of Mayorga, Baird, with another, by that of Valencia de San Juan, where there was a ferry-boat to cross the Esla river.

Can any further evidence be required as to the fact that the 5th 60th was not, could not have been, with those who retreated on Corunna? Hardly; and yet there is more to be gathered from Davy's papers. In the circumstances of the case, there was much to cause any good officer much chagrin and vexation; and feeling that for his own sake and those with him a respectful memorial was due to themselves, he did send such an one, and has entered with his own hand in the letter book:

The following answer was received from the adjutant-general of the army under the command of Lieutenant-General Sir John Moore to the memorial of the officers under the immediate command of Major Davy, forwarded from Ciudad Rodrigo on the 13th December, 1808.

And then the following letter is entered:

Headquarters
Castro Nuovo
Dec. 19th, 1808
Sir,
I have had the honour to lay your letter of 12th instant, and the memorial of the officers of the detachment of 5th battalion 60th Regiment under your command, enclosed therein, before the Commander of the Forces, and I am directed to desire that you will inform them, that his Excellency's motives for sending the detachment back arose from the inexpediency of keeping the battalion divided, and not from any idea of the nature they apprehend.
While his Excellency laments that circumstances have rendered it necessary to remove the detachment from the present scene of action, he desires that you will observe to the officers, that their station in Portugal is by no means uninteresting, and that their exertions there may he most usefully directed.
I have the honour to be, Sir,
Your most obedient humble servant,
(Signed) *H. Clinton,* A.G
To Major Davy
Commanding 5th Battalion 60th Regiment

It must be repeated then, 'the 5th battalion were not at

Corunna;' and no one could wish to claim a share in an action in which they could take no part, being far away. The 5th battalion had plenty of opportunities of showing that if there were leaven it had not 'leavened the whole lump;' and the present place will not be amiss for speaking of the enlistments that had taken place, and the steps which were taken for the purification of the battalion. The backbone of the battalion was German, and when it sailed from Cork one of the lieutenants (Hoffman) was recruiting in Germany. But it can hardly be believed, and yet it is true, that (though not 'composed principally of Frenchmen,' as Napier says) they had had a number of men from the French prison-ships sent to them for service! On the 16th of September, 1808, Davy had received the following letter in reply to one from himself:

Headquarters
Dragos
Sept. 16th, 1808
Sir,
I am desired by the commander of the forces to acknowledge your letter of yesterday's date, with an enclosure from Major Davy commanding the 5th battalion of the 60th Regiment desiring permission to enlist deserters, and I am to acquaint you that his Excellency does not approve of deserters from the enemy being enlisted in a corps destined to do the duty of advanced posts; nor does he think it expedient, at this moment, to allow Hanoverians to be enlisted by any other corps than those composing the infantry of the German Legion, for the recruiting of which instructions have been received from home.
I have the honour to be, Sir,
Your most obedient humble servant,
(Signed) *H. Clinton,* A.G.
To Lieutenant-General the Right Hon. Sir Arthur Wellesley

One cannot but be surprised at Major Davy having made the proposition he did; but it must be remembered that deserters from the French were not necessarily of the same class as men from the prison-ships. There were many who were under compulsion in the ranks of the French army, and there was at any rate in their desertion an evidence of their having no goodwill towards that service.

And yet another thing may have weighed with Major Davy. De Rottenburg was still on the strength of the battalion as lieutenant-colonel, and with him his loyal major had always been '*d'accord.*' Now in writing to him from England on the 15th of August, 1808, he had said to Davy:

> You will have many opportunities to get excellent recruits from the Germans in the French service, and I suppose they won't object to supernumeraries; in which case a good batch might be obtained from our best behaved for the 5th battalion of the 60th.

The commander of the forces however thought differently. On the 6th March, 1809, Woodgate rejoined regimental headquarters at Belem; and at once the active commanding officer set to work to purge that wing, as he had begun to do with the other under the directions of Sir John Cradock; and the following letters will show how carefully this was done. Without the light of these letters thrown upon the subject it would not have been possible to understand the meaning of the 'Remarks' placed against so many names in the muster roll of December, 1809, which is preserved among the Davy papers, and in which the phrase is constantly repeated of 'sent to England suspected:'

Headquarters
Lisbon
Jan. 8th, 1809
Sir,
The commander of the forces has directed me to trans-

mit, for your information and guidance, the enclosed copy of a letter from the secretary to his Royal Highness the Commander-in-Chief directing a selection to be immediately made from the battalion under your orders of such men as were taken from French prison-ships, and whom you may consider as subjects not to be confided in, in order that they may be sent to England to be disposed of in the rifle companies of the 60th Regiment serving in other stations.

You will be pleased to take the earliest practicable measures to obey the instructions of H. R. H., and as soon as you have selected the men that come under the description specified you will immediately transmit to Sir John Cradock a descriptive list of them conformably to the latter paragraph of Lieutenant-Colonel Gordon's letter; when his Excellency will furnish you with orders respecting the mode in which they are to be conveyed to England.

I have the honour to be, Sir,

Your obedient humble servant,

(Signed) *Thomas Reynell*

Lieutenant-Colonel and Military Secretary

To the officer commanding the 5th Battalion 60th Regiment

Letter alluded to above:

Horse Guards

Dec. 7th, 1808

Sir,

I have it in command from the commander-in-chief to desire that you will be pleased to cause such men of the 5th battalion of the 60th Regiment as may have been taken from prison-ships, and are considered unfit to be trusted, to be selected and sent to England by the earliest opportunity in order to their being placed in the rifle companies of the same regiment serving on other stations; and you will be pleased to cause an accurate description return of such men to be sent with them.

I have the honour to be, Sir,

Your obedient humble servant,

(Signed) *J. W. Gordon*

To Lieutenant-General Sir John Cradock

Portugal

Belem

March 7th, 1809

Sir,

I have the honour to acquaint you that the five companies of the 5th battalion 60th Regiment, under the command of Major Woodgate, have yesterday joined the other five companies here. It is my duty to state to you that from immediately after the action of Roleia on the 17th of August last the battalion has been divided into detachments which were attached to the several brigades of the army, and have thus gone through the arduous service of riflemen during the campaign, and since that period the battalion has never been united.

The arms, accoutrements, appointments, clothing, &c. have suffered materially by the nature of the service peculiar to light troops; and the interior economy has necessarily been deranged by so many detachments.

To establish that regularity without which no regiment can serve with credit, and to supply those deficiencies which have taken place, I think it necessary to request that some time may be allowed before the battalion is sent on actual service. I shall not lose a moment to effect these objects, but I think one month, or at least three weeks, will be required.

I have the honour to be, Sir, &c, &c.

(Signed) *W. G. Davy*

To Brigdadier-General Sontag, &c, &c.

Belem
March 9th, 1809
Sir,

In conformity to the instructions of his Excellency the Commander of the Forces, bearing date 10th January 1809, transmitted to me by Lieutenant-Colonel Reynell, together with an enclosed copy of Lieutenant-Colonel Gordon's letter to his Excellency the Commander of the Forces, Horse Guards, 7th Dec. 1808, I have proceeded to select such men as are therein alluded to, and enclose a list of the same, and request your instructions with regard to the ships on board which they are to be sent. The accounts of these men will be made up to the 24th inst., and balances paid if the money can be procured from the paymaster for that purpose. A description return shall be forwarded to you as soon as possible, and I also enclose a list of those who from debility and disease are considered as unfit to serve in a light battalion, in order that a board may be directed to inspect them, that they may be sent to the Army Depot, Isle of Wight, there to be discharged or transferred as the inspector may think fit.

I have the honour to be, Sir,
Your obedient humble servant,
(Signed) *W. G. Davy*
To the Deputy Adjutant-General
Lisbon

Lisbon
March 20th, 1809
Sir,

I have the honour to acquaint you that agreeably to the commands of the 7th Dec. 1808 of H. R. H. the Commander-in-Chief, communicated to me through you by letter bearing date 8th January 1809, forty-four men of suspected character have been selected, and sent on board ships to be conveyed to England.

The number of deserters, prisoners on board ships, amounts to 110, amongst which by Major Woodgate's report (ninety-three of them belonging to the companies detached under his command on 21st Sept. 1808) there are some he has reason to believe of good character, who may have been misled by the bad conduct of others; but in order to hold forth to the battalion a striking example (at this moment so particularly necessary) of the consequences attendant upon desertion, I have refrained from making any application to his Excellency to have them given up to the regiment.

'The clothing of the men having suffered much, from the nature of the service in which the battalion has constantly been employed, and his Excellency having been pleased to say that he would afford us his assistance to have the clothing for the present year forwarded, permit me to request the influence of his Excellency to get it expedited to this country with as little delay as possible. The battalion having been on the Irish establishment, the clothing will come from thence through Messrs. Armit and Borough, Army Agents, Dublin.

I have the honour to be, Sir,

Your most obedient humble servant,

(Signed) *W. G. Davy*

To the Military Secretary to his Excellency the Commander of the Forces

Lisbon

We will close this account of difficulties which the commanding officer had to struggle with in the recruiting of his battalion by letters of this same year, though of rather later date.

After the 'suspected men' had been selected, the new arrangements of the army under Sir Arthur Wellesley were made, and he (who had witnessed their behaviour) expressed his fullest confidence in them.

Again they were tested, by the hardest test to which a battalion can be subjected, namely, that of constant detachments; but they will be shown to have maintained at the 'passage of the Douro' and the battle of 'Talavera de la Reyna' all the qualities which at Roleia and Vimeiro gained them the high reward of praise from Sir Arthur.

But losses in these actions, to say nothing of sickness and invaliding, lost them many men; and Major Davy again addressed a letter to the commander of the forces on the important topic of enlistment.

A month later, when he was trying to complete his strength of riflemen, and wanted to promote some, and add others to the list of non-commissioned officers, he was met by an order for reduction of establishment; and then he addressed an able letter to the Under-Secretary for War. But it was returned to him by Lord Palmerston with directions to apply to the commander-in-chief, and then, on the 13th of December 1809, he forwarded a duplicate copy of the same to Lieutenant-Colonel Betham for the consideration of the commander-in-chief. The following are copies of these letters:

Badajos
Sept. 13th, 1809
Sir,
Feeling exceedingly anxious to get the 5th battalion 60th Foot, now so much reduced, completed to its establishment, I take the liberty of requesting you to propose to his Excellency to write to England for that purpose. An opportunity is now offered of obtaining some most excellent recruits from among the prisoners taken at Flushing, but I am aware, that, unless the strongest instances are made to the contrary, we shall be filled up with a class of men who might again put the reputation

of the battalion to hazard. I beg leave to mention that this was one of the objects which dictated my application to his Excellency for leave, in order that I might have it in my power to select men fit for the service, and therefore request he will mention that the Austrian-Hungarians, together with all Germans north of the Rhine, particularly Hessians, are those upon which we can place the most dependence.

I last year brought at some hazard from Oporto with me 200 fine Swiss recruits, who had served as Voltigeurs in the French army, and were particularly calculated for our arm, but have been much disappointed to find that they have, since, all been given to the 2nd battalion 60th Foot destined for the West Indies.

I have the honour to be, Sir,

Your most obedient humble servant,

(Signed) *W. G. Davy*

To Colonel Bathurst

Military Secretary to his Excellency the Commander of the Forces

In the following month Major Davy wrote a long letter to England, to the Secretary of War, on the same subject.

Badajos

Oct. 17th, 1809

Sir,

Having this day only received a duplicate of a letter dated the 29th March 1809 (original never came to hand) from Messrs. Greenwood and Cox acquainting me that a reduction of the 5th battalion 60th Foot had taken place from the 25th Dec. last to the establishment of one S. M., one Q. M. S., one O. S., one P. M. S., forty S., forty C, eighteen D., three F. 750 P., I beg leave to submit to your consideration some reasons respecting the same as relative to a Rifle Corps, in the situation and of the composition of the 5th battalion 60th Foot, such as I trust will justify me in requesting that the number of N.C.O.'s. may be kept up to its present strength.

I beg leave to mention that the battalion embarked from Ireland for foreign service with not less than eighteen or twenty officers, including vacant commissions, short of its establishment, and the consequent injury to the service so deeply felt, and conspicuously instanced in this corps, may in some measure be attributed to this cause.

It is evident that a Rifle Corps acting as this has done (having constantly been employed during both, the campaigns in Spain and Portugal by detachments not only of companies, but of subalterns' and serjeants' parties, and covering an extended chain of outposts—one I recollect of more than ten miles—as well as performing the duties of light troops) cannot fairly admit of a parallel with the situation of regiments of the line, nor of an application of those regulations which are more particularly referable to the latter: and, if this in a general point of view may be thought to merit consideration, I cannot but conceive that it bears with still greater force when applied to a regiment of foreigners, acting in a foreign country in whose service many of the subjects composing the corps have received pay, and against an enemy from whose armies a no less proportion have also deserted, and obviously demonstrates the necessity of having (independently of other considerations) a greater number of officers, and N.C.O.'s. to preserve that control which is requisite, and restrain the dispersion (inherent to light troops, particularly Tirailleurs) which in the field after the firing of the first shot I should otherwise apprehend would take place.

The service of these corps has been so imperfectly understood in England (I trust I may be pardoned the observation) that they have, generally speaking, been modelled upon the system of regiments of the line, which is as generally inapplicable to them; and manifold inconveniences and difficulties have resulted from hence.

And here I beg leave to remark that, though by the creation of a serjeant a regiment of the line loses a musket, a Rifle Corps suffers no diminution in this respect in its strength; on the contrary, the serjeants are considered as the best marksmen, and by their example and instructions to others may make themselves conspicuously useful. I should willingly give up ten bugle-men for a similar augmentation of this class of N.C.O., the former being comparatively unnecessarily numerous, and of little service, and the latter by far too few for the important duties they have to discharge.

It was a maxim of the late Sir John Moore, and which he several times repeated to me, that "one rifleman should be deemed an equivalent, when posted, to three sentries of the line, and that the parties must in all cases be commanded either by an officer or N.C.O."

It would be impossible to adhere to it unless an adequate proportion of the latter is admitted, and so many economical and interior duties have the N.C.O.'s of this corps (by an ill-judged interference with them) to discharge in conjunction with the line, that we really sometimes experience much difficulty in executing them.

Many observations might be added upon these heads, but I fear I have rendered an apology necessary for trespassing on your time with those already stated. I have the honour to subjoin a return of the present strength, and beg leave to conclude with remarking that though, for a considerable time, I did not fill up vacancies from a wish to select the men best qualified for the situation, yet after the action of Talavera (the necessity of rewarding those who had, by their conduct, entitled themselves to it, and the diminution of the officers by wounds, and sickness, and capture, one of the companies being now commanded by an ensign, and many having no more than one officer actually present) I felt it my duty to meet these circumstances by appointing N.C.O.'s to the full establishment, having received no directions to the contrary, and trust they will be allowed to continue in their respective situations.

I shall however fill up no vacancies that may hereafter occur until I have the honour to receive your orders.

I have the honour to be, Sir,

Your most obedient humble servant,

(Signed) *W. G. Davy*

Major commanding 5th Battalion 60th.

To the Right Hon. the Secretary at War

Strength of 5th battalion 60th Regiment: fifty-four serjeants, fifty corporals, fourteen buglers, 561 privates.

Copy sent to Military Secretary to the Commander-in-Chief.

This letter was acknowledged by Lord Palmerston, the then Under-Secretary at War, who wrote to Major Davy from the War Office on the 8th of November 1809, referring him to the commander -in-chief, 'with whom the arrangements for altering the military establishments originate,' and in consequence of this reply Major Davy forwarded a copy if this letter to Lieutenant-Colonel Betham on the 13th of December 1809.

We have exhausted the argument of dates in analysing the routes of Sir J. Moore and the 5th battalion 60th, and it must be said that Napier is in the main right, and Mr. Carter quite wrong as regards the 5th 60th. But Mr. Carter's mistake is natural; he probably had access to returns showing the formation of Moore's army, but had nothing to point out to him the facts relating to a withdrawal of the 5th battalion just before the concentration of the forces near Astorga. Who did know these details until now? The Davy papers have cleared up what even Sir William Napier only imperfectly knew.

Mr. Carter says that '2nd battalion 60th were at Corunna under Lieutenant-Colonel Codd,' and this we believe to be quite true. They came out with Sir David Baird's force. They were only 270 strong, and were left at Corunna in garrison. They returned 212 in number, and being a weak battalion and on the spot, were perhaps placed on board the transports among the very first embarked on the 14th and 15th of January 1809. At any rate they never have been named as being in the battle, and probably never fired a shot in Spain.

The 2nd battalion then could have no claim to the honours of of repulsing Soult; and the 5th battalion were far away; and two such negatives will not, I think, make an affirmative to the claim of a share in the honours of 'Corunna.'[2]

We have alluded more than once to the muster roll of December 1809, and (as we shall not refer to it again) let us here pick out one of the plums from it (and there is much interest in the whole).

In No. 2 (B), or Captain de Salaberry's company, there is a corporal named John Schwalbach, against whose name is written the remark—'Discharged by order of Lieutenant-General Sir Arthur Wellesley, 14th June 1808.'

At first sight it might be understood that he was a 'suspected' man, but it was far otherwise. John Schwalbach was a man

2. In Hart's *Annual Army List for 1862* p. 27, the note at the bottom page is No. 119, and states—'Major General MacArthur was present at the Battle of Corunna as an ensign in the 60th regiment.' Major Morrah of the 60th Rifles was then Adjutant of 2nd battalion 60th at Portsmouth, having just returned with them from the north of China. He wrote to General MacArthur on the subject, who told him in reply that it was the 2nd battalion 60th he was serving with, and that they were in reserve; but where the reserve was is still left unknown.
It is stated also in the *Royal Military Chronicle,* 1813, vol. 6. p. 311, that the 2nd battalion 59th and do. 60th (or Royal American) were allowed to carry Corunna on their colours, and appointments in commemoration of the action of January 16th, 1809.

of mark; he had already attracted the notice of his regimental superiors, and his commanding officer had promoted him to the rank of corporal, and (unable to do more as his strength was to be reduced) had appointed him lance serjeant.

It was presumably to employ him in one of the Caçadores regiments that Sir Arthur directed his discharge, and good use he made of his opportunities. From 1809 to the end of the war he had a fine 'school of arms,' and the best of schoolmasters. For the remainder of his days Schwalbach made Portugal his adopted country, and rose high in its service. In 1839 he was a major, and employed as a special commissioner, as there was Brazilian trouble for the Portuguese; and in 1847 he was a general commanding in the royal army, and had been ennobled for his services.

There appeared a sketch of him in January, 1847, in the *Illustrated London News*, with a woodcut portrait of him and his rival general. From this sketch we extract the following landmarks of his career:

Johan Schwalbach is one of the commanders of the royal troops at present operating with Marshal Saldanha against Das Antas and the Insurgents. As is evident from his name he is a German; but he has been for many years in the Portuguese service. He was a favourite officer of Don Pedro, who raised him from the rank of lieutenant to that of general, and gave him the title of Baron von Setabal. His latest achievement is the occupation of the place from which he takes his title (an important town). He is much dreaded by the democrats, and they evacuated it—popular forces, junta, and all—three hours before he arrived. Schwalbach is a brave soldier and an able general; he is a military commander and nothing else; never having mixed himself up with politics at all. It is difficult to foresee what will be the issue of these convulsions. Constitutional government is impossible: for no one can be trusted with power, and the mass of the people neither comprehend nor care for political principles.

It is worthy of note that Saldanha, the Queen's general, under whom Schwalbach was serving, and General das Antas his opponent, and the leader of the insurrection in Portugal, both served under Lord Wellington against the French, Das Antas having been a subaltern, and afterwards a captain, in the 7th battalion of Cacadores.[3]

---

3. See *Illustrated London News*, January 2nd, 1847.

CHAPTER 5

Douro & Talavera: 1809

After the retreat to Corunna there remained in the Peninsula about 8000 English under Cradock, chiefly in and about Lisbon, who were raised to 14,000 at the end of February, by the arrival of reinforcements; the Portuguese troops were not more than 9000. The affairs of Spain were still more, unpromising. Blake had only 8000 or 9000 ragged and half-starved troops in the Galician mountains; Castanos, who had been reinforced from Andalusia, had 25,000 at Toledo, and 10,000 more were at Badajos. The Arragonese and Catalonians were fully occupied within their own pounds; and altogether there were not more than 120,000 men, scattered all over the Peninsula, to resist a French force amounting, even after the departure of the Guards to Germany, to 280,000 infantry and 40,000 cavalry. General Beresford, appointed a marshal in the Portuguese service, had raised 20,000 new levies to be taken into British pay, but the greatest encouragement arose from the landing of Sir Arthur Wellesley with fresh troops at Lisbon.

The British Government had resolved not to abandon Portugal. They had consulted Sir Arthur on the placing the Portuguese army under a British general, and asked him for a plan of operations; he recommended Beresford for the command mentioned, and to the second question he replied by an exceedingly well drawn up *Memorandum on the Defence of*

Portugal (dated London, March 7, 1809; *vid. Wellington Despatches*); and the public voice having already marked him out as the most fitting man to be entrusted with the chief command of the army, the Corunna army was sent speedily back to the Tagus, as fast as the regiments could be made efficient, and on the 22nd of April he arrived himself in Lisbon and was made marshal-general of the armies.

The 22nd of April, 1809, is indeed an important epoch, a day to be remembered, a day from which the annals of the Peninsula, instead of a confused and involved narrative of separate operations, begin to present a connected and consecutive stream of events. He immediately infused new life into every department, military and civil, and gave courage and assurance to the direction of affairs.[1]

On the 27th of April the following order was published:

General Order
Adjutant-General's Office
Lisbon
April 27th, 1809
His Majesty has been pleased to appoint Lieutenant-General Sir Arthur Wellesley, K.B., to be Commander of his Forces in Portugal; and his Excellency having arrived in this country to assume the command, all reports, applications, &c. are henceforth to be addressed to him through the usual channels. His Excellency having appointed the following officers *aides-de-camp*, they are to be obeyed accordingly.
Lieutenant-Colonel Bathurst
60th Foot, Military Secretary
Staff of the Forces in Portugal
Captain Francis Cockburn, 60th Foot, D. A. Adjutant-General. Lieutenant-Colonel James Bathurst, 60th Foot, Assist.Q.-M.-Gen.

---

1. See *Epitome of Alison*, and Sir E. Cust's *Annals of the Wars*.

On the same day orders were issued for the collection and march of the troops upon Oporto, and in about a week the whole force destined for the north of Portugal was assembled at Coimbra. The following are extracts from the orders of that date:

Coimbra
May 6th, 1809
1. The commander of the forces recommends the companies of the 5th battalion of the 60th Regiment to the particular care and attention of the general officers commanding the brigades of infantry to which they are attached; they will find them to be most useful, active, and brave troops in the field, and that they will add essentially to the strength of the brigades.

Major Davy will continue to superintend the economy and discipline of the whole battalion, and for this purpose will remain with that part of the army which will be most convenient to him with a view to that object.

Coimbra
May 4th, 1809
2. The light infantry companies belonging to, and the Riflemen attached to each brigade of infantry are to be formed together on the left of the brigade under the command of a field officer, or captain of light infantry of the brigade, to be fixed upon by the officer who commands it. Upon all occasions in which the brigade may be formed in line, or in column, when the brigade shall be formed for the purpose of opposing an enemy, the light infantry companies and Riflemen will be of course in the front, flank, or rear, according to the circumstances of the ground and the nature of the operation to be performed.

Major Davy having received his instructions from Sir

Arthur proceeded to distribute his battalion again in the same way that the general had adopted the previous year on disembarking at Mondego Bay; and, thanks to the regimental order book, an extract from it will enable us to know what companies were detached and to what brigades.

Regimental Orders
Coimbra
May 4th, 1809
Agreeably to the general order of this day, the battalion will be divided in the following manner:
Major Davy and staff to Major-General Tilson's brigade, with:
Major Galiffe's company,
Captain de Salaberry's company,
Captain Andrews' company,
Captain Schoëdde's company,
Captain Blassiere's company.
Captain McMahon's[3] company to Brigd.-General A. Campbell.
Captain Hames' company to Brigd.-General F. Campbell.
Captain Wend's company to Major-General Hill.
Captain Wolf's company to Brigd.-General Cameron.
Captain Prevost's company to Brigd.-General Sontag.
Major Woodgate will remain to superintend these five companies, and take measures to obtain instructions from the adjutant-general relative to the subsistence for them.

And the following orders to the battalion, letter of instructions to Major Woodgate, and Major Davy's own memoran-

3. Captain McMahon could not have marched with his company, for on April 15th be had met with an accident, the effects of which he felt for many years, if not the whole of his remaining life. The Commander of the Forces had desired, by a 'General Order,' that all officers commanding companies of Rifle regiments should be mounted; and on that date, the 5th battalion being halted on the line of march, Captain McMahon received a sudden order to advance quickly with his company, when in attempting to spring into his saddle he snapped the 'tendon Achilles.'

dum as to his placing himself in such position as best to supervise the whole, will be of interest to read before we follow the army to the field.

Regimental Orders.
Coimbra
May 5th, 1809

1. The detachment under command of Major Woodgate, and the officers commanding companies attached to the several brigades, will send all returns and reports to their respective brigadiers. Duplicates of the weekly states, and monthly returns, together with the muster rolls, to be sent in sufficient time to the commanding officer to enable him to make out the general returns at the stated periods, addressed to 'The Adjutant-General's Office at Headquarters,' by those companies which have immediate communication with the commanding officer.

The daily states of those companies within the reach of the commanding officer will be sent to him as usual.

2; All standing, or such orders as may be given during the division of the battalion, must be strictly and rigidly executed, as the commanding officer will frequently visit the companies attached to the several brigades, and expects to find no deviation from them.

3. All requisitions must be made through the respective brigades, and reported by the first opportunity, as well as all extraordinaries, to the commanding officer.

4. The major trusts that every officer of the battalion will use his best endeavours, in conjunction with himself, to keep up the interior economy and discipline of the battalion under circumstances in which he is well aware there are great difficulties to be encountered; but he trusts their zeal and attention will surmount them.

5. Ensign Fürst will act as adjutant to Major Woodgate's detail.

6. Lance-Serjeant Schwalbach[4] to be attached to Captain Wend's company.

Coimbra
May 5th, 1809
Sir,

As the headquarters of the battalion for the present is attached to one of the companies brigaded with the army, you will be pleased to consider yourself as commanding officer of the detachment of the five companies of the battalion now with you and act accordingly.

You will of course send in the regular returns, as required by general orders, at the stated periods to your brigadier, and duplicates of the same to me, addressed to the "Adjutant-General's Office," in sufficient time to enable me to make out the general states, &c. of the regiment.

You will of course also comply with His Majesty's regulations concerning the mustering of the companies; or, if divided, enjoin the several officers commanding companies to do the same, the muster rolls to be of course transmitted to me.

I have not been able, with every representation to Sir A. Wellesley himself, to procure more than a certain proportion of pay upon the estimates of the current month, of which Captain Andrews will be the bearer, and distribute it agreeably to my directions.

Ensign Fürst will also accompany Captain Andrews, and will, for the present, do the duty of adjutant to the detachment (Lieutenant Franchini's presence being absolutely required with his company). It will also be necessary for you to appoint an officer to act as quartermaster should you deem it requisite. Mr. Kemmeter will do duty as adjutant with me.

---

4. For notice of this N. C. O., see end of last chapter.

You will be pleased to use your utmost endeavours to keep the clothing as much in repair as its condition will admit, and see the men as much as possible provided with necessaries. I am aware that you will have, as well as myself, considerable difficulties to encounter in the situation in which the battalion has been placed since its landing in Portugal, almost unprecedented in the army; but I doubt not that you will, as well as myself, use your utmost endeavours for the best of the battalion and the service.

Referring to the authority already given by the adjutant-general, I conceive you to be entitled to draw the allowances for the acting adjutant and quartermaster of your detachment should you deem it necessary to have officers in those situations.

I have the honour to be, Sir,

Your most obedient, humble servant,

(Signed) *W. G. Davy*

To Major Woodgate

Memorandum by Major Davy

The foregoing letter and orders were occasioned by the general orders of yesterday, 4th May 1809, by which the regiment was again broken up into detachments; five companies proceeding, under the command of Major Woodgate, with Major-General Tilson's army, and the remaining five companies brigaded with the army, as follows:

Captains Andrews', Salaberry's, McMahon's, Schoëdde's, and Blassiere's companies, under the command of Major Woodgate, to Major-General Tilson's brigade, attached to Marshal Beresford.

Major Galiffe's to Brigd.-General A. Campbell.

Captain Hames' to Brigd.-General H. Campbell.

Captain Wend's to Major-General Hill.

Captain Wolff's to Brigd.-General Cameron.

Captain Prevost's to Brigd.-General Sontag.'

In consequence of which I immediately addressed a letter to the adjutant-general representing the necessity of my being allowed to attach myself to either brigade as circumstances might require, and waited upon Sir Arthur to state the difficulties and consequences which I apprehended would ensue from the battalion being divided, he replied thus:

Adjutant-General's Office
Coimbra
May 4th, 1809
Sir,
I am directed by the Commander of the Forces to acquaint you that he approves of your idea of attaching yourself to such part of your regiment where you may conceive your services most necessary.
I am likewise to desire you will communicate immediately with Marshal Beresford relative to the five companies which are to march tomorrow.
I have the honour to be, Sir,
Your obedient humble servant,
(Signed) *Charles Stewart*
Adjutant-General
To Major Davy,
5th Batt. 60th Regtiment

One cannot read Major Davy's orders without admiring his great attention to details; nothing seems to escape him that can tend to the comfort of those under him, or the efficiency of his battalion.

Their pay, their subsistence, their arms and ammunition are absorbing his constant attention. He was most particular about daily parades on the line of march in camp; no excuse must be taken. With or without clothes, come the rifleman must. One cannot but smile at the following order when on the march in Portugal:

> On halting-days the officers commanding companies will inspect their men at eleven o'clock roll-call, and they will pay particular attention to the state of the arms, ammunition, and accoutrements. The blue pantaloons which have been torn upon the march are immediately to be repaired, and those men who are under the absolute necessity of wearing their white drawers must appear with them well washed and cleaned. The stocks are to be worn, and the rosettes and bugles which have been torn out of the caps are to be replaced, etc.[5]

The insisting that riflemen should parade, even without their 'blue pantaloons,' reminds one of the lessons on 'duty before decency' which Mr. Midshipman Easy gave to Mr. Biggs the boatswain, when he made him come up the side and on to the deck of H.M.S. *Harpy*, without any clean white drawers though to confine his shirt-tail which was fluttering in the breeze.

Joking apart, it is as necessary an order now as it was then, that no regiment or detachment should omit its daily parade for inspection, however hard and long may have been the day's march over, or the next day's march to come.

These arrangements having been made on the 5th, on the 7th May Marshal Beresford was detached with a mixed force, 6000 being Portuguese, to the upper Douro, to operate from the side of Lamego. This force, be it remembered, had five companies of the 5th 60th included in it.

The same day the main body of the British army advanced from Coimbra towards the Vouga river. Two divisions of infantry, one the advanced guard consisting of the King's German Legion and Brigadier-General R. Stewart's brigade,

---

5. In another place necessity forces him to authorise the men cutting away the skirts to patch the upper part of their jackets.

with a brigade of six and another of three-pounders under Lieutenant-General Paget; the other comprising the Guards, Brigadier-Generals Campbell's and Sontag's brigades, with a brigade of six-pounders under Lieutenant-General Sherbrooke, marched by the high road to Oporto, accompanied by the cavalry under Brigadier-General Payne; while a third division of infantry, composed of his own and Brigadier-General Cameron's brigades, and a brigade of six-pounders, under Major-General Hill, took the road to Aveiro, situated at the southern extremity of the Lake of Ovar which runs parallel to the coast.

These halted on the 8th, to afford time to Marshal Beresford with his corps to arrive upon the upper Douro.

Soult was then at Oporto, Victor at Merida, but the frontier insurrection debarred all intercourse between them; and it was against Soult that the British troops were directed. Their strength was 16,000 men (of which 1500 were cavalry), with twenty-four guns under the personal command of Sir Arthur Wellesley.

The advanced posts met on the 11th of May, but the French, retreating rapidly, crossed the Douro and burned the bridge of boats; and Sir Arthur Wellesley says in the despatches:

It was important, with a view to the operations of Marshal Beresford, that I should cross the Douro immediately; and I had sent Major-General Murray in the morning with a battalion of the King's German Legion, a squadron of cavalry, and two six-pounders, to endeavour to collect boats, and if possible to cross the river at Avintas, about four miles above Oporto; and I had as many boats as could be collected brought to the ferry immediately above the towns of Oporto and Villa Nova.

Before eight o'clock on the morning of the 12th the British army was secretly concentrated behind a rocky height, on which stood a convent immediately facing Oporto. The

Douro rolled in front, deep, swift, and more than 300 yards wide, and 10,000 veterans guarded the opposite bank; and moreover, unless the river be passed, the French might secure a retreat, and defeat Beresford in passing, being able with two marches to reach the Tamega.

But Soult was unsuspicious and negligent. Suddenly a large unfinished building called the Seminary caught Sir Arthur's eye, having easy access to the water, and a high wall extending on each side to the bank of the river and enclosing space for two battalions.

Colonel Waters discovered a poor barber who had come over the river the night before in a small skiff, and readily agreed to go back: accompanied by the Prior of Amarante, Waters crossed unperceived and returned with three barges.

Eighteen guns were placed in battery on the convent rock. At ten o'clock, the French being tranquil and unsuspicious, the British wondering and expectant, Sir Arthur was told that one boat was ready. 'Well, let the men cross,' was the laconic reply; and a quarter of an hour afterwards an officer and twenty-five soldiers of the Buffs were silently placed on the other side of the Douro in the midst of the French army[6].

The Seminary was thus gained, all remained quiet, and a second boat passed. With the crossing of the third boat the tumult began, and secrecy was no longer valuable. The army crowded to the bank; Paget and Hill's divisions pressing to the point of passage, Sherbrooke's to where the bridge had been cut away the night before. Paget passed in the third boat, but was badly wounded; Hill took his place. The force accumulated; the fight waxed hotter; the (English battery on the convent rock swept the enclosure, and the struggle was such that Sir Arthur was only restrained from crossing by the remonstrances of those about him and the confidence he had in Hill. Soon however some citizens were seen bringing over several

6. See Sir William Napier's account.

94

great boats to Sherbrooke, while a prolonged shout from the streets and the waving of handkerchiefs from the windows gave notice that the enemy had abandoned the lower town.

We may not follow Napier, much as one is tempted to do so, into all the details of this brilliant feat of arms. The French were forced to a hasty retreat, abandoning their sick and great part of their stores; and so complete was the surprise that Wellesley sat down to the dinner prepared for Soult.

Sir Arthur at this minute was unaware of what Beresford had done, but he had performed great service, even of more importance than was at first apparent. He, and half of the 5th 60th with him, had attacked Loison, who on the 10th had fallen back from Pezoa de Regoa on the Douro when Beresford crossed that river.

Beresford was then in the position required for turning Soult on to the Chaves road. On the 11th he followed up Loison briskly, while a Portuguese insurgent force under General Sylveira closed on his flank. The 12th his outposts were driven into Amarante, and next day he abandoned that place.

On the 14th Sir Arthur moved forward himself, and the 15th had reached Braga; Beresford was near Chaves, Sylveira marching toward Salamonde, and Soult's capture seemed inevitable to his pursuers; he was however beyond their toils, having by a surprising effort extricated himself from perils as great as ever beset a general.

Driven across the Sousa, he passed Valonga, and crossing the mountains arrived at Carvalho d'Este, thus gaining a day's march and baffling the combination to surround him.

But on the 16th Sir Arthur Wellesley, quitting Braga in the morning, overtook Soult's rear-guard in the evening at Salamonde before it had crossed the Ponte Nova. Some light troops turned the French left, Sherbrooke assailed their front, and after one discharge they fled by the right to the Ponte Nova; but ere they could cross the bridge the British artillery was up and crushed them cruelly.

The passage of the Douro must ever be considered one of the most brilliant acts of war, and those who were with Beresford, as well as those with Sir Arthur, might be proud at having joined in such an operation.

On the 13th May, 1809, General Hill published the following 'Brigade Order':

> Major-General Hill is happy to embrace the earliest opportunity of acknowledging the highly distinguished conduct of the brigade under his command in the action of yesterday. Their cool and determined behaviour in passing the Douro, their subsequent advance to take up and occupy a post on the high ground above that river, and their ready and gallant conduct in receiving and repelling the attack of the enemy, taking their guns, and afterwards completely driving them, although much superior in number, from all the towns and suburbs of Oporto before any reinforcement came up, were never surpassed on any occasion.
>
> The Major-General therefore feels the highest satisfaction in returning his best thanks to Lieutenant-Colonel Drummond and Captain Wend, and the company of the 60th attached to his brigade, and begs that the same will be conveyed to the officers and men of these gallant corps accordingly.

After this brilliant opening of the campaign, Wellesley returned to Oporto, where he was detained above a month by the want of money, and not less by the necessity of enforcing order among his troops, whose conduct to the natives (as he himself said) was 'worse than that of an enemy.'

Sir Arthur had however in this short campaign of twenty-eight days recovered the second city of the kingdom of Portugal and driven the invader ignominiously across the border, with his army, as Jomini said, 'in a far worse condition than Sir John Moore's had been.' Having beaten Junot first, and then

Soult, the Marshal of highest reputation in the French army, he now prepared to try his strength with Marshals Jourdan and Victor. The latter had advanced his outposts as far as Castello Blanco, but on hearing of Soult's misfortunes and Wellesley's approach fell back on Almaraz and Torremocha.

Sir Arthur had gone to Aveiro, and from Aveiro he proceeded to Coimbra, where his head-quarters were established on the 28th May; and on the 8th June he was at Abrantes. His progress was slow from the difficulties which he encountered, but he used the time to send an able staff officer, Lieut.-Colonel Burke, to Cuesta's head-quarters to arrange a plan of campaign.

At this period there were about 250,000 French troops of all arms. Within hundred miles round Madrid were 100,000 men, King Joseph occupying the capital with 5000. Mortier with some 18,000 was two marches from Toledo, at Villa Castin; Sebastiani at Toledo with 12,000, and Victor at Cassares with 28,000. Soult had rapidly refitted at Lugo and advanced to Salamanca, where being joined to Ney he could bring into line 30,000 men.

Wellesley had at Abrantes 19,000 excellent troops; Mackenzie was at Alcantara with 8000, of which 2000 only were English; Sir Robert Wilson among the mountains of Estremadura with 4000 partisans, Beresford at Almeida with 15,000 Portuguese, and the Duque del Parque with 12,000 Spaniards in and about Ciudad Rodrigo.

Cuesta had 40,000 ill-armed and ill-disciplined Spaniards between Medellin and Cassares; while Venegas, with 26,000, lay among the mountains of Toledo.

The English broke up from Abrantes, and on the 18th July effected their junction with Cuesta at Oropaga.

On the 22nd Wellesley entered Talavera, a mile or two beyond which Victor with 22,000 men had taken up a position.

In consequence of the arrival of reinforcements in July, a new distribution of the regiments and brigades look place at Placentia, and that of the 5th 60th became as follows:

One company was now with Brigadier-General Campbell (Guards), 1st division under Lieutenant-General Sherbrooke. One company with Cameron's brigade, 1st division under Lieutenant-General Sherbrooke. One company with General Tilson in 2nd division, Major-General Hill. Five companies with Colonel Donkin, 3rd division, Major-General Mackenzie.

One company with 1st brigade and one company with 2nd brigade of 4th division, Brigadier-General A. Campbell.

Sir Arthur seeing the faulty position of Victor on the 22nd would have attacked him on the 23rd, but Cuesta would not fight, and Victor retired at his leisure across the Alberche towards Toledo; where in the course of the 24th, 25th, and 26th, Joseph having united his own force with that of Sebastiani, joined him, and Joseph found himself at the head of 50,000 combatants.

No sooner did Victor retire than Cuesta, who would not fight on the 23rd, now persisted in spite of Wellesley's protestation against the rash act, followed him, and on the 26th Victor met Cuesta at Alcabon and completely defeated him. Back came the Spaniards in confusion, and on the 27th Cuesta placed his army entirely at Wellesley's disposal.

It was now clear to Sir Arthur[7] that a general action might be expected, and he resolved not to decline it, but proceeded to take up as good a position as he could on ground he had already selected and strengthened with some field-works on a line perpendicular to the Tagus.

The country in front was a plain, open near this position, but beyond it covered with olive and cork trees up to the Alberche. A series of unconnected hills, steep, yet of moderate height, and running parallel with the Tagus at a distance of two miles, bounded this plain on the left, and half a mile beyond them was a mountain-ridge from which they were separated by a rugged valley.

---

7. See Alison's *Epitome*, Napier's *Battles and Sieges* and Gleig's *Life of Wellington*.

The Spanish infantry were posted on the right in two lines, having their flanks resting on Talavera which touched the river. Their left was closed by a mound crowned with a large field redoubt, behind which a brigade of British cavalry were posted.

The British were drawn up on the open and rugged ground to the left, whence a rivulet ran along the front of the whole position.

The combined armies then, with 44,000 infantry, 10,000 cavalry, and 100 pieces of artillery, offered battle to King Joseph coming on with 80 guns and 50,000 men, 7000 being cavalry.

On the 27th, before daylight, the French were on the march to attack, and at one o'clock Victor reached the heights of Salinas overhanging the Alberche, whence he could see the dust raised by the allies taking up their position, though the forest masked the dispositions.

Victor first marched on the Casa de Salinas, a house situated in the plain below. To reach it he had to ford the Alberche and penetrate two miles through the forest; yet the position of M'Kenzie's division was indicated by the dust, and as the British cavalry had sent no patrols, the post was surprised. Sir Arthur himself, who was reconnoitring from the house, very hardly escaped capture; and the French charged so hotly, the English brigades were separated, fired on each other, and were driven in disorder through the forest into the open plain. In the midst of this confusion the 45th, a stubborn old regiment, accompanied by some companies of the 60th riflemen, kept good array, and on them Sir Arthur rallied the others and checked the enemy, covering his retreat with cavalry; yet he lost 400 men, and the retrograde movement was hastily made in the face of both armies.[8]

M'Kenzie with one brigade now took post behind the Guards' centre; but Colonel Donkin (who had with his brigade five companies of 5th 60th), seeing the hill on the ex-

8. See Napier's *Battles and Sieges*.

treme left unoccupied, crowned it with the other brigade and filled the position.

Victor issuing from the forest in martial order crossed the plain, crowned the hill opposite to Donkin, and opened a heavy cannonade. Sebastiani pushed forward his light cavalry and attacked the Spaniards, who fled disgracefully. But the left of the English line displayed the greatest intrepidity. The round hill at the extremity was of easy ascent in rear, but steep and rugged towards the French, and was also protected there by the deep watercourse at the bottom. Nevertheless Victor, seeing Donkin's brigade was not numerous and the summit of the hill still naked of troops, thought to seize the latter by a sudden assault.

The sun was sinking, but the twilight and the confusion amongst the Spaniards appeared so favourable to the French Marshal that, without acquainting the King, he directed Ruffin's division, supported by Villatte, to attack, and Lapisse as a diversion to assail the German Legion.

Donkin beat back the French, but Hill, who had been ordered to support him, was nearly taken prisoner, and lost his Brigade-Major Fordyce. Hill however brought up the 29th regiment, the 48th and some detachments reinforced them, and Donkin presented a formidable front. Still Victor persevered; the fighting became vehement, in the darkness the flashing musketry showed how resolutely the struggle was maintained, the enemy's broken troops went down once more into the ravine below, and Lapisse abandoning his false attack on the Germans, the fighting of the 27th ceased.[9]

The British had lost 800 men, and the French 1000. On this day the 5th 60th lost three riflemen killed. Captain Wolff was wounded (severely) with four men, and nineteen were missing. With regard to the fighting on the 27th Sir Arthur reported thus to Lord Castlereagh (extract):

9. See Napier's *Battles and Sieges*.

At about two o'clock on the 27th the enemy appeared in strength on the left bank of the Alberche, and manifested an intention to attack General M'Kenzie's division; the attack was made before they could be withdrawn; but the troops, consisting of General M'Kenzie's and Colonel Donkin's brigades, and General Anson's brigade of cavalry, and supported by General Payne with the other four regiments of cavalry in the plain between Talavera and the wood, withdrew in good order, but with some loss, particularly by the 2nd battalion 87th Regiment and 2nd battalion 31st Regiment, in the wood.

Upon this occasion the steadiness and discipline of the 45th Regiment and 5th battalion 60th Regiment were conspicuous, and I had particular reason for being satisfied with the manner in which General M'Kenzie withdrew his advanced guard.

At daybreak on the 28th Ruffin's troops again menaced the British hill.

King Joseph consulted with Jourdan and Victor, who embarrassed him with opposite opinions. He inclined to Jourdan: but hearing that Soult could not come up, and that other combinations were threatening Madrid, his judgement was overpowered; and rejecting the better counsel he resolved first to try the chance of a battle.

On the renewal of the battle on the 28th the assault was repeated in the same quarter with the same ill success, and Joseph at length ordered a general charge of the whole line. But now was apparent the disadvantages of the attack in column against a steady opponent: torn by a rolling fire on each flank, and charged with the bayonet by Campbell's division, the French were repulsed with the loss of ten of their guns, while Ruffin and Villatte were once more foiled in an attack on the left; though some of the British cavalry pressing the pursuit too far were severely handled by the Polish lancers.

The centre meanwhile, where the Guards and German Legion were posted, was galled by the fire of fifty heavy cannon, under cover of which the division of Lapisse rushed up the hill with shouts of victory. But the assailants were bravely met and hurled back by the Guards. And though they, disordered by success, were in turn charged and broken by the French reserve, the advance of the 48th restored the battle; and the French, beaten at all points, drew off in good order across the Alberche.

The French loss in this great battle was put at 9,000 men. The British loss was 6,268.

The casualties of the 5th 60th on the 28th were—Captain and Brevet-Major Galiffe and Captain Andrews, slightly wounded; Lieutenants Zuhleke, Ritter, Mitchell, and Ensign Altenstein, all severely wounded; one bugler and six riflemen killed, one serjeant and twenty-four riflemen wounded, and two serjeants and ten men missing. There is one anecdote of the battle which must be here repeated, 'because it shows the coolness and intrepidity of the troops.'

> During the action of the 28th, and at the time the enemy's guns were playing on the British left, a solitary hare was started on the plain by a bursting shell; when it was discovered a shout was set up by the men, much to the annoyance of the general officer; it was ultimately shot by a soldier of the 60th Rifle Battalion.

Poor fellow, his name has not been recorded in history; but as the Spaniards kept Sir Arthur's troops starving, though on full rations themselves, the hare was probably of more value than many medals to the rifleman and his comrade in their bivouac after the battle.

The Commander of the Forces did full credit to his army in his despatches to Viscount Castlereagh; and on the 29th of July he published the following order of the day:

General Orders
Headquarters
Talavera de la Reyna
July 29th, 1809

The Commander of the Forces returns his thanks to the officers and troops for their gallant conduct on the two trying days of yesterday and the day before, on which they had been engaged with, and beaten off, the repeated attacks of an enemy of a superior number.

He has particularly to request that Lieutenant-General Sherbrooke will accept his thanks for the assistance he received from him, as well as for the manner in which he led on the division of the infantry under his command to the charge with bayonets.

Major-General Hill and Brigadier-General A. Campbell are also entitled in a particular manner to the acknowledgement of the Commander of the Forces for the gallantry and ability with which they maintained their posts against the attack made upon them by the enemy. The Commander of the Forces has also to acknowledge the ability with which the late Major-General M'Kenzie (whose loss the Commander of the Forces laments) withdrew the division under his command from the outpost in front of the enemy's army on the 27th; as well as to Colonel Donkin for his conduct on that occasion.

The Commander of the Forces likewise considers Lieutenant-General Payne and the cavalry, particularly Brigadier-General Anson and his brigade, who were principally engaged with the enemy, to be entitled to his acknowledgements; as well as Brigadier-General Howorth and his artillery, Major-General Tilson, Brigadier-General Stewart, and Brigadier-General Cameron, and the brigades under their command respectively.

He had opportunities of noticing the gallantry and discipline of the 5th battalion 60th Regiment, and 45th, on the 27th instant, and others on the 28th, and requests (among other commanding officers) that Major Davy will accept his particular thanks.

Colonel Bathurst (60th Regiment) also is among those of his staff who are specially thanked.

Proud and happy now might be Davy and his battalion. They had proved themselves equal to any other regiment, nay had one special praise, and it was to the commanding officer that much of it, most of it, was owing. His constant watchings, his warnings and rebukes when necessary, had borne fruit, and he had found room for satisfaction and commendation already. He had put the following in orders on the march:

Regimental Order
Castello Branco
July 2nd, 1859
The commanding officer in expressing his satisfaction to the officers and men of the detachment under the command of Major Woodgate on the favourable report he has received of the good behaviour of that part of the regiment corresponding with what he witnessed on the march to Guico, and return to Guarda, is happy at the same time to communicate to them that the companies attached to the several brigades of the army have been equally distinguished by the regularity of their conduct; and in participating with them the satisfaction he feels upon this occasion, doubts not that they will use every exertion to uphold the good name which the battalion has so justly acquired.

Major Davy had previously written to the colonel commandant of the battalion, General Sir George Prevost, giving an account of the 5th 60th, and in due course received the following pleasing reply:

Halifax
Nova Scotia
Oct. 16th, 1809
Dear Sir,

I received a few days ago your letter from Abrantes of the 25th June, and at the same time the newspapers announced the great and glorious victory of Talavera. From the report of Sir Arthur Wellesley, I have the satisfaction to learn the 5th battalion of the 60th Regiment did its duty, and in consequence, the apprehensions respecting the bravery and loyalty of the corps are replaced by confidence and admiration. Experience has taught me to ascribe, with few exceptions, to the commanding officer of a regiment its perfections and imperfections. On the present occasion you have my congratulations, and the battalion has my thanks for having rendered itself worthy of being considered a British regiment.

I shall have much satisfaction in receiving your particulars of a battle, which appears to have afforded the general a noble opportunity of displaying his science. I hope Major Galiffe and Captains Wolf and Andrews, and the subalterns who were wounded on that glorious occasion, have recovered.

I am, dear Sir, yours faithfully,
George Prevost

The two armies slept on the ground the night of the 28th, and still faced one another on the 29th. King Joseph, alarmed at the rumours of Wilson's advance on Madrid, broke up his bivouac and marched away, placing Victor on the farther bank of the Alberche, to crush the allied rear should Soult force them to retire.

Meanwhile Wellesley was well pleased at receiving the reinforcement of Crawfurd with the famous Light Division, who had marched sixty-two English miles in twenty-six hours (leaving only seventeen stragglers), but had arrived just too late for the battle.

On the 2nd of August Wellesley received information which determined him to double back and fight Soult, whom he believed to have but 15,000 men. With this view he marched on August 3rd to Oropesa, where he learnt for the first time that not 15,000 but 35,000 French troops were in the valley of the Tagus. There was not a moment to spare. Directing Crawfurd to pass and seize the mountains, and to destroy the bridge at Almaraz, which he made haste to do while Mortier loitered who might have prevented him, Wellesley turned towards Arzobispo; but he had not proceeded far when he met Cuesta with the Spanish army, who, alarmed at the rumours of Soult's advance, had abandoned his position on the Alberche, leaving the sick and wounded in Talavera to their fate. Thus it was that Captain Wolf, with the other officers and men who were wounded in the battle, became French prisoners.

That night and the following day (the 3rd and 4th) the English crossed the Tagus, and were safe.

Disregarding Cuesta and his Spaniards, Sir Arthur made for Deleytosa, where, during the 7th, 8th, and 9th, the scattered portions of his army were re-assembled; and on the 11th he established his head-quarters at Jaraicejo, on the great road through Estremadura towards Badajos and Lisbon. There he remained nine days. His eye was now steadily fixed upon Portugal, as Soult had recommended Joseph to march against Lisbon. The King however, not adopting the suggestion, broke up his army into portions; and Wellesley was thus enabled to fall back at his leisure upon Badajos, in the villages round which he placed his weary and worn army to recruit.

Wellesley, while these things were in progress, received from his own and the Spanish Government the rewards he had earned. He was created Baron and Viscount Wellington, by which immortal name we must henceforth designate him. The Duke of York and the English Minister of War wrote him letters of congratulation. The Parliament, when it met, voted its thanks to him and to his army, but the Opposition and a large party in the country could find no words but those of abuse and condemnation, and clamoured for the abandonment of the contest.[10]

Lord Wellington henceforth turned his attention almost entirely to the defence of Portugal. Early in October he paid a hasty visit to Lisbon, ostensibly to consult with Mr. Villiers about the resources of the kingdom, but really to consider the defence of the place; and with Colonel Fletcher he planned and ordered the execution of the lines of Torres Vedras. The operation was kept a profound secret, and when their existence and value were discovered in the following year, the 'lines' were almost as much a surprise to the English as they were to 'the darling Child of Victory.'

Wellington arrived in Lisbon on the 9th, quitted it on the 27th. On the 2nd November he was at Seville conferring with Lord Wellesley, and two days after accompanied him to Cadiz, whence he returned to Badajos.

By this time Major Davy also was expecting his well-earned promotion. He had been somewhat sore at his services, not having been recognised after Vimeiro, and had addressed a letter to Sir Arthur on the subject, which he had forwarded with the following communication to Colonel Gordon:

Abrantes
June 17th, 1809
From Lieutenant-General Sir Arthur Wellesley
To Colonel Gordon
Military Secretary to the Commander-in-Chief
My dear Colonel,
I enclose a memorial which has been given into my hands by Major Davy, which I beg you to lay before the commander-in-chief.

---

10. See Gleig's *Life of Wellington*.

I believe that H. R. H. the late Commander-in-Chief had intended to promote all the majors commanding battalions in the late service in Portugal, and certainly if the services of any battalion could give to their commanding officer a claim to promotion, the conduct and services of the 5th 60th Foot entitled their commanding officer to this advantage.

I have had every reason to be satisfied with them again upon this occasion (passage of the Douro), and I shall be very much obliged to you if you would recommend Major Davy to the favourable consideration of the commander-in-chief.

(Signed) *A. Wellesley*

But before his promotion arrived Davy had plenty of occupation: he was worried with a very bad paymaster, which caused much extra trouble to be thrown upon himself, and he had to place the office in the hands of Captain Andrews, from whom it was afterwards taken over by Captain Schoëdde; and he also was troubled with a Lieutenant Steitz.

During September, October, November, and December, Davy's letters are dated from Badajos; but in the last month of the year the battalion was moved to Montemor-o-Novo, as appears from a memorandum of his written at the former place, and a regimental order from the latter place of 13th December, 1809.

Memorandum by Major Davy

3rd December, 1809. The battalion by the detached companies, &c. commenced its march to Montemor-o-Novo.

4th December. Major Woodgate's detachment of five companies marched to Estremoz. I directed Major Woodgate, upon his arrival at Montemor on the 7th, to lend the quarter-master to Lisbon for the clothing.

10th December. The battalion was this day united at

Montemor-o-Novo, having been separated in detachments since 4th May.

The distribution of these detachments in November, 1809, may be of interest; it was as follows:

One company at Badajos with the brigade of Guards.

One company with Brigadier-General Cameron's brigade (1st division).

One company at Montijo with Major-General Tilson's brigade (2nd division).

Five companies and head-quarters with Colonel Donkin's brigade (3rd division) at Campo Mayor.

Two companies at Olivença (with the 4th division), and one attached to General Coles', the other to Colonel Kemmis' brigade.

On the 13th December, 1809, the regimental orders directed that, 'As it must appear absolutely necessary that a Rifle corps should always be prepared to act by detachments of companies or otherwise as the nature of the service on which they are employed may point out,' every officer is to make himself acquainted with the forms of Weekly States, Monthly Returns, Adjutant's. Rolls, Pay-lists, and those for Drawing Provisions and Camp Equipage; and officers commanding companies are to produce them at monthly musters, made out by their subalterns as if on detachment.

The companies of the battalion also were numbered:—

	No.		No.
Brevet-Major Galiffe's	1	Captain Hames'	6
Captain McMahon's	2	Captain Prevost's	7
Captain Andrews'	3	Captain Wolff's	8
Captain Blassieres'	4	Captain Schoëdde's	9
Captain Wend's[11]	5	Captain de Salaberry's	10

Strength fit for duty:—two majors, six captains, ten lieutenants, eight ensigns, six staff-sergeants, 470 riflemen.

---

11. This name sometimes appears as 'de Wendt.'

At the time of the move Davy was very anxious to be in England, and on December 5th, 1809, he addressed a private letter to Lord Wellington, requesting that 'after I have reported the battalion completely equipped for service your Lordship's permission to proceed to England' may be granted; and ending thus:

I confess that my former and present applications have not been uninfluenced by private motives of a nature of no mean consequence to me as an individual, but your Lordship will recollect with indulgence that I never lost sight of that which I considered as the most important, and the only apology which I can now offer to your Lordship for repeating it is by assuring you that there is no private interest, or inclination, which I shall not feel myself bound to sacrifice to your Lordship's commands.

Wellington acknowledged his reasons and granted his request, but whilst Davy was preparing to hand over his command to Woodgate, Lord Wellington's recommendation for promotion was being attended to, and at the end of the month he was gazetted a lieutenant-colonel in the '7th Veteran Battalion.'

He left the regiment for which he had done so much; but to us he yet lingers a little longer through his letters from Woodgate, Galiffe, Andrews, and others. And amongst those letters none perhaps would please him more than the spontaneous expression of regard for his riflemen which he received from General Cameron at the time of the move of the battalion to Montemor-o-Novo. He writes from Lobau thus:

Lobau
Dec. 4th, 1809
My dear Sir,
My little company of the 60th, under your command, marched from hence yesterday morning agreeable to

route. I was sorry to part with it, as consisting of the best behaved men I ever had attached to me in any military situation. There has been no instance of a complaint against any one of them since under my command. And should a similar distribution take place upon any future occasion I hope you will favour me with the same company back again. My interpreter Paylin came to me yesterday to know whether any allowance was made for interpreters under his circumstances. To which I replied in the negative. At least, that I did not know of any, but that you would be able to find out for him. He wishes to join his company and I send this by him. I believe he is a very steady honest man; and I hope you will promote him. At your convenience I shall be glad to hear that you enjoy good health and spirits, and I remain,
My dear Sir,
Yours faithfully,
Alan Cameron
Brigd.-General.
Major Davy
Commanding 5th Batt. 60th Regt.
Badajos

CHAPTER 6

Busaco: 1810

In December, 1809, the British army broke up from its position on the frontier of Estremadura, and took up another in Upper Beira, between the Mondego and the Tagus.

The Portuguese army was in a state of well nigh inefficiency, and it was therefore placed in cantonments in the interior of the country, with a determination not, if possible, to remove them until their re-formation and re-equipment had taken place.

So well was this matter attended to that by the first week in April Lord Wellington could bring into line, and place considerable reliance on, twelve battalions of regular infantry and four of chasseurs. These (estimated at 14,000 men) raised his force in Beira to 30,000; besides Hill's corps amounting to 12,000.

Whilst Wellington, desirous to provide securely for the future, kept his forces in cantonments, Colonel Fletcher was meanwhile busy in the rear on the famous lines of Torres Vedras.

In 1810 Napoleon sent 120,000 men from the Wagram army into Spain, who raised the forces of the French to 366,000.

Joseph, Soult, and Mortier, with 60,000, marched on Seville and besieged Cadiz.

The three corps of Regnier, Ney, and Junot were placed under the command of Massena, Napoleon himself supplying the plan of operations, leaving Massena only so much liberty of discretion as would enable him to feel he had an independent command.

He disposed of these forces in the following proportions:— 86,000 were to conquer Portugal; 20,000 with Drouet were to be in reserve at Valladolid; 15,000 under Serras covered the right towards Galicia.[1]

Before however we resume the sketch of military operations we will see what we can learn about the 5th battalion 60th from the letters to Davy from his officers.

As soon as they were united at Montemor-o-Novo orders were given to send an officer to Lisbon to bring up the clothing, and settle arrears of pay, about which there was much trouble.

Captain Andrews, who was acting-paymaster, was sent on this duty, and from Lisbon he wrote back to Major Davy. This is one of the last letters he got before leaving for England.

Lisbon
Feb. 1st, 1810
My dear Colonel,
From inaccuracy, not intended, my letter communicating your promotion withheld half your good-fortune. The account I gave was received from the town-major here, whom I questioned so particularly that I did not conceive a mistake possible; however I beg leave to give you the abstract from the Gazette which I have seen:

London

December 30th, 1809

7th Garrison Battalion, Major Wm. Gr. Davy, from the 60th Regiment, to be Lieut.-Colonel, vice Powlet removed to the 12th Veteran Battalion.

I was not much pleased with them for putting you off with a W. I. R. (as I supposed); but it would not have been kind to have commented on it. The thing is now

---

1. See *Epitome of Alison's History*, and Gleig's *Life of Wellington*.

Picton

done well, and you will have the whole army nearly at your option of choice, should you resolve to continue in the service; and indeed at your time of life, and advanced rank, it would be a great sacrifice to retire. Let such notions be reserved for beings like me, doomed to be drudges in the military drama of life.

I had the pleasure to receive your letter yesterday with the estimates, &c, and immediately proceeded to Hunter, who started a difficulty I could not anticipate. He objects to issuing the money without a warrant, which, he says, his instructions from the Treasury positively require; and, on the other hand, Colonel Peacocke says "he cannot, dare not, sign a warrant out of Lisbon;" but on my stating the whole affair he promises to make Hunter obey the letter received by Colonel Darrock in answer to mine from the adjutant-general at headquarters. But as all is bustle today landing troops I am put off till tomorrow, when I have no doubt of success, as Colonel Peacocke seems determined not to have the public service any longer trifled with on this head; so that at the latest I shall be able to leave this on Sunday or Monday, and as I wish on every account to get the two months' pay I shall act upon Colonel Pakenham's authority rather than on Colonel Bathurst's, which will be taking no advantage.

I have great pleasure to inform you of the success of your recommendation of poor Zuhleke; he is promoted in the 'Gazette' of the 15th *ult.*, *vice* Farrar of the 3rd battalion deceased. Your commissions shall be all punctually attended to. Please be so good as to remember me to Major Woodgate, and say that I shall not forget his Winsor-soap, &c.

I remain, dear Major,

Most faithfully yours,

A. Andrews

Mem. P.S.—Arrived at Lisbon on 31st and 1st, and landing this day the following regiments and detachments,
&c.:—74th, 79th, 94th Regiments; detachments of 300
men of the 11th, 45th, and 57th Regiments; a strong
detachment of artillery, and 400 recruit-horses for the
cavalry; making in all upwards of 4000 men brought out
by Generals Picton and Stuart.

General Tilson is here sick, but expects soon to join.
Report says a large part of our battalion is to be attached to General Hill's division to form the army of
the Tagus.

To Lieut.-Colonel Davy
Commanding 5th Battalion 60th Regiment
Montemor-o-Novo

'Poor Zuhleke' was one of those wounded and left behind
with Captain Wolf and others at Talavera; they had become
prisoners to the French, and he, unknowing of the promotion
in store for him, had just then written to his commanding officer a letter which was received on the 10th of January, 1810:

Madrid
Dec. 20th, 1809
Sir,
I had the honour of addressing two letters to you from
Talavera. The first, Mrs. Zuhleke writes me, came to
hand, and I hope the second, in answer to your favour
of the 26th Sept., has reached you likewise; it was inclosed in a pack forwarded by an officer of the Cold-
stream Guards under the address of Mrs. Z., with the
annotation, "to be transmitted to you in case Mrs. Z.
had left Portugal." The pack also contained a letter for
Captain Andrews.

Since about the 1st of November I left Talavera. Most of
the officers and men have been sent to France. Of the
regiment under your command nobody but Captain

Wolf and me are here now; and in the whole of the British only eighteen officers—five captains and thirteen subalterns.

Captain Wolf desires to be most respectfully remembered to you; he is recovering, one of his wounds healed up, but has lost his martial attitude. My wounds have I good appearance, but there are still rags or bones in them which retard the healing.

We inhabit the cells of the convent "St. Francis" converted into a hospital, are well treated, and might live comfortable if the monthly supplies of money with which his Lordship the Commander of the Forces hitherto favoured us will not be withheld. For we have no opportunity here of drawing any bills, and shall not I apprehend receive any allowance in cash as prisoners till we arrive in France.

I take the liberty of enclosing a letter for Mrs. Zuhleke. She gave me hopes of being soon exchanged: may they not be disappointed, Lord Wellington's kind endeavours not fail, and I soon in person have the honour to testify my respects to you as,

Sir,

Your most obedient humble servant,

G. H. Zuhleke

Lieutenant, 5th battalion 60th

P.S. 25th Dec. The money which our noble commander his Lordship sent us has been paid into our hands yesterday.

Zuhleke did not wait for an exchange. He effected his escape on 26th April 1810, and on arriving in Lisbon asked Lord Wellington to place him in the Portuguese service. On the 22nd October he was appointed major in the 2nd Caçadores, and served as major in 1810-11-12-13. He was present in the lines of Lisbon, engaged at Fuentes d'Onor, sieges of Badajos and Ciudad Rodrigo, and battle of Salamanca; defended with a detachment the bridge of Valladolid on the 28th October; was in an action near the village Munhoz 17th November, at the battles of Vittoria and the Pyrenees. In November 1812 the command of the 2nd Caçadores devolved on him. He was on the 30th July 1813 promoted Brevet Lieutenant-Colonel, and on 27th August effective Lieutenant-Colonel, and in that position served at the battles of Nivelle, the Nive, Orthes, and other actions, till April 1814. He was made C.B. for his services, which he began in 1794. First he was *Fahmenjunker* in the Guards of Hesse Cassel, and was employed in Germany and the Netherlands in the army under the King of Prussia, and afterwards under the Duke of York in 1795. He was appointed to 5th battalion 60th as Ensign when it was raised, 25th December, 1797, served with it in Ireland at Goff's Bridge, near Horse Town, and in Wicklow; and from 1799 to 1802 in the West Indies, and at the taking of Surinam.

Lieutenant-Colonel Davy, as he now must be styled, left the Peninsula for England, and the next letter he got was from Major Woodgate, who succeeded to the temporary command of the battalion until the arrival of Colonel William Williams:

Coimbra
March 6th, 1810
My dear Davy,
I received your letter from Lisbon at Alcontri, but as I thought you would have sailed the next day I did not answer it from thence. "Thus far into the bowels of the land have we marched without impediment," and, until the last two days, without rain, but now it pours down in torrents. Galiffe and I dined yesterday with General Fane. His brigade of cavalry is stationed here. He begs me to send his remembrances to you when I write. I extract the general orders of the 22nd *ult.*, as I know they will please you.

No. 4. A company of the 5th battalion 60th Regiment is to be attached to each of the brigades of the army according to the plan directed in the orders of the 4th May 1809.

The Commanding Officer 5th battalion 60th Regiment will detach three companies to Lieutenant-General Hill's division as soon as he will receive this order and a route from the quartermaster-general for the purpose. And as the general officers commanding' brigades have invariably expressed the highest satisfaction at the uniform good conduct of this invaluable body of men, which has always continued effective under many trying circumstances, the Commander of the Forces desires that, as far as possible, the same companies may be detached to the same brigades as formerly.

You see, my dear Sir, his Lordship will not desert us, and although he has divided us more than last year, I trust we shall again be conspicuous if an opportunity offers. The orders go on to state:

Two companies will be attached to Sir J. Sherbrooke's division—one for the brigade of Guards, and one for Brigadier-General Cameron's brigade. Two companies to the 4th division; being one for Major-General Cole's and one for Brigadier-General Campbell's brigade; and three companies with the head-quarters of the regiment to the 3rd division.

The third division is commanded by your friend General Picton[2], and contains our old brigade of Colonel McKinnon, and another of General Lightburne; Crawfurd has a division called "the light division," and is out

---

2. General McKenzie, who had commanded the 3rd division, had been killed at Talavera.

of our way. I have complied with his Lordship's di-rections about sending the same companies, although against my wish, but after the compliment the general have made, I could not do otherwise. I much wished to keep Wend with me for many reasons, but as General Hill also asked for him, I sent him there again. I send Schoëdde to the Guards, and keep Hames at head-quar-ters; and, as he now has become one of the committee of paymaster-ship, his presence with us will be neces-sary when Andrews is away. I keep Andrews', Hames's, and Salaberry's companies with me.

I sent Wend's, McMahon's, and Blassiere's companies to Portalegre, where General Hill is, from Rio Maior. The other seven companies march with me tomorrow to Vi-seu, where I shall crave admittance to his Lordship and thank him for his kindness, &c., &c. This place is very full. Your old patron very kindly received me.

I have promoted those you wished, and filled up other vacancies, I believe according to merit, at least I hope so. You may tell General de Rottenburg I am not very much obliged to him for sending out Colonel Williams, but I trust we shall have a bloody fight before he comes.

Believe me, dear Davy,

Your sincere friend,

William Woodgate

Addressed to Lieutenant-Colonel Davy (at)

Messrs. Gosling and Co., Bankers

Fleet Street

Another letter from Major Galiffe may here be introduced:

Cerdeiva

Near Guarda

April 2nd, 1810

Dear Colonel,

You left us so abruptly that I had not even time to take

leave of you, and really I expected that, as you had always been kind to me, you would have told me your resolution to leave us without saying anything. However I hope your friendship for me is not altered, and that you will still remember your friends of this battalion; and really situated as I am you can be of very great service to me, in assisting my getting the majority vacant by your promotion. Lord Wellington has been pleased to second it, and yet there is no answer made to my memorial.

I don't know if there has been any obstacle thrown in my way; and nobody could better know what it is than you, as you are at head-quarters.

I would beg you, dear colonel, when you see Colonel Torrens to ask him if he has been kind enough to answer the memorial and what I am to expect. I am sure at the same time that your own recommendation will have great weight with him; and I have no doubt but what everything will succeed to my satisfaction if you will have the goodness to assist me.

Since you sailed we have been separated again, but, instead of five, seven companies are detached. McMahon, Wend, and Blassiere are with General Hill at Portalegre; Wolf with General Cameron at Mengualda; Hames with the Guards at Viseu; Provost's and mine, both under my command, with General Cole at Guarda and neighbourhood; and Andrews, Schoëdde, and Salaberry's, with the staff, are attached to General Picton's division at Trancoso.

Major Woodgate is very unwell, he has a kind of rheumatism in the head; his face is much swelled, and I believe he will be under the necessity of going to Lisbon for some time.

On our march from Coimbra to Viseu, Banes of my company, who belonged to the band, deserted in the night at Malliada during a most terrible storm, and he was supposed to have been drowned in the same place where last year (if you recollect) we lost two Swiss in coming from Oporto; but lately one of our serjeants passing by Coimbra found him in a gentleman's dress walking snugly through the streets; he is now at head-quarters, where he will have a severe punishment.

The men in general behaved very well, and they are the spoiled children of the division, in fact we are much more liked than the 95th.

The headquarters are going to be removed from Viseu to Cea, half way to Coimbra on the road from Guarda to this place. Everybody here says that we are to retire; in a little time we will be under the necessity of doing so, even without an enemy before us, for we begin to feel the scarcity of provisions, and already there is almost no forage for our horses.

The French have retired also to Salamanca and Astorga; Ney has left that army to go to Paris, and they say that as there is to be war with Russia no reinforcements will come from France, and for that reason they are going to concentrate their forces near Madrid, and will act upon the defensive; and as we are in the same situation we may remain so the whole of the campaign.

Be so kind as to write sometimes to me, and be per-suaded of the sincere consideration with which I have the honour to be, dear colonel,

Your most obedient servant,

John Galiffe

All our gentlemen beg to be kindly remembered to you.

To Lieutenant-Colonel Davy

7th Garrison battalion

To the care of Messrs. Cox and Greenwood

Army Agents

London

These letters help us through the difficulty of knowing where our riflemen have got to. For, though the generals ever bore testimony to their good character and usefulness, the single detached companies were often not specially mentioned; and the 60th rifleman who wants to know what his predecessors are about must, as he reads, look for and keep in mind the names of Hill, Picton, Beresford, Cole, Cameron, Tilson, Donkin, Sontag, and other brigades to which from time to time a company of riflemen were attached.

The following is an order of this period with regard to detaching companies which may here find its place:

Regimental Order
Coimbra
May 4th, 1810
Captain McMahon's company will be attached to the five companies, directed to proceed tomorrow morning with Marshal Beresford, in place of Major Galiffe's, which will be attached to that brigade to which Captain McMahon was before.
Major Galiffe will be pleased to conform to the directions given to Major Woodgate. Ensign Fürst will for the present do duty with Major Galiffe's company.
The band agreeably to his Majesty's regulations will join their respective companies.
The instruments are to be delivered to the quartermaster, who will endeavour to make such arrangements as circumstances will admit for their security.
All servants must march with their respective companies.
Officers commanding the companies attached to the several brigades will send in tomorrow morning a return of their respective companies, to the brigade-major of the brigade to which they are attached, and henceforward report regimentally to Brevet-Major Galiffe.

To return however to a consideration of the general position of affairs in the beginning of the year 1810. Lord Wellington's army was in cantonments; the Portuguese troops were being drilled and disciplined; and Colonel Fletcher was at work at Torres Vedras.

In the first week of February intelligence reached Lord Wellington's head-quarters that Soult was entering Estremadura from Talavera, and that Mortier from Andalusia was moving to support him. On the 12th the two corps having united arrived in front of Badajos. Just about the same time Ney's advanced guard summoned Ciudad Rodrigo, and Victor began his siege operations at Cadiz.

Lord Wellington at once executed a counter-move. On the 12th Hill was put in motion from Abrantes, and with his own division of British infantry, two brigades of Portuguese infantry, a brigade of British and a regiment of Portuguese cavalry, one battery of German and two of Portuguese guns, marched upon Portalegre.[3]

It was on the 22nd of February that Woodgate was directed in general orders to detach three companies to Hill; and we have learnt from his letter to Davy that he had sent the companies of Wend, McMahon, and Blassiere to join him at Portalegre; and that he himself with the other seven companies marched for Lord Wellington's head-quarters of March 7.

This move was intended to bring Hill into communication with the Duque del Parque, who was supposed by this time to have crossed the Tagus; but although this object was not attained another was, for the enemy no sooner heard of Hill's arrival at Portalegre, than they retired from before Badajos; part under Mortier moving towards the south, part under Regnier to his old quarters at Merida.

From this time till the middle of March no important movement was made by either party.

Early in April Massena, with his instructions from Napoleon, but, it is said, against his inclination and with a heavy

3. See Gleig's *Life of Wellington*.

foreboding of failure, commenced his arrangements; formed magazines at Salamanca, moved up Junot, and pushed on Ney's corps (30,000 strong) to blockade Ciudad Rodrigo on the right of the Agueda.

Crawfurd, with the splendid Light Division, the 95th Rifles, 43rd and 52nd Regiments, repeatedly asked leave to make a forward movement, but as often was restrained by the Commander of the Forces. Wellington, as soon as he heard of Ney's advance, moved forward the British army, and taking up a new line, with his head-quarters at Celorico, communicated easily from the left bank of the Agueda with the town. On the 1st of June he found that with all his forces he could bring into line about 32,000 men, as opposed to 57,000—being the strength of the united corps of Ney and Junot.

The only thing regarding the 5th 60th at this moment to be noticed is the regimental order just given, showing that on the 5th of May five companies were detached to Marshal Beresford's force, and a change in the companies of Brevet-Major Galiffe and Captain Wend.

Fighting there had been at the outposts, but not for the 60th. There was a sharp attack on the 19th of March by General Ferey near the bridge of San Felices.

Ferey waited till night, passed the narrow bridge, bayoneted the sentries, and went fiercely fighting into the village of Barba del Puerco. Here were the riflemen however of the 95th; and, as Sir William Napier says:

.... their Colonel Sydney Beckwith, conspicuous by his lofty stature and daring actions, a man capable of rallying a whole army in flight, urged the contest with such vigour that in a quarter of an hour the French column was borne back and pushed over the edge of the descent.

On the 1st of June Massena took Ciudad Rodrigo, and Crawfurd assumed a fresh position a mile and a-half from

Almeida, and demanded two more battalions as a reinforcement. Lord Wellington replied that 'he would give him two divisions if he could hold his own ground, but that he could not do so;' and repeated his former orders, 'not to fight beyond the Coa.'

On the 11th of July Almeida surrendered. But still Crawfurd, though he fell back, would not pass the Coa. He was not satisfied with having for three months, with a weak division, kept his ground within two hours' march of 60,000 French.

On the 24th of July Ney suddenly fell on him with 24,000 infantry, 5000 cavalry under Montbrun, and thirty guns; endeavouring to interpose between him and Almeida, and to drive him into the deep valley of the Coa. The fight was really useless, though it served only as another proof of the grand valour of the 'light division;' for at a great expense of life, though without losing a gun, by sheer dint of hard fighting, he gained the bridge of Almeida, and stopped the enemy from crossing after him. That night however Lord Wellington withdrew him, causing the 3rd division which occupied Pinhel to fall back at the same time; and the army was placed in a new line between Guarda and Trancoso.

The 60th shared not in the honour won by the 95th Riflemen that day, though the opportunity was offered if Sir William Napier were correct in saying that during the fight General Picton came up from Pinhel alone; and when Crawfurd asked him for the support of the '3rd division,' he refused, and 'they separated after a sharp altercation:' and also that he 'considers that, although Crawfurd was fighting contrary to repeated orders, still Picton should have assisted him under circumstances of such extreme danger.'[4]

Undoubtedly he should have done so had the circumstances been as Napier has represented them. But it was not so, and could not have been so. Sir William gives no author-

---

4. See Napier's *History of Peninsular War.*

ity for his statement. He neither saw the meeting himself, nor has any writer ever mentioned even the rumour of such a meeting.

Sir John Burgoyne was actively employed in the immediate neighbourhood, and in his diary gives an entry of the combat on the Coa; and in allusion to the small amount of dependence at that time to be placed on the Portuguese troops, states that General Picton, who was quartered with his division in and about Pinhel, was riding out that day, and lost his way, but found a number of the Portuguese Caçadores regiments, both officers and men, skulking away in the rocky and broken ground where chance had led him; and Burgoyne's biographer places a foot-note saying that Napier was a 43rd man, and that the Light Brigade were very sore at being so roughly handled by the French on the 24th July, and were ready to throw the blame on others indiscriminately.

But the matter is fully discussed in Robinson's *Life of Sir Thomas Picton,* vol. 1. p. 289, where it is pointed out that it is nowhere stated—

.... what were the private instructions which General Picton had received from Lord Wellington at this time.

These may have been as positive as those to Crawfurd, and have compelled a refusal even had a request for co-operation been made; and after a temperate discussion of the question the evidence of one of Picton's own staff is adduced. This officer states of his own knowledge that 'any attempt to bring up the third division in time to support the light division (unless information had been sent to General Picton when General Crawfurd commenced falling back) would have been ridiculous, as the country could not have been traversed by infantry in less than three hours.' With regard to any personal ill-feeling existing between Generals Picton and Crawfurd, he says:

I can only say that I never knew the former to express himself in any but the most friendly terms of General Crawfurd. I certainly upon one occasion heard him observe, "That fighting fellow Crawfurd will some day get us into a scrape;" but this was not uttered at all in an unfriendly tone; on the contrary, I think that he had a great respect for the daring courage in General Crawfurd's character, at the same time that he always regretted his want of prudence and consideration.

This testimony is valuable; the officer's means of information were favourable, for he was on the spot and speaks of his own knowledge. It is true that he says he does not think 'Picton was half a mile from Pinhel' that day, and that he seldom rode out alone, 'certainly not on this day;' which does not agree with Burgoyne's expression; but he does state positively:

. . . . we heard firing in the direction of General Crawfurd's position; but as this was so common an occurrence, it was thought but little of. And, farther, I can state that the first intimation which we received at Pinhel of the serious affair which had occurred at the bridge, was by the body of an officer who had been killed at the bridge being brought back on the following day; this officer had left us early in the morning of the 24th, and was brought back dead on the 25th, having fallen during the fight.

Before proceeding with this sketch we will give two other letters written by Captain Andrews (who was with Picton's division) from Pinhel and La Rosa.

Pinhel
May 19th, 1810
My dear Colonel,
Shortly after the date of my former we moved up here to protect the front, from Almeida on the right to Ciu-

dad Rodrigo on the left. General Crawfurd's left connects with us, extending his right to Gallegos and the villages perpendicular to Guarda.

About the 28th *ult.* the enemy moved a column from Salamanca to near Ciudad Rodrigo, which caused our second line to close up upon the first, when head-quarters removed at an hour's notice from Viseu to Celorico; but tranquillity soon prevailed again, and the advanced posts of both armies are on speaking terms, and only separated in one place by a small river.

All the late accounts induce a belief that the enemy will not be in a condition to make a forward movement till very considerable reinforcements arrive which are not yet on the road; this promises a lingering existence to us. Within these last few days past we have had five recruits join us: Colonel Williams, Doctor Drumgold, and Ensigns Kruger, Larbusch, and Burghaagen, of whom I shall remark in rotation.

Colonel Williams is a short man looking in profile at a short distance like Dumoulin (assistant-surgeon), but on nearer inspection in front much resembles Captain White, late lieutenant in this battalion. His manner is quick, peremptory, and at the same time courteous; he speaks with rather a studied tone of voice, something between the agreeable and the commanding; he bows like a statesman entering into office, and from all I have observed doubt not that General De Rottenburg has entrusted him with the talisman so essential to command this corps.

Our doctor is a promotion from the 2nd West India Regiment to the 79th Regiment, from which he was exchanged to us. He is a being with a circular head fixed on between his shoulders, without any neck. The deficiency is so well recompensed by the rotundity and size of his body that without any violation of language we may apply the old adage, *things are as broad as they are long.* "Caledonia gave him birth."

With respect to the three ensigns, I fear more interesting matter will deprive me of noticing them at present. De Bree is still in Lisbon, very unwell; I believe he is to be sent home to recruit.

Schoëdde has been confined for three weeks with fever; an application has been this day made to send him to Lisbon; his constitution will not stand this kind of life any longer.

I most kindly thank you for the manner in which you mention the military object of my wishes. When you have seen General de Rottenburg possibly you may be able to let me know his opinion; from which, and your own, I shall make up my mind how to act.

Major Woodgate is recovering fast; he presents his kindest regards, as does Schoëdde, Galiffe, and Fürst.

Wishing you every success and happiness,

I remain, faithfully yours,

(Signed) *A. Andrews*

To Lieutenant-Colonel W. G. Davy

Gosling & Sharpe, Bankers

London

La Rosa

Sept. 12th, 1810

My dear Colonel,

About the 29th of July the army moved to the rear of Celorico, except the light brigade and cavalry.

Our station was in a village half way up the Sierra de Estella, where, although the climate was uncommonly fine, we got more sickly than ever I knew, as out of our three companies we had near fifty in hospital; and I believe, even bad as this appears, we were more fortunate than the rest of the army.

The sick of the whole army are immediately sent off to Coimbra and Lisbon, and everything kept in a state In facilitate a movement in that direction.

Our head-quarters at present is at Gavio, a considerable town at the foot of the Estrella, four leagues behind Celorico. Cavalry at the latter place, light brigade at Minho, Cole's division at Pincencos, Picton's at Galines, La Rosa, etc.; and the first division at the Ponte de Marcell, about four leagues from Coimbra; we are all in houses of some sort.

Our corps has been going on in the old way for a long time; the only change is that Prevost has arrived from America and now commands his company. Schoëdde has rejoined, quite well; we have only had one officer-recruit for some time, a Lieutenant O'Heir from Brunswick, a genteel-looking man, an Austrian of Irish parents.

Ever faithfully yours,

(Signed) *A. Andrews*

To Lieutenant-Colonel Davy

Gosling & Sharpe, Bankers, London

With regard to his own promotion, about which he has written to Davy, Captain Andrews became major at the commencement of the following year (17th January, 1811), and became a lieutenant-colonel 14th December, 1815.

With regard to Schoëdde, his first prognostication was fortunately quite wrong. Andrews himself in his second letter states that he had already returned to his duty.

It, is true that he was very ill with ague for three months, and had to be sent to Belem, where, by his own account, he had recovered under a regimen which an old Portuguese army doctor recommended: the treatment ordered was, 'the best of living, and at least two bottles of Madeira *per diem.'*[5]

---

5. Schoëdde related the circumstances of his illness and the old Portuguese doctor's treatment and cure to Sir H. C. Daubeney.

Whether this would prove successful in all cases of ague, who shall say? It succeeded with Schoëdde. With this exception, he was never absent from the front. He had, previously to joining the 5th 60th in 1801, served in Egypt, and distinguished himself; and was one of the very few who embarked at Cork in 1808, and disembarked at Cove from H.M.S. *Clarence* on 25th July, 1814.

The fall of Almeida was a great annoyance to Wellington, but was accepted by Massena as a fortunate event, as it secured him an excellent base for future operations, which he lost no time in entering upon, stating his intentions of 'driving the leopards into the sea.'

Instead however of keeping to the left of the Mondego, and pressing the English, who had begun at once to fall back, he turned off at Celorico, and made (by a longer and indifferent road) through Viseu towards Coimbra.

Wellington calling in Hill and Leith, who were watching the course of the Tagus, got together 50,000 of all arms, of which 24,000 were British, and felt strong enough to fight a battle; so he seized on the position along the ridges of the Sierra de Busaco, and there determined to make a stand.[6]

The position consisted of a range of precipitous heights, intersected with valleys, through one of which runs the great road from Viseu to Coimbra, the entire extent of ground being about seven to eight miles. From the convent of St. Anthonio on the right to a village called Metheada on the left was about four miles, an advantageous position for purely defensive purposes, but too extensive for the whole of Wellington's army united; and on September 25th (although on the 21st he had effected his junction with Hill) only half his troops were in line, and it presented many gaps. Ney would have taken advantage of this. He had 40,000 men under him. Hill had by forced marches reached the Murcella, Spencer

---

6. See Gleig's *Life of Wellington*.

had not come in, Leith was only passing the Mondego, and scarcely 25,000 men were in line on the position which Wellington had chosen and prepared.[7]

The Prince of Essling was about ten miles in rear, but the officer sent by Ney to ask his assent to an attack was kept two hours without an audience, and then sent back with orders to await the prince's arrival; and thus the opportunity was lost, when there was unavoidable confusion in taking up the position, and great intervals between the divisions.

Ney and Reynier wrote in the night to Massena advising an attack at daybreak; yet he did not come up until midday with Junot's corps and the cavalry, and then proceeded leisurely to examine the position. But it was now completely manned. Hill had the extreme right, Leith was next in line, Picton next to Leith, Spencer in reserve on the highest crest. Crawfurd with the light division, and Cole with his, closed in the left, covered flank and front, by impassable ravines. The artillery was disposed on all salient points, and skirmishers covered all the accessible ground. Portions of the 5th 60th were with Hill and Cole both to right and left and in other parts but the companies with regimental head-quarters, Andrews', Hames', and Salaberry's, under Colonel Williams (who had now joined), were formed by Picton into a light corps by adding the light companies of 45th, 88th, 74th, and 94th Regiments; and Picton threw the whole of these into the ravines of St. Antonio de Cantaro, to the right-front of the position. Other companies were with Sherbrooke attached to the brigade of Guards and Cameron's brigade, one with Cole, and one with Brigadier-General Campbell.

Ney now strongly objected to an attack;[8] Reynier advised one, and the Prince of Essling made dispositions for the next morning. Ney was to assail the light division on the left; Reynier was to fall on Picton on the right. Massena could

---

7. See Sir William Napier.
8. See Sir William Napier and Sir E. Cust.

only employ 40,000 men in his attack; his enemies numbered 60,000, but from the great extent of ground, and the impossibility of making any counter attacks, they were the weakest at the decisive points.

Before daybreak on September 27th five columns of attack were in motion, and Reynier's troops, having comparatively easier ground, were soon in the midst of Picton's picquets and skirmishers, and, in spite of a vigorous resistance and showers of grape from six guns, in half-an-hour were close to the summit of the mountain. The French forced back part of the right of the third division; Lord Wellington immediately opened two guns with grape upon their flank, Picton launched the 88th and 45th at them; they charged furiously, and the French, exhausted by their efforts, opposed only a straggling fire, and both parties went mingled together down the mountain side with a mighty clamour and confusion, their track strewed with the dead and dying even to the bottom of the valley.

We transcribe these passages from Napier regarding the repulse of the French[9] by Picton because the head-quarters of the 60th were with him. But one is tempted to write the whole of these things from Napier and Sir E. Cust. The latter describes the battle-scene well: how (when in Reynier's attack Generals Merle and Grain d'Orge and Colonels Desgramois and Merle were struck down, and the French troops wavered) General Foy brought up to the top of the road the advance of Hendelot's division and kept firm; but Leith with the 38th and 9th under Colonel Cameron ran in upon the French Grenadiers as they came up, and without a shot being fired by the British down in a moment went Colonel Demoutriers and General Foy: 2500 were now *hors-de-combat*, and Reynier retired. The discipline shown by the troops too was excellent; it restrained them from pursuit lest the crest of the position should be lost, and Hill only arrived at the summit in time to pour in some telling volleys upon the retreating columns. At this very moment Wellington came up to the spot and exclaimed, "If they attempt this again, Hill, give it them in volleys, and charge bayonets, but don't let your people follow them far down the hill."

We may not also copy Napier's picture of the fiery Crawfurd standing alone upon a crag watching the French attack and preparing to repel it. Suffice it to say that Ney's attack had no better success than Reynier's. Crawfurd had concealed the 43rd and 52nd in a ravine, and at the opportune moment ordered them to charge. A horrid shout startled the brigade Ferey, and the 1800 British bayonets drove them in headlong flight down the hill-side, leaving General Simon wounded and a prisoner on the summit.

Brigadiers Ferey and Maucune endeavoured to renew the action. Ney heading the attack, longed to storm the convent where the head-quarters of Wellington were, but found himself obliged to withdraw from the attempt, and, like Reynier on the other flank, to rest and wait for further orders from the Prince of Essling.

The loss to the French, including Generals Grain d'Orge, Simon, Merle, Loison, and Maucune, is stated at 4500 men.

The British loss, according to the official statement, was 197 killed and 1072 wounded and missing, one half of the whole loss being in Picton's division.

The casualties of the 60th Rifles were Colonel Williams and Captain Andrews (slightly) wounded, Lieutenants Joyce and Eberstein (severely), Lieutenant Franchini (slightly), sixteen riflemen wounded, and five missing;.

The battle of Busaco produced a prodigious moral effect at the period. To the British it was not only a triumph, but it established perfect confidence in the Portuguese, and dispelled any desponding feeling in the usefulness of those comrades in future fights.

Massena and the French army were deeply mortified at this

---

9. See Sir W. Napier and Sir E. Cust.

failure; Reynier hung his head, Ney blustered, but Massena preserved his erect bearing, and feeling he had erred enough in risking the attempt of forcing such a position, resolved to push on for Lisbon in spite of the check he had received. His endeavour was to push his army along the coast into Coimbra. Wellington had sent Trant to watch and occupy the communication, but General Sylveira, without his knowledge or sanction, ordered Trant and his troops back to Oporto.

The road therefore being now open to Massena's march, Wellington gave orders to his army to quit the mountains at Busaco, and make the best of their way through Coimbra, marching as direct as possible upon Torres Vedras.

The French army followed close. Junot, leading, entered Coimbra as the British left it. Massena marched out of Coimbra on the 4th of October to Condeixa, and followed Wellington on the road by Pombal and Leyria; and at the latter place, incredible as it may appear, learned, for the first time, the shelter which the English general had been for twelve months carefully preparing for the reception of his troops and the protection of Portugal. Within these 'lines' he withdrew, sweeping in with him the Portuguese population of all ranks, nobility and gentry travelling according to rank, and a horde of peasantry with their families, flocks and herds, and household stuff; and on the 7th, having retreated nearly 200 miles without losing a straggler, a gun, or an article of baggage, his business was complete.

When Wellington entered the 'lines' they consisted of 126[10] closed works, defended by 29,751 men and 247 pieces of cannon. The interior works opposite to St. Julien, to cover the point of embarkation, required 5350 men and ninety-four guns. Wellington further called in the Marquis de Romagna with 6000 Spaniards on the 20th of October. Altogether, including followers, 130,000 persons received daily rations at

10. The number of redoubts and cannons was increased from time to time, and the totals will be found to differ much in various writers.

British cost at this period; besides the multitude of fugitives who had followed the allied armies, who numbered nearly 400,000 souls, all of whom received sufficient subsistence. The military annals of no age of the world record such an incident; and the entry into the 'lines' was as unexpected to the British as the French armies. Both were astounded at the foresight evinced by the British General, and at the skill which had rendered the position not only impregnable but unassailable.

Massena was stopped; in vain he and his comrades reconnoitred from one flank to the other; there was no joint in Wellington's harness where an arrow might find entrance. The Prince had no supplies. The French soon ate and destroyed what little had been left by the population, who with their flocks had followed their shepherd within his fold of earthworks. By the 14th of November the Prince of Essling was forced to break up his army from before the 'lines of Lisbon;' and instead of 'the leopards being driven into the sea,' Wellington was informed that morning that 'not a man was to be seen in his front, either at the outposts or along the whole position.' Ney was quietly drawn back on Thomar in the morning; at nightfall, Junot, followed by Reynier, fell back on Santarem; while Massena had quietly moved his head-quarters to Torres Novas.

Accordingly, on the departure of the French army from his front, Hill's division crossed with all speed to the south bank of the Tagus, to move up to Abrantes, while the bulk of the British army moved forward by the great road to Cartaxo, where head-quarters were established on the 16th, and the troops placed in cantonments at Alcoentre, Rio Mayor, and Villa Franca, with the cavalry outposts as far advanced as Caldas.

From Alcoentre we have an important letter from Woodgate to Davy. Picton had been left as a measure of precaution to hold the lines of Torres Vedras, and the 5th 60th had been looking forward from the 27th of September (when they had the hard day's fighting in the ravines of St. Anthonio) to know 'what they said in England' of the victorious repulse of the French army at Busaco.

The English mail had arrived with newspapers and copies of Lord Wellington's despatch. Special mention had been made of Picton and his division, the regiments under him, and their commanding officers; but, for the first time, there was no mention of the 5th battalion of the 60th, although special recognition of Colonel Williams and his day's work at St. Anthonio de Cantaro had been made by Picton in divisional orders. Great—naturally great—was the chagrin of colonel and battalion. Williams appealed to Picton; Picton wrote him a handsome letter, and luckily Woodgate copied it and sent it with one from himself to Davy. Davy preserved it, and after seventy years it now sees the light.

Why the explanation was never made before is quite inexplicable. But it has now been given, and the testimony of Woodgate's and Picton's letters has induced her Majesty to give her gracious permission to the 60th to add the word 'Busaco' to the others on their regimental badges; and the only one of Wellington's great battles which has been so long wanting is now to be found filling its proper place. These letters must ever have a great interest to every 60th rifleman.

From Major Woodgate
To Lieutenant-Colonel Davy
Alcoentre
Dec. 24th, 1810
My dear Davy,
Since my last to you we have had much to do, although by the papers and the mangled accounts of the affair of Busaco you might fairly conclude we had nothing to do in that business.
The omission of our regiment among the number of those which distinguished themselves was owing to

General Picton not making a written report of the conduct of his division. The fact is Lord Wellington was present during the whole affair, and on its termination thanked General Picton and said, "You need not make any report to me, I have seen the whole myself, and shall mention your division particularly."

You may suppose we were much astonished, on the arrival of the despatch, to find that the efforts of the "Americans" had escaped his Lordship's notice. Colonel Williams, who was in the thickest of the fight, and was twice wounded, was of course particularly annoyed, as he had a very fine command of light infantry who were engaged the whole day; and consisted of our three companies[11], the 45th, 88th, 74th, and 94th. He applied to General Picton, who of course expressed his sorrow for the omission, and wrote to him the letter which I shall transcribe on the other part of this paper.

I trouble you on this subject as I trust you still feel an interest for some of those who are still in the battalion, and that this unusual omission of the 60th may be accounted for.

(Signed) *W. Woodgate*

Copy of General Picton's letter to Colonel Williams:

Cordoceira
Oct. 30th, 1810
My dear Sir,
On reading over the *Gazette* account of the action of the 27th *ult.* at Busaco I was much disappointed and concerned not to find your name among those of the

---

11. Picton formed a light corps for divisional purposes of the head-quarters and three companies of the 5th battalion 60th and the light companies of the other regiments under him. And throughout the whole of the Peninsular War the light troops, or light battalion, of the third division were constantly engaged, and as constantly mentioned by Wellington in his despatches.

commanding officers of corps in the third division who were particularly noticed on that occasion. You cannot have any doubt of my sentiments, as they were expressed in the Division Orders of that day; yet I fear that I must take the blame to myself for the omission, having neglected to make a written report of the circumstances of the day to his Excellency the Commander of the Forces, who, being present on a commanding situation, and immediately contiguous to that part of the position defended by the third division, I conceived to be fully acquainted with the merits and services of each particular corps; but, on reflection, I find the post you defended (with the light corps of the division) with so much gallantry, for so many hours, was situated so low in the ravine of St. Antonio d'Alcantara[12], that he would not probably have seen your situation, or witnessed your exertions; but you may be assured that I will take an early opportunity of mentioning to his Lordship that no commanding officer of any corps had more claim to public notice on that occasion than yourself.

I am, dear Sir,

Your faithful servant,

(Signed) Thos. Picton

Major-General

Commanding 3rd Division

To Lieutenant-Colonel Williams

Commanding Light Corps, 3rd division

But it was not only on account of the 60th that Picton had to regret that he had not put in writing the exploits of his division. Lord Wellington had given him credit for directing the charge of the 45th and 88th Regiments, and as he was not on the spot he was vexed that those who should have had the credit of it had not been mentioned. Moreover, a private let-

---

12. The spot is called, in his despatch, by Wellington, 'Antonio de Cantaro.'

ter of his to the Duke of Queensberry (in which he described only his own portion of the day's work at Busaco, touching but lightly on what the light and other divisions had done) had been surreptitiously obtained and published in the papers, and when these came out to Spain great was the indignation of many who fancied Picton claimed the whole credit for himself; great too was Picton's anger at what he considered a breach of confidence, though he acquitted the Duke of being a party to such a proceeding. He therefore wrote a letter to Lord Wellington giving a minute detail of the disposition and conduct of his division, and fortunately a copy of this was found amongst the manuscripts of the general, and is here copied from Robinson's life of him, vol. 1. pp. 330-337.

Cadaceira
Nov. 10th, 1810
My Lord,
In consequence of an extraordinary report, which has been circulated with a good deal of assiduity, it becomes necessary that I should make a written detailed report to your lordship of the circumstances which preceded and attended the action which took place upon the height of Busacos on the morning of the 27th of September, inasmuch as they relate to myself and the troops I had the honour of commanding on that occasion.

Major-General Lightburne, with the Fifth and Eighty-Third regiments, was detached to the left, and did not act under my orders.

On the evening of the 35th, by orders from your lordship, I occupied that part of the Sierra de Busacos which is immediately connected with the pass of St. Antonio de Cantara with Colonel Mackinnon's brigade, consisting of the Forty-Fifth, Seventy-Fourth, and Eighty-Eighth Regiments, amounting to about one thousand three hundred rank and file; and with the Ninth and

Twenty-First Portuguese Regiments under Colonel de Champalimand: upon the whole about 3000 men.

All the movements of the enemy during the 26th indicating a determination of attacking the position early in the following morning, I made what dispositions I judged necessary for the defence of the post that evening; and there being an unoccupied space of considerably above a mile between my left and Sir Brent Spencer's division, immediately after sunset (when it could not be observed by the enemy) I detached Lieutenant-Colonel Wallace, with the Eighty-Eighth Regiment, to take up an intermediate position, and communicate with the hill of Busacos and the main body of my division at the pass of Saint Antonio.

The troops in the immediate neighbourhood of the pass were visited by me on their respective posts by daybreak; and immediately after, Colonel Mackinnon returned from visiting the Eighty-Eighth Regiment, and reported that the enemy was collecting in the ravine, opposite the position occupied by that regiment; in consequence of which I immediately detached Major Gwynne, of the Forty-Fifth Regiment, with four companies, to reinforce that post.

A few minutes after, when the day began to clear up, a smart firing of musketry was heard on the left, apparently proceeding from the point where the Eighty-Eighth Regiment had been stationed; and after a short suspense a violent cannonade opened upon the pass of Saint Antonio, and at the same time a heavy column compelled the advanced picquet of the division to fall back, and pressing forward with great impetuosity, endeavoured to push up the road and force the pass. The light corps of the division, unable to resist such a superiority of numbers in front, was most judiciously thrown in upon the flank of the advancing column by Lieutenant-Colonel Williams; and it was received with so steady and well directed a fire by the Twenty-First Portuguese Regiment of the line, and three companies of the Seventy-Fourth Regiment that moved up to their support on the left, that after a long struggle, and repeated desperate attempts to effect their object (during which they suffered much from the well-directed fire of the Portuguese artillery, under Major Arentschild), they were ultimately under the necessity of desisting, though a severe firing of cannon and musketry still continued.

About this period the fire of musketry on the left appearing to increase and draw nearer, I directed Colonel Mackinnon to take the immediate command of the troops at the pass of Saint Antonio, and rode towards the left, with the Assistant Adjutant-General, Major Packenham; leaving my *aide-de-camp*, Captain Cuthbert, and the Assistant Quartermaster-General, Captain Anderdon, to bring up as fast as possible one battalion of the Eighth Portuguese Regiment, and the five remaining companies of the Forty-Fifth Regiment.

On reaching the high rocky point about half-way between the pass of Saint Antonio and the hill of Busacos, I found the light companies of the Seventy-Fourth and Eighty-Eighth Regiments retiring in disorder, and the head of the enemy's column, already in possession of the strong rocky point, deliberately firing down upon us, and the remainder of a large column pushing up the hill with great rapidity. Whilst endeavouring to rally the light infantry companies with the assistance of Major Packenham, I was joined by Major Smith of the Forty-Fifth Regiment; and we succeeded in forming them under the immediate fire of the enemy, not more than sixty yards distant. Major Smith most gallantly led them to the charge, and gained possession of the rock, driving the enemy before him; but I am concerned to say, fell in the moment of victory, for which we were chiefly indebted to his animating example.

The assistant quartermaster-general having fortunately brought up a battalion of the Eighth Portuguese Regiment, commanded by Major Birmingham, at this critical period, I personally led and directed their attack on the flank of the enemy's column; and we completely succeeded in driving them in great confusion and disorder down the hill and across the ravine.

Not being able to discover any enemy upon the ridge to my left, I immediately returned to the pass of Saint Antonio, where the firing of musketry and cannon still continued with little apparent abatement. On my arrival I learned from Colonel Mackinnon that the enemy had not been able to make any impression during my absence.

At this moment Major-General Leith's *aide-de-camp* came to report the arrival of that general and his division; upon which I rode from the port of Saint Antonio to the road of communication, and directed the leading regiment of the brigade to proceed without loss of time to the left, as I had no occasion for assistance. General Leith's brigade in consequence marched on, and arrived in time to join the five companies of the Forty-Fifth Regiment under the Hon. Lieutenant-Colonel Mead, and the Eighth Portuguese Regiment under Lieutenant-Colonel Douglass, in repulsing the last attempt of the enemy.

Your lordship was pleased to mention me as directing the gallant charge of the Forty-Fifth and Eighty-Eighth Regiments; but I can claim no merit whatever in the executive part of that brilliant exploit, which your lordship has so highly and so justly extolled. Lieutenant-Colonel Wallace of the Eighty-Eighth, and Major Gwynne, who commanded the four companies of the Forty-Fifth engaged on that occasion, are entitled to the whole of the merit, and I am not disposed to deprive them of any part. I was actively engaged at the time in repelling the attack upon the post with which I was principally charged, though I provided, as far as the means I had at my disposal would allow, for the safety of every part of the position within my reach; and the moment I could with propriety and safety to the service quit the principal point of my command, I immediately proceeded to the post where my services were most necessary, and was at all times to be found where his Majesty's service and my own honour required that I should be.

I shall not say anything of the conduct of the troops under my command during the whole of the trying service of the day: it was beyond eulogy, and can receive no additional splendour from my feeble praise.

With many apologies for troubling your lordship with such long details, in which I am necessarily so much concerned,

I have the honour to be, with high respect,

Your Lordship's very faithful, humble servant,

(Signed) *Thomas Picton*

To Lieutenant-General Lord Viscount Wellington

Commander of the Forces

It will be seen by anyone, who will compare this interesting report with Napier's *History*, how much the two accounts are at variance. Napier places Sir Brent Spencer on Picton's left, but makes no mention of the great gap which he perceived and did his best to stop 'after sunset.' Napier make erroneous statements also as to the 45th and 88th. he says that the enemy's column 'scaled the mountain so swiftly and with such astonishing power, that they overthrew everything that opposed their progress;' and that 'the right of the 3rd division was forced back, the 8th Portuguese Regiment was broken to pieces, and the hostile masses gained the highest part of the crest just between the 3rd and 5th divisions.' Here is a confusion of the 8th and 21st Portuguese. And then he makes a further confusion about the driving out 'the leading battalions' by the '45th and 85th.' Why, the latter regiment and four companies of the former were defending themselves at this time from an attack more than half a-mile on the left of Picton's division! the remainder of the 45th being in reserve. And he would imply that Leith too was at work on the right, when we see by the above report that he moved to his own left to Picton, and passed on even to his left by the rear of the 3rd division.

Napier's account of this portion of the battle of Busaco must be pronounced very confused and inaccurate. If anyone doubts this let him carefully compare Sir William on his own side and Sir Thomas on his.

CHAPTER 7

Fuentes d'Onor: 1810-1811

At the end of 1810 the three Marshals, Massena, Ney, and Junot, had found themselves foiled by 'the lines,' and fallen back on Santarem and Torres Novas, whilst Lord Wellington had at once pushed Hill to the south of the Tagus, and cantoned his army about Rio Mayor, Alcoentre, and Villa Franca, with head-quarters at Cartaxo, and Picton holding the lines of Torres Vedras.

The distribution of the 5th 60th at that time was as follows: 1st division, with brigade of Guards under Stopford, one company; General Cameron's brigade, 2nd bn. 24th, 2nd bn. 42nd, 1st bn. 79th, one company. 2nd division, Major-General Hon. W. Stewart's brigade, 3rd, 2nd bn. 31st, 2nd bn. 48th, 2nd bn. 66th, one company; Hoghton's brigade, 29th, 1st bn, 48th, 1st bn. 57th, one company. 3rd division, light infantry corps, head-quarters and three companies. 4th division, with Kemmis's brigade, 3rd bn. 27th, 1st bn. 40th, 97th, one company. 6th division, General Campbell's brigade, 2nd bn. 7th, 1st bn. 21st, 2nd bn. 53rd, one company.

This distribution was however somewhat altered early in 1811, and we find that on April 3 in that year the distribution was—1st division, Stopford's brigade (Guards), one company; Nightingale's (late Cameron's) one company. 3rd division, Mackinnon's brigade, 45th, 74th, and 88th, one company; Colville's brigade, 1st bn. 94th, 2nd bn. 5th, 83rd, and 88, one company; light corps of 3rd division, head-quarters, three companies. 4th division, Kemmis's brigade, 3rd bn. 27th, 1st bn. 40th, and 97th, one company. 6th division, Hulse's brigade, 1st bn. 11th, and 1st and 2nd bns. 61st, one company; Burn's brigade, 1st bn. and, and 36th, one company.

The opening movement of the year cannot be better summarised than they are in the Duke's own memorandum of what he had done, written at the end of 1811.[1]

Immediately upon receiving information of the entry of the French into Estremadura, General Hill was put in motion on the 12th of February with his own British division, two brigades of Portuguese infantry about 4000 strong under General Hamilton, Slade's cavalry about 1000 British and one regiment Portuguese cavalry, and one German and one Portuguese brigade of artillery.

Hill was ordered in the first instance to Portalegre, to co-operate with the Duque del Parque, then supposed to have crossed the Tagus; and to prevent if possible any serious operation against Badajos. The enemy retired from that place as soon as they heard of General Hill's arrival at Portalegre.

Ney, with two divisions of his corps, summoned Ciudad Rodrigo, but he retired again upon the Tonnes upon finding the advanced guard of the British army crossing the Coa.

From this time till towards the middle of March no movement of importance was made by either party, when the French corps in Estremadura broke up, and Mortier marched to the southward; and Reynier, with Soult's corps, remained in the neighbourhood of Merida.

On the 5th of March the enemy retired from their position at Santarem apparently intending to collect a force at Thomar. On the morning of the 6th the British army was put in motion to follow them, and a considerable body of troops (part of Marshal Beresford's corps) under Major-General the Hon.

1. See *Wellington Despatches.*

W. Stewart marched upon that town, with the 4th, 6th, and part of the 1st divisions of infantry, and two brigades of British cavalry.

On the 9th, in front of Pombal, the cavalry under Arentschild had a brilliant affair with Montbrun's cavalry.

It was not till the 11th of March that a sufficient body of troops were collected to commence an operation on the enemy. On that day the 1st, 3rd, 4th, 5th, 6th, and light divisions of infantry, and General Pack's brigade, and all the British cavalry, joined upon the ground immediately in front of the enemy, who had commenced their retreat from their position during the night; and Wellington pressed their rear-guard considerably. An attempt was made to hold the ancient castle of Pombal, but the French were driven from it, and in the night retired on Redinha, where Ney took up a strong position at the end of a defile, with his right in a wood upon the Soure river, and his left extending towards some high ground on the river Redinha, with the town in their rear.

Wellington attacked them there on the 12th with the 3rd and 4th divisions of infantry, Pack's brigade, and the cavalry, the other troops being in reserve.[2]

The post in the wood on their right was first forced by Sir W. Erskine with the light division.[3] The troops could then form in the plain beyond the defile, and the 3rd division under Picton were formed in two lines, in the skirts of the wood upon the right; General Cole's division (the 4th) in two lines in the centre, with Pack's brigade on the right in support and communicating with the 3rd division and the light division in two lines on the left. The rest in reserve.

The formation was made with great accuracy and celerity, and Sir Brent Spencer led the line against the heights, from which position he immediately drove the enemy with great loss.

---

2. See *Wellington Despatches*, and Cust's *Annals of the Wars*.

3. General Crawford was absent from illness: he rejoined on the field of Fuentes d'Onor, when the light division received him with a spontaneous shout.

There was but one narrow bridge, and a ford close to it, over the Redinha, over which our light troops passed with the enemy. But they commanded the passage with cannon, and it took some time to pass over sufficient troops and make a fresh disposition to attack the heights on which they had taken post.

The 3rd division however crossed, and manoeuvred on their left flank, while the light infantry and cavalry, supported by the light division, drove them upon their main body at Condeixa. The light infantry of General Picton's division, under Colonel Williams of the 60th Rifles, and the 4th Caçadores, under Colonel do Rego, were principally concerned in this operation; and the spirited description given by Sir William Napier must not be omitted, as it specially describes the operation in which the 60th Rifles took so important a part.

Ney, keenly watching the progress of this grand formation, had opposed Picton's foremost skirmishers with his left, while he withdrew the rest of his people, and with such rapidity that they gained the village before even the cavalry could touch them; the utmost efforts of Picton's light troops and the horse artillery only enabled them to gall the hindmost of the French with their fire. One howitzer was however dismounted, but the village of Redinha was in flames between it and the pursuers; and the Marshal wishing to confirm the courage of his soldiers at the commencement of the retreat, ordered the French Colonel Brüe to cover it with some infantry, while in person he superintended the carrying off the injured piece; this was effected, yet with the loss of fifteen or twenty of Brüe's men, and with great danger to Ney, for the British guns were thundering on his rear, and the light troops of the 3rd division, chasing like heated bloodhounds, passed the river almost at the same time with the French. The reserves of the latter then cannonaded the bridge from the heights beyond, but a fresh disposition of attack was made by Lord Wellington, the 3rd division continued to press the left, and Ney fell back upon the main body at Condeixa, ten miles in the rear.

The British lost twelve officers and 200 men killed and wounded in this combat, and the enemy lost as many. Wellington had gained complete success in both the combats of Pombal and Redinha, and indeed, in Napier's opinion, he might at the latter place have destroyed his enemy, but that he paid the Duke of Elchingen too much respect.

On the 13th the allies renewed the pursuit, and before ten o'clock discovered the French army in order of battle, excepting the and corps, which was at Espinhal.

The crisis of Massena's retreat had arrived. The defiles of Condeixa leading upon Coimbra were behind him, and those of Miranda de Corvo leading to the Puente de Murcella were on his left, but in the fork of these two roads Ney was seated on a strong range of heights covered by a marsh, and his position was only to be approached by the high road, which led through a deep hollow against his right; and trees were felled, a *pallisado* barred the hollow, and breastworks were thrown up on each side, for here Massena designed to stop the allies, while Montbrun seized Coimbra.

But the same man, Trant, who had captured Coimbra after the battle of Busaco, now held and saved it. Montbrun finding such resistance sent an exaggerated report early on the 13th to Massena, and he, too readily crediting the account of Trant's strength, relinquished the idea of passing the Mondego.

Lord Wellington finding Ney so strongly posted at Condeixa, moved Picton through the mountains on his left to turn the position. Massena, with Ney in possession of Condeixa, made further dispositions, as if he judged his own position secure, and showed as confident a front as if he had gained Coimbra. Wellington however saw Massena's baggage filing off by the Murcella when he first came upon Condeixa, instantly comprehended the true state of affairs (that Coimbra was safe), and as instantly detached the 3rd division by a very difficult path over the Sierra de Anciao to turn his extreme left.[4]

For some time all was quiet in the French lines. Towards three o'clock however Picton was descried rounding a bluff end of the Anciao Sierra some eight miles off, and as he was already beyond their left there was confusion in the French camp. Thick smoke arose from Condeixa, which Ney set fire to, columns were seen hurrying towards Casal Nova, and the British troops pushed forward, The felled trees and fires impeded the advance; hence the skirmishers and some cavalry could alone close with the rear of the enemy, but this they did so rapidly as to penetrate between the division at Fonte Coberta and the rest of the French, and it is said that the Prince of Essling only escaped capture by taking the feathers out of his hat and riding through some of the light troops.

Condeixa thus gained, the British cavalry pushed on towards Coimbra, opened the communication with Trant, cut off Montbrun and took some of his men.

The army kindled their fires, the light division planted pickets close to the enemy, and fancying the French were in full retreat, Sir William Erskine put them in motion next morning and committed them to the combat of Casal Nova. The morning of March 15th was foggy, and the troops nearly captured Ney; but the 52nd had been plunged into the mist and the body of the enemy, and the Rifles were following them, when the fog lifted, and the 52nd were seen closely engaged and without support. Lord Wellington came up at the moment. It was his intention to turn the French left, and the 4th division was already marching on Panella. Between the 4th division however and Casal Nova the 3rd division was more directly turning the enemy's left flank, and the main

4. See Napier's *Peninsular War.*

body was coming up in front; but Erskine's error forced on the action, and the light division were pushed forward to succour the 52nd Regiment.

The front was so extensive, and the French skirmishers so thick and easily supported, that soon the line stretched out in one thin thread, all engaged, and without any reserve; nor could it even thus present an equal front until Picton sent the riflemen of the 60th to prolong the line.[5]

The fighting was vigorously maintained among the stone enclosures on the mountain side, and the right was partly turned, yet the main position could not be shaken until Picton and Cole had turned it by the left. Then the attack was strong and general on the centre, and Ney commenced his retreat, covering it with artillery and light troops, and retiring from ridge to ridge with admirable precision.

For some time his loss was small; about midday the British guns and skirmishers got within range of his masses, and his retreat became more rapid and less orderly; yet he finally gained the strong pass of Miranda de Corvo, which had been secured by the main body of the French, and here Montbrun rejoined the army.

Massena, fearing that Cole and Nightingale would gain his rear, fired the town of Miranda and crossed the Ceira in the night. His whole army was now compressed and crowded in one narrow line; destroying ammunition and baggage he pressed his retreat, desiring Ney to cover his passage with a few battalions, but not to risk an action. But Ney disregarding his orders provoked the combat of Foz D'Aronce on the 15th, where he was sorely worsted, losing not less than 500 men, one half of whom were drowned in the Ceira, whilst the British loss was only four officers and about sixty men; and an eagle was found in the bed of the river when the waters subsided.

Thus terminated the first part of the retreat from Santarem,

5. See Napier.

conducted by the French with more atrocious cruelty than any part of the war. Even if the destruction of Redinha, Condeixa, Miranda de Corvo, and the villages *en route* could find any justification on military grounds, that of Leiria and the convent of Alcobaça must be pronounced unjustifiable, and a part of the extravagant outrages then committed which utterly revolt the reader of their story.

The river Ceira was very full, and the supplies were running very short, and Lord Wellington was not unwilling to halt a few days to rest his troops, who had all had much work, though a very large proportion of the severest toil and hard fighting had fallen to the share of Picton's third division and the light division.[6]

In the despatch of 16th of March describing the operations of the 13th and succeeding days he especially mentions that:

> .... the light troops of General Picton's division under Colonel Williams (60th Rifles) and those of General Nightingale's brigade were principally engaged on the right; and the 95th Regiment in front of the light division; and the troops behaved in the most gallant manner.

In the fighting on the 13th, Lieutenant Joyce of the 60th Rifles was wounded; and on the 15th another, Lieutenant Sawatsky, an officer of merit and future promise, was amongst the killed.

The position assumed by Massena on the 18th behind the Alva was strong, and Junot, Ney, and Reynier had judicious orders given to them, had they but obeyed them. Reynier took himself off through the Sierra de Moita in pique, which caused Massena to leave his position in haste and make the best of his way to Celorico, where he arrived, unpursued, on the 21st; whence he continued his retreat to Guarda on the 22nd. Marshal Ney's insubordination was so great that Masse-

---

6. See Napier's *Peninsular War* and Sir E. Cust's *Annals*.

na had no choice but to dismiss him, and having ordered him to the rear placed his corps under the command of Loison.

The city of Guarda has the reputation of being the highest inhabited town in Europe: situated on the summit of one of the loftiest branches of the Sierra de Estrella, it obtains the name of *Guarda*, 'watch-tower,' from its position, and has always enjoyed the military reputation of being the 'key of Portugal.' The Prince of Essling resolved to stop his retreat here and to rest his army, but he was dislodged by one of Wellington's masterly combinations—a pressure on his flanks. On the 28th of March Picton's division drove the French out of Freixadas, while Trant and Miller, bringing up their *ordenanzas*, secured Pinhel and cut off communication with Almeida.

The French officers, little apprehensive of an assault in such an eyrie, relaxed their accustomed vigilance, and, to their utter confusion, were suddenly pounced upon by five columns of attack, consisting of infantry and cavalry, which had ascended the mountain by roads, the lengths of which, as they wound in numberless sinuosities along the sides of a precipice overspread with trees, were difficult to calculate. It was intended that the columns should reach the summit almost at one and the same moment without having been discovered, but Picton with the 3rd division was much earlier on his ground than the others. The brigade Maucune, posted considerably in front of the city, with difficulty escaped being cut off, but all were driven hastily from Guarda with the loss of 300 men.[7]

7. Sir E. Cust says that time and distance were so well calculated that the different columns were simultaneous in their arrival; but this was not so, as will he seen in Major Woodgate's letter to Davy describing these operations; and Picton himself expressed surprise that such 'a famous general (Massena) showed so little determination or talent on the occasion.' Picton's position was strong and commanding, hut his force very inferior, and Massena allowed him to remain for two hours within four hundred yards of his main body without attacking him.
As the columns came up staff-officers made constant use of their glasses, and one, pointing to an unfinished fort, remarked to Sir Edward Pakenham, 'We shall have some sharp work there; that place is full of men.'

Disappointed of rest and driven from Guarda, Massena still clung to the sterile hills of Portugal. The Emperor had ordered him not to quit it, yet he felt he could no longer maintain himself there. He also required time to supply the strong places he had won, Almeida and Ciudad Rodrigo. On the 29th he placed the Coa between himself and his adversary, with his right at Rovina and his left at Sabugal.

On the morning of the 3rd April the attack was made. The position itself could only be forced by turning the left, and the light division with Slade's cavalry crossed the upper stream by a wide circuit; Dunlop's division crossed at the bridge of Sabugal; and Picton with the third division supported these attacks.

The attack commenced in a frightful storm of rain, rendering things invisible and causing confusion. The early part of the fight fell on the light division and Beckwith's brigade. Admirable was the conduct of the 95th Rifles and the 43rd, who took a howitzer, and strenuous were the endeavours of the French to recapture it: the 52nd,however, came up and assisted them to retain it. Reynier put all his troops in motion and outflanked the British left, when at that moment the fifth and third divisions passed the bridge in the teeth of showers of grape, the British cavalry appeared on the hills, while Picton, resolutely opening fire, decided the fate of the day.[8]

(continued from previous page) Sir Edward fixed his glass on the spot, and after a short time replied—'Full of men; yes, it is full of men—but they're all red jackets!' It was Picton's division which had thus early got possession of the fort, after driving the enemy out with such precipitation that they actually left their kettles on the fires, containing their meat, which thus became a most acceptable prize to Picton's soldiers. Robinson's *Life of Sir Thomas Picton.*
8. It was the leading brigade (Colville's) of the fighting division which came up led by Picton; and an officer of one of the regiments describes their progress to the point of attack thus:—'As we advanced up the hill we formed line. General Picton rode up in front of us, with his stick over his shoulder, exposed to the heavy fire of the enemy, as composed as if he had been in perfect safety. "Steady! my lads, steady! and don't throw away your fire until I give you the word of command," he said. And not a shot was

The trophy of the howitzer cost the lives of nearly 200 men, and it was around this that the real battle was decided. The 1st 52nd, supporting the 43rd, had got it into an enclosure, when, as Wellington says in his despatch:

> The enemy were making arrangements to attack them again in this post, and had moved a column on their left, when the light infantry of Major-General Picton's division, under Lieutenant-Colonel Williams (60th Rifles), supported by Major-General the Hon. C. Colville's brigade, opened their fire on them.
>
> At the same moment the head of Major-General Dunlop's column crossed the bridge of the Coa, and ascended the heights on the right flank of the enemy, and the cavalry appeared on the high ground in rear of the enemy's left; the enemy then retired across the hills towards Rendo, leaving the howitzer in the possession of those who had so gallantly gained and preserved it, and about 200 killed on the ground, six officers, and 300 prisoners in our hands.

He adds, that in his opinion—

> .... the action was one of the most glorious that British troops were ever engaged in. . . . the enemy had retreated over the Spanish frontier on the 4th, and had continued their retreat, until on the 8th the last of them crossed the Agueda.

(continued from previous page) fired until within a few yards of the enemy's right; but then a volley was poured in close and true. A cheer at the same moment was caught up by Beckwith's tired soldiers, and the attack was renewed with fresh energy.'

Picton was in the constant habit of riding with a stick in his hand, and even in the heat of battle he sometimes retained it. When the firing commenced he might be observed tapping the mane of his horse, or a favourite cob, at measured intervals, in proportion to its rapidity; as it became quicker and the fight grew warmer, this movement of the stick would be increased both in rapidity and force until at length the animal became restive. But this seldom drew Picton's attention off, as his firm seat saved him from all apprehension of a fall.

The loss of the 60th at Sabugal was two riflemen killed, and one serjeant and one rifleman wounded.

Before tracing the further action of the army we will here give the last letter written by one of the 60th Rifles actually engaged in all these various combats, as the result of which the French were driven out of Portugal. On the 23rd of April, 1811, Major Woodgate wrote to his old friend and commanding officer as follows:

My dear Davy,

I can date this letter from no particular place, as I am not aware that the few houses we occupy are sufficient to create a village, or be called by any name; but we are between Almeida and Ciudad Rodrigo, near Alamadilla, having followed the enemy thus far "without impediment." I shall not attempt to give you a history of their retreat and our pursuit, as the despatches will tell you all, and with more accuracy than I can. I shall only say that your friend General Picton's division (and of them entirely the light companies, and our three companies, brigaded as before under Williams), together with the light division, were almost the only part of the infantry of the army engaged. We lost a few men and Sawatzky, whom, as an attentive and useful officer, I much lament.

There are about 1500 Almeida who are destined, by our arrangements, to fall into our hands, not by besieging that place, but we purpose starving them out, and for that purpose have surrounded the fortress; but the opinion is that the French, after getting themselves a little refreshed, will march a considerable force to their relief, which may, if we choose to stand, bring on what has been so long postponed, something like a general engagement.

On the retreat we never could bring them to stand. Their rear-guard, and that of great strength, 20,000 strong, under Reynier, was the only part of their army we could engage with, and they only fought because they were overtaken.

Every town on the road, Leiria, Pombal, Condeixa, &c., &c, has been burnt to the ground, and the road strewed with dead bodies of all ages, horses, mules, and baggage of every description.

We had two fine views of the enemy. We saw about 30,000 men march out from Condeixa, and at Guarda about 16,000 marched out, while our division was within 600 paces of them. The whole army was intended to have met there, and, cooperating, to have attacked them; but it so occurred that we, who had marched over the mountains, were the only people who arrived at the appointed time, and the enemy retiring on our first appearance, we had a fine opportunity of seeing them move off: as our force consisted of not more than 4000, we could do no more than quietly to march into the town when they marched out of it, which we did that evening.

Lord Wellington has left us for a week to go to the Alemtejo, to the camp there, and will probably attempt to retake Badajos, which you know has surrendered in the true Spanish way. General Hill's late division and General Cole's are on that side, with numerous Portuguese, under Marshal Beresford's command, who has been thought slow and dilatory. I think however we shall hear something good from that quarter soon.

You must have seen Andrews' promotion. He leaves us in a few days, having just come up to settle his pay-mastership accounts to March.

De Bree has not left England yet to join us, as Andrews hears from him last mail. He has most officiously (as usual) been sending out recruits to us without the least authority or leave from Colonel Williams; we received sixty-four of his selection lately, the greater part of whom were taken six months ago in this country. This is not giving the men or the regiment a fair chance. You will see him in London, as I am sure he will endeavour to find you out, on his way to join, when you can arrange the business about the stores.

I trust your plan of getting employed will succeed; I mean in the Guards, because I well know many lieutenant-colonels on full pay would be glad to exchange with you, but I think with you the Guards more eligible. Thinking of you the other day, it struck me that if you wished something immediately, while your other engagements are going on, that it would suit to be on this staff as assistant adjutant-general, which I have no doubt you could procure with much ease.

You will doubtless see Austin in London; tell him I received his friendly letter from Martinique, and now I know he is in England I shall write to him. We are going on much the same, only I am heartily tired of this concern, and I must at all events come over for a few months before winter.

After our last skirmish near Sabugal, I found the French *Ordre du jour* of the 1st April, which stated that a *feu de joie* would be fired on the following day, in consequence of the Empress of France having been delivered of a son, the King of Rome, on the 20th of March. It was the first news we heard of it, which we find confirmed by the papers; and I only mention it to show the expedition with which the intelligence reached the French army. I understand they have telegraphs from the Pyrenees to Madrid.

Steitz has been removed to the 1st battalion, and Gilse has resigned the adjutancy, and Broetz is appointed.

I am, my dear Davy,

Your faithful friend,

Wm. Woodgate

There was a short rest for the soldier, but none for the chiefs who conducted affairs. Massena was getting more anxious, and fearful of the Emperor's displeasure. That Emperor had given him stringent orders which he had been unable to carry out. That Emperor, having given these orders, had left him five long months without a communication. And when on breaking up from before 'the lines' he had sent General Foy to Paris to report and ask for instructions, supplies and reinforcements, that officer was detained until February, and then returned with the answer that none could be sent, all were wanted for Russia; but the Prince of Essling was to concentrate different corps, and to call on the Duke of Dalmatia for co-operation. But Soult was not much more obedient than Ney, whom he had now dismissed. He pleaded inability to march as directed on Abrantes; but though he refused point-blank to do this, he had so far put restraint upon himself as to convert the siege of Cadiz into a blockade, and to penetrate with 15,000 or 16,000 men into Estremadura.

He began this operation on the 31st December 1810, and Merida and Olivença opened their gates to him. His next move was on Badajos, but he approached it with great caution; and on the 19th January 1811, having beaten the Spanish army, he might have completed the investment of it, but still he delayed; and the Governor, *Don* José de Imar, held out until the 11th of March, when, though no practicable breach had been effected, and though he had received intelligence through Elvas that an English corps was approaching near for his relief, he surrendered at discretion!

Lord Wellington knew the value of Badajos and was mortified; and his chagrin was the greater as he had proofs that the base Spaniard had been bribed to a betrayal of his trust, and it would take the lives of a vast number of brave men to regain the fortress. Still it must be done; and we must take a glance at Beresford and his work, which had been carried on whilst the operations ending at Sabugal were in progress, because (though unsuccessful) the first siege of Badajos was, as Alison asserts, the real turning-point of the Peninsular War, and we have the interests to watch of four detached companies of the 5th 60th, three of which were engaged at Albuera.

At the end of 1810 Lord Hill had been forced by illness to go to England, and Beresford had been put in charge of the force on the left bank of the Tagus, which was considerably augmented by Portuguese troops, and amounted to about 14,000 men. It was composed of eighteen guns, two divisions of infantry, and five regiments of cavalry, Portuguese and British.

Beresford was successful in the recovery of Campo Mayor, and early in April he recovered Olivença; which he summoned on the 9th, but the governor refused to surrender, when the army encamped round the place and preparations were made for the siege. On the 11th however intelligence arrived that the French under Latour Maubourg had retired to Llerena, when Beresford started after them.

The garrison of the fort was nearly 500 men, and General Cole with the 4th division was employed in its reduction. In this division one company of 60th Rifles attached to Kemmis's brigade was present, and the fort surrendered at discretion on the 15th of the month.

The small loss of the British (only four men killed and ten wounded) was attributed by General Cole to the fire kept up by the British light companies and the rifle companies of the 60th and Brunswick regiment under Majors Pearson and Birmingham. By the capture of the place nine Spanish officers and eighty men, prisoners of war to the French, were released, and the garrison, consisting of twenty-eight officers and 357 men (effectives) with ninety-six sick and wounded in hospital of the French artillery, were made prisoners.

But though successful at Campo Mayor and Olivença, Beresford was in difficulties on the Guadiana, and Wellington, for whom there was no rest, set off in haste to apply a remedy. Speeding from Villa Formosa he was at Elvas by April 20th, and on the 22nd reconnoitred Badajos in company with Beresford himself, fixed on Albuera as the spot on which a battle should be fought if forced on by Soult, and gave detailed instructions for the conduct of the siege of Badajos.

But Wellington did not assume the command of the army on the south side of the Tagus. Scarcely had he dismounted when a despatch was put in his hands that Massena was again about to take the field, and it was necessary for him to hurry back to the north.

On the 25th April Wellington was back with his army on the Coa, with which he was blockading Almeida and watching any movement of the French. Massena had not been able to supply Almeida, and he was now anxious to do so. He had abundantly supplied Ciudad Rodrigo, and had been feeding his army from those supplies.[9]

Lord Wellington's despatch to the Earl of Liverpool from Villa Formosa on the 8th May, 1811, will give the clearest account of what took place. He says:

> The enemy's whole army, consisting of the 2nd, 6th, and 8th corps, and all the cavalry which could be collected in Castille and Leon, including about 900 of the Imperial Guard, crossed the Agueda at Ciudad Rodrigo on the 2nd inst. The battalions of the 9th corps had been joined to the regiments to which they belonged in the other three corps, excepting a division consisting of battalions belonging to regiments in the corps doing duty in Andalusia, which division likewise formed part of the army.
>
> As my object in maintaining a position between the Coa and the Agueda, after the enemy had retired from the former, was to blockade Almeida, which place I had learned, from intercepted letters and other information, was ill-supplied with provisions for its garrison, and as

---

9. See Cust's *Annals* and Gleig's *Life of Wellington*.

the enemy were infinitely superior to us in cavalry, I did not give any opposition to their march, and they passed the Azava that evening. They continued their march on the 3rd in the morning towards the Dos Casas in three columns.

The allied army had been cantoned along the river Dos Casas, and on the sources of the Azava; the light division at Gallegos and Espeja. This last fell back upon Fuentes de Onoro, on the Dos Casas, with the British cavalry, as the enemy advanced; and the 1st, 3rd, and 7th divisions were collected at that place.

Shortly after the enemy had formed on the ground on the right of the Dos Casas, on the afternoon of the 3rd they attacked with a large force the village of Fuentes d'Onor, which was defended in a most gallant manner by Lieutenant-Colonel Williams[10] of the 5th battalion 60th Regiment, in command of the light infantry battalion belonging to Major-General Picton's division, supported by the light infantry battalion of General Nightingale's brigade, and that of Major-General Howard's brigade, the light infantry battalion K. G. L., with the 5th and 2nd 83rd Regiments.

The troops maintained their position, but observing the repeated efforts which the enemy were making to obtain possession of the village, I reinforced it successively with the 71st, 79th, and 24th regiments. The 71st, under Colonel Cadogan, charged the enemy and drove them from a part of the village of which they had obtained a momentary possession. Nearly at this time Lieutenant-Colonel Williams was unfortunately wounded, but

---

10. The spirited conduct of Lieutenant-Colonel Williams of the 60th, who commanded the light troops of Picton's division on this occasion, and who in the most gallant manner defended the village against the repeated attacks of the enemy, called forth the warmest eulogiums from General Picton and the whole army. It was not until after he was wounded that the light troops were arrested in their successful opposition. Robinson's *Life of Picton*.

I hope not dangerously; and the command devolved upon Lieutenant-Colonel Cameron, 79th.

The contest continued until night, when our troops remained in possession of the whole.[11]

Napier calls the fighting of this day the 'combat' of Fuentes d'Onor; the 'battle' was on the 5th May.

Massena, dissatisfied with the results of the day's fighting, and not having as he designed made himself master of the Castel Bom road, spent the 4th in reconnoitring, and on the 5th he attacked.

The British were drawn up on the level summit of a plateau, between two deep ravines accessible only by a neck of land on their right, and against this point the attack of the French was directed. So vehement was their onset that the British were driven back, and Montbrun with 4000 Cuirassiers (covered with the glories of Wagram, and to whom the allies had only 1200 horse to oppose), instantly taking advantage of the confusion, turned and broke the right wing. Wellington now fell back at right angles to his former position, a perilous movement, but executed by his troops with invincible steadiness in the face of the enemy, and the desperate combat continued without decided advantage till nightfall, when the French drew off. Wellington, wearied as his troops were, spent the night in throwing up field-works, which when the morning dawned the enemy showed no disposition to assail.[12]

The loss on either side was about 1500 *hors-de-combat,* of which the loss of the 5th 60th was—

On the evening of the 3rd May, three riflemen killed, Lieutenant-Colonel Williams (severely) and Lieut. Duchastelette (slightly) wounded, nine riflemen wounded, and eight missing.

---

11. See *Wellington Despatches.*
12. See Alison's *History*, Gleig's *Life of Wellington,* Carter's *Medals of the British Army*

On the 5th May, Major Woodgate and Lieutenant Wynne wounded, one serjeant and eleven riflemen wounded, and one missing.

The battle of Fuentes d'Onor, though less decisive than perhaps any other in which Lord Wellington ever commanded, served every purpose for which it had been hazarded.

On the 8th May the enemy retired to the woods between Espeja, Gallegos, and Fuentes d'Onor, in which position the whole army was collected by the following day, with the exception of that part of the second corps which continued opposite Alameda; but during the night of the 9th the whole broke up and retired across the Azava, covering their retreat by their numerous cavalry, and on the following day the whole crossed the Agueda, leaving Almeida to its fate. Unable to relieve it, he sent orders to the governor to blow up the works and evacuate the place, which was done in the night of the 10th. Four hundred of the garrison were made prisoners in the attempt to escape, and thus the soil of Portugal was cleared of the enemy.

Colonel Williams was specially mentioned in Lord Wellington's despatch.

When the Prince of Essling retired to Ciudad Rodrigo, he found Marshal Marmont, Duke of Ragusa, had arrived there on the 7th, with orders from the Emperor to supersede him and assume the command of the army. Thus Massena, Ney, Junot, and Loison quitted the Peninsula for France all about the same time, and the military career of the old Marshal arrived at its close, though his life was continued for some years. We must now turn to the force under Marshal Beresford, where we have four companies of the 60th Rifles attached respectively to the brigades of —

2nd division, Major-General Hon. W. Stewart:
Colonel Colborne, one company
Major-General Hoghton, one company

Colonel Abereromby, one company

4th division, Major-General Lowry Cole:
Colonel Kemmis, one company

It was the 4th of May before Badajos could be invested towards the south. Its communications with the open country towards the north were not cut off till the 8th. The besiegers were ill-furnished with artillery, ammunition, and stores; and their guns, served chiefly by Portuguese recruits, made little impression. They could not open fire upon Fort St. Christoval earlier than the 11th, when intelligence of Soult's approach came in. He had collected about 19,000 infantry and cavalry at Seville, and was advancing with rapid strides to relieve the place. Beresford upon this sent away his siege guns, destroyed such of the stores as he could not remove, and marched with the main body of his force to meet the enemy, and on the 15th drew up at Albuera.

The allies had 30,000 men in all;[13] but 16,000 were Spaniards and 8,000 Portuguese, 7,500 only were British; 3,000 were cavalry, and they had thirty-eight guns.

The action began early on the 16th by a movement of the French against the bridge of the Albuera rivulet, which was opposed by the Portuguese and Hanoverian brigade; but the real attack was made on the right, where a range of heights was held by the Spaniards.

Blake, with characteristic obstinacy, at first refused to change his front to receive the enemy; and when the evolution was at last ordered, the unwieldy masses of the Spaniards were charged in the midst of this critical movement by an overwhelming body of the enemy; and after a short and sanguinary struggle were driven in confusion from their vantage-ground, which was immediately occupied by the French artillery. Beresford perceiving the danger ordered the British divisions from the centre; but as the leading brigade were

13. See Cust's *Annals* Gleig's *Life of Wellington*.

deploying to charge, they were assailed in flank and rear by the French Hussars and Polish Lancers, who had got round them under cover of a mist, and were almost all slain or taken. All seemed lost; but the 31st stood its ground, and Hoghton's brigade came up to the front. Hoghton fell nobly leading the 29th, and the fire of the British began to slacken for want of ammunition, while a deep gully prevented their reaching the enemy with the bayonet.

Colonel Hardinge on his own responsibility, while Beresford was preparing for a retreat, ordered Cole's division to mount the hill on the right, while Abercrombie with the reserve ascended on the left. The French were thus assailed on both flanks in the position into which their advance in the centre had led them. The Fusilier brigade, incessantly pressing on, retook six guns which had been captured by the Polish Lancers, and the French were at length driven headlong down the hill, on the summit of which 1,500 unwounded men, the remnant of 7,500 unconquerable British soldiers, stood triumphant. The Portuguese and Germans pressed the pursuit, and the French, though covered by the fire of their artillery and by Montbrun's gallant Cuirassiers, were driven in headlong confusion from the field of battle.

Kemmis's brigade, with the company of 60th Rifles, which had done good service at Olivença, were not up in time for the battle, but arrived next day by a forced march from Jerumenha. The morning of the 17th showed both armies in their respective situations; but in the evening these reinforcements arrived, and two divisions, the 3rd and 7th, were hurrying up from the Coa, which Wellington had sent to Beresford's support. Soult therefore gave up all idea of renewing the contest, and on the 18th retreated.

The 60th lost on the 10th, when they repulsed a sally from Badajos—one captain (Prevost) and seven riflemen wounded, besides three who were wounded in the trenches on the 5th. And in the battle of the 16th they had one sergeant and one rifleman killed, and Lieutenant Ingersleben, two sergeants, and sixteen riflemen were wounded.

On the 21st Lord Wellington arrived. Hill also returned from sick-leave and resumed his command. Beresford went to Lisbon to reorganise the Portuguese army, and Wellington resumed supreme direction of affairs on the Alemtejo.

Badajos was invested anew on the 25th of May, and the engineers broke ground on the 31st as a false attack against Pardaleras, under fire of which 1,200 men successfully opened a trench on the night of 30—31st, and another against the castle at 800 yards.

On the night of the 6-7th of June the breach in San Christoval was deemed practicable, and an assault was attempted, but the stormers were beaten off with the loss of 100 men. Again, on the night of the 9-10th another assault was ordered, but was again unsuccessful; and as the troops could not form for the attack of the castle breach until Fort Christoval was taken, it remained unassailed, and the second attempt on Badajos ended. For on the 10th an intercepted despatch informed Lord Wellington that Marmont and Soult intended to concentrate their whole force in Estremadura, and that Reynier, with Marmont's advance, would be at Merida on the 15th; in consequence of which the siege was stopped on the 12th. But Wellington, who had studied his ground, had determined that the hill country from Campo Mayor to Portalegre would afford him a good position to canton his army during the hot season, and he therefore called in Hill and marched his army away, concentrating on the 17th on both banks of the Caya. The two marshals, in spite of their enormous superiority of force, were deceived by the boldness of his attitude, and entered Badajos together, where they gave their hands to its noble defender, Philippon.

Wellington determined then to return to much the same position he had formerly held on the Coa, maintaining a blockade of Ciudad Rodrigo, which he thought was only supplied till the 20th of August, not having learnt that Marmont had thrown fresh supplies into the place before moving southwards; he was therefore much mortified when, in the first week in August, he placed the fortress in complete blockade, to find they had two months' more provisions than he had calculated.

In September Marmont became anxious about Ciudad Rodrigo, and desirous of opening communications with it. Leaving one division on the Tagus, he crossed the Guadarama with the rest of his army. Dorsenne made a simultaneous movement on the 22nd, and the army of the north, consisting of 14,000 or 15,000 admirable troops, escorted a convoy which threaded its way through the English posts with skill and celerity, and the place was revictualled for eight months.

The proceeding was more prompt than was expected, and the British army was sickly and scattered; to risk a battle therefore beyond the Agueda was hazardous, and Wellington fell back upon El Bodon and took up a position there.

The position was not strong, nor the cavalry numerous; while Montbrun had thirty or forty squadrons, fourteen battalions, and twelve guns. Wellington had a difficult card to play. In his despatch to Lord Liverpool of 20th September, 1811, he says:

> The 3rd division and that part of Major-General V. Alten's brigade of cavalry which was not detached occupied the range of heights which are on the left of the Agueda, having their advanced guard under Lieutenant-Colonel Williams of the 60th on the heights of Pastores, within three miles of Ciudad Rodrigo, the light division on the Agueda. General Graham on the left on the Lower Azava. On the 23rd the enemy appeared in the plain, but retired again after a short time. On the 24th they advanced again in considerable force, and before evening had collected their army beyond the hills which surround the plain of Ciudad Rodrigo.[14]

14. See *Wellington Despatches*.

The portion of Picton's division about Pastores was too far distant to take immediate part in the beautifully-managed retreat that then took place; the allied infantry formed into squares to resist the charges of Montbrun's cavalry; these driven off, they remained still in their square formation, and retired in the utmost order on Fuente Guinaldo, the enemy never attempting to charge them a second time, but following them and firing on them with artillery.

Lieutenant-Colonel Williams (of the 60th) with his light infantry, and Lieutenant-Colonel the Hon. R. Trench with the 74th Regiment, retired from Pastores across the Agueda, and thence marched by Robleda, where they took some prisoners; recrossed the Agueda, and joined at Guinaldo in the evening.

The enemy brought up a second division of infantry in the afternoon of the 25th; and in the course of that night, and of the 26th, they collected the whole of their army in front of our position at Guinaldo; and not deeming it expedient to stand their attack in that position I retired about three leagues. On the 27th the French detached a division of infantry and fourteen squadrons of cavalry to follow the retreat by Albergueria, and another of the same strength followed by Forcalhos.

The former attacked and drove in the picquets at Aldea da Ponte. Pakenham attacked them with his brigade of the 4th division, supported by Lieutenant-General Hon. L. Cole (with 4th division), and by Sir S. Cotton's cavalry; the enemy were driven through Aldea da Ponte back upon Albergueria, and the picquets of the cavalry resumed their station.

But the enemy, having been reinforced by the troops which marched from Forcalhos, again advanced about unset and drove in the picquets of the cavalry from Aldea da Ponte, and took possession of the village.

Lieutenant-General Cole again attacked them, and drove them through the village; but night coming on he evacuated it, and the enemy occupied it during the night.

On the 28th Lord Wellington formed the army on the heights of Soito, about a league in rear of his position on the 27th. The enemy also retired from Aldea da Ponte, and had their advanced posts at Albergueria.

Marmont's opportunity had escaped him, and his troops were beginning to suffer from want of provisions. So he returned to his cantonments. Ciudad Rodrigo was safe, but Wellington had escaped from his toils, and quietly withdrew to a better position between the Coa and the Agueda.

On the 27th Captain Prevost of the 60th Rifles, who had been slightly wounded at the repulse of the sortie from Badajos on May 10th, was again wounded, and this time 'severely.'

The brilliant campaign of 1811 was now at an end as regarded the main army, but Hill had in October a separate and most successful affair in the surprise and capture of Arroyo Molinos; and as he had two companies of the 60th Rifles with him, whose services gave him great satisfaction, the event must be recorded before closing this portion of our sketch.

Lieutenant-General Hill gave his report of the affair in a despatch to Lord Wellington, dated Merida, 30th of October, 1811.[15] From this it is seen that he had 'been instructed to drive the enemy out of that part of Estremadura which lies between the Tagus and the Guadiana.' He therefore commenced his movements on the 22nd. On the 23rd the head of the column reached Albuquerque. On the 24th he had a portion of his force at Aliseda, and the remainder at Casa de Castillana, about a league distant. On the 25th he made a cavalry reconnaissance and drove the enemy from Arroyo del Puerco, who retired to Malpartida. On the 26th he followed to that place, but the enemy had left, and Hill halted his troops

---

15. See *Wellington Despatches*.

for the night. He put them in motion again next morning; and hearing that the enemy had only left Torremocha that morning and had halted his main body at Arroyo Molinos, he made a forced march to Alcuescar that evening, placed his troops out of sight, and allowed no fire to be made.

Finding the French ignorant of his approach and off their guard, General Hill determined to attempt a surprise before the enemy should march in the morning.

The troops moved from their bivouac near Alcuescar about two o'clock on the morning of the 28th, right in front, direct on Arroyo Molinos.

Major-General Howard's brigade, 1st 50th, 71st, and 92nd Regiments (with one company 60th Rifles), led; Colonel Wilson's brigade, 1st 28th, 2nd 34th, and 39th, with another company 60th Rifles, followed; and then his Portuguese and Spanish infantry and cavalry. They moved in this order until within half-a-mile of the town of Arroyo Molinos, where, under cover of a low ridge, the column closed and divided into three columns—Howard to the left, Wilson to the right, the cavalry in the centre.

The advance was unperceived by the enemy. One brigade of Girard's division had already marched by the road of Medellin, the brigade of Dombrowski and the dragoons of Briche were falling in to follow them, and General Girard was in his quarters waiting for his horse. Hill's men stood waiting for his order, and he with them maintaining the calmest demeanour. Suddenly he drew his sword, gave a loud hurrah, spurred his horse, and leading the men with an animation and enthusiasm which astonished those who knew the man, burst into the street, whilst 'Hey, Johnny Cope, are ye wauking yet' from the bagpipes of the Highlanders rose above the storm. The surprise was complete. Girard himself scaled the rocks and escaped. Generals Brun and D'Aremberg, with 1300 prisoners, three guns, and the whole of the baggage fell into the hands of the victors.

The affair filled all the French divisions with an eager desire to revenge it. But again, about two months later, Hill was too much for them, and he nearly captured the division of Dombrowski: only, getting a hint of his danger, that general quitted Merida in the night, leaving a magazine of bread and wheat to the allies.

Hill gave ample and well-deserved praise to the brigades of Howard and Wilson; and the order with his thanks to the troops, dated Portalegre, 9th of November, 1811, whilst it 'begged them to accept his best thanks generally and individually,' also 'noticed in terms of the highest approbation the conduct of Captain Blassiere, 5th battalion 60th, for the close reconnaissance he made of the enemy's position on the night preceding the action.'

CHAPTER 8

Ciudad Rodrigo, Badajos, Salamanca: 1812

The Spanish authorities wished Wellington to make a winter campaign, but he could not be induced to do so. His men had simply no clothes, his horses were dying for want of fodder, and there was great sickness among the troops, partly from fatigue and exposure during the operations of 1811, and in some measure from the return of Walcheren fever amongst those who had served in that expedition. He therefore allowed the troops to remain quietly in cantonments; but he himself was by no means idle, but actively, though quietly, preparing for the execution of the great plans he had formed.

He was desirous of carrying the war into Spain, but he would not let go his hold on Portugal which he had now secured, nor could he attempt an advance without first obtaining possession of Ciudad Rodrigo and Badajos.

If these two important fortresses were to be taken it must be in the shortest possible time, so that Marmont should not relieve Rodrigo, nor Soult Badajos; so Wellington spent the winter in preparations for the spring he was about to make at the beginning of the new year.

He had had no proper guns or material for carrying on the first and second attempts on Badajos. The trenching tools supplied to the army were so infamously bad that the working parties used to struggle for those tools which had been captured in Fort Olivença; and the state of things gave rise to Picton's grim joke that 'Lord Wellington was suing Badajos in *forma pauperis.*'

Wellington however had at length received a siege train from England, which had been brought up the Tagus and placed in Almeida, the breaches of which he had repaired; and where he had collected all his material for a siege, and the parts of a trestle-bridge to be put together when required, and had even built 600 wagons of a lighter pattern, of his own planning, to improve the transport of his stores.

He knew that what he had to do must be done quickly. He had good information as to the position of the French troops, whilst they were in ignorance of his intentions; and finding Marmont supine, and that Napoleon was still withdrawing troops for the Russian campaign, he resolved on his endeavour to take Rodrigo almost by a *coup-de-main.* He directed Hill, who was stationed at Portalegre with 15,000 men, to create alarm in Andalusia by demonstrations in the direction of Seville; and on the 7th of January, 1812, in spite of frost and snow, passed the Agueda and closely invested Ciudad Rodrigo.

The outworks, a lunette and the fortified convents of Santa Cruz and San Francisco, were stormed and carried, and the batteries which were opened on the 14th had by the 18th made two breaches which were declared practicable.

Lord Wellington now made a close personal observation of the state of the wall, and was satisfied that the assault might be given with success. Sitting on the embankment of a field-work, amid the roar of artillery, he wrote the order for attack on the night of 19th-20th, precise and circumstantial in detail.

This order contained the words 'Ciudad Rodrigo must be stormed this evening;' and the brave fellows' comment on the decree when the order was given out was only 'We will do it.'[1]

---

1. See Alison's *Epitome* and Sir E. Cust's *Annals.*

The assault was ordered for seven o'clock. The main breach was assigned to the third division, (Picton's), Crawfurd with the light division was to attack the lesser.

General Picton marched the left brigade of his division to the convent of Santa Cruz, situated on the right of the batteries, where the officers and men were made acquainted with the duties which they had to perform, the remainder of the division being formed in the first parallel. The night was calm, and the heavens studded with stars; and a young moon shed a faint light upon the earth, which seemed to mock by its tranquillity the wild and sanguinary scene which was about to ensue.

Colonel O'Toole with the light company of the 83rd Regiment and the second Caçadores was directed to cross the Agueda by the bridge, and make an attack upon the outwork in front of the castle ten minutes before the time appointed for the general assault; his instructions being to destroy two guns planted in this outwork which might be the means of annoying the assailants by flanking the entrance to the ditch. At half-past six the division was ready, when General Picton trotted up, pounding the sides of his hog-maned cob, and accompanied by his staff.[2]

Mackinnon's brigade was to take the lead, composed of the 60th Rifles (five companies), the 45th Regiment, the 74th Regiment, and the 88th Regiment. Lieutenant-Colonel Campbell, in the absence of General Colville, commanded the left brigade in support, composed of the 5th, 77th, 94th, and 83rd Regiments, the whole being directed against the principal breach.

---

2. From Robinson's *Life of Sir Thomas Picton*. To each regiment Picton said a kindly word. When he came to the 88th Regiment his words were, 'Rangers of Connaught! it is not my intention to expend any "powder" this evening; we'll do the business with the "could iron"!' which were received by those whom he called his 'brave rascals' with a shout of determination.

At 7 p.m. the signal was given. The assailants reached the walls and cleared the counterscarp; at the foot of the great breach they were met by a terrific discharge of grape and musketry at a few yards' distance; shells and grenades were rolled down, which burst in the midst of the throng; and when they had at last won the summit a mine was fired under their feet, and the most forward, among whom was the gallant Mackinnon, were blown into the air. Still they held the ground they had gained.

The lesser breach had been stormed after a severe struggle, in which Crawfurd was mortally wounded on the glacis.

The Portuguese also had scaled the walls on the opposite side of the fortress, and it was won.

The total loss to the allies during the siege and at the assault amounted to 178 killed, 818 wounded, and seven missing: of these the losses of the 5th batt. 60th were two riflemen wounded on the 18th, and at the assault on the 19th one serjeant was killed, and Captain Levington and three riflemen were wounded. Of the French garrison who survived, 1500, including sick and wounded, became prisoners of war, and all Marmont's battering train and immense stores were taken.

So prompt had been Lord Wellington (now made an Earl) in his operations, and so imperfect was Marmont's intelligence, that he never heard until the 15th that the English had taken the field; and though he calculated on collecting his scattered forces on the Agueda by the 26th or 27th, the astounding intelligence of the capture of Rodrigo was received by him on the 21st at Fuente il Santo, and he had to find a new *point-d'appui* as near the Portuguese frontier as was safe, and Salamanca was the spot chosen for the purpose. It was put into a state of defence by fortifying three convents, which stood at the three angles of a triangle, and inclosed among them a considerable space of ground.

The third division were highly and specially complimented by their general, who in his despatch to Lord Liverpool says:

The conduct of all parts of the third division, in the operations which they performed with so much gallantry and exactness on the evening of the 19th, in the dark, afford the strongest proof of the abilities of Lieutenant-General Picton and Major-General Mackinnon, by whom they were directed and led.

Lord Wellington at once set to work to repair the breaches and improve the defence of his captured fortress, but he was interrupted by stormy weather. On the 28th such heavy rain set in that the trestle-bridge at Marialva could not stand; the stone bridge was two feet under water, and the place was exposed for several days to recapture but for the ill-judged operations of Marmont.

Badajos was anxiously looked to, and a pontoon-bridge with military artificers and some Portuguese seamen were ordered from Lisbon to Abrantes, where draft bullocks were collected to draw it to Elvas; and Major Dickson gave his whole energies at Lisbon to arrangements for bringing up ship's guns, which had been applied for from Admiral Berkeley. Through his energy the guns, fifty-two in number, and the pontoons were parked at Elvas early in March, and gabions and fascines were piled in great numbers.

Marmont's wishes and suggestions had been sharply refused by Napoleon, who ordered the protection of Badajos to be left to Soult; so he drew to a head on the Tormes, and transferred at the same time his head quarters from Valladolid to Salamanca.

Wellington desired nothing better. Whilst Marmont kept four divisions near the Tagus his designs were suspended; but he no sooner heard of their removal than he resumed his project, and putting his army in motion he arrived at Elvas on the 11th March.

This march from the Agueda to the Guadiana was as perilous an enterprise as Wellington ever attempted. His men were all but naked, and, for lack of means to bring the clothing up to them, he was obliged to detach regiment after regiment to points on the Tagus where the clothing at the moment happened to be. Had the enemy been a more enterprising one he probably would never have run such risks; but no evil came of it, nor were his working parties at Rodrigo or Almeida molested, and on March 16th he established his bridge on the Guadiana, two leagues above Elvas, and on the 17th Badajos was invested.

Ground being broken the same night, the first parallel was drawn; and from hour to hour the works went on with all the vigour of which officers and men were capable, stoutly opposed as they were by a garrison of 5,000 men under the resolute and skilful General Philippon.

The capture of Rodrigo was completed in twelve days, one half of the time which might have been expected; that of Badajos took twenty days, and even then was much hastened; and we may not follow siege operations from day to day in detail.

On March 17th the trenches were opened.

On the 19th the French made a sortie which, though repulsed, caused a great loss to the English in trenching tools, which they could ill-spare. Heavy rains set in, the trenches were flooded, the pontoon-bridge over the Guadiana was carried away, provisions ran short, and all, except Lord Wellington, grew despondent.

The bridge was restored, the trenches baled out, and on the 25th the batteries opened. There was no time for regular approaches; as soon as an outwork was breached it was stormed.

On the night of the 25th-26th the Picurina lunette fell, and the ravelin of San Roque was next attacked; and then upon two bastions, the Trinidad and the Santa Maria, fresh batteries were opened.

On the 5th of April Wellington visited the trenches and directed the fire on the curtain.

On the evening of April 6th he formed three columns of

attack for the assault to be delivered at 10 o'clock that night (of 6th and 7th); and faithful to the appointed hour the troops moved on.

The 4th and light divisions, together nearly 10,000 men, were to assault respectively the breaches of the Trinidad and Santa Maria bastions, while attempts were to be made by escalade by Picton and Kempt on the castle, and by Leith on the distant bastion of San Vincente.

As soon as it was sufficiently dark to prevent detection by the garrison the two British brigades of the 3rd division moved from their encampment in columns right in front. They were composed as follows—the right brigade, under Sir James Kempt, was formed of the 45th, 74th, and 88th Regiments; the left of 2nd battalion 5th, 77th, 83rd, and 94th, under Campbell of the 94th; the seven light companies of these regiments and three companies of the 5th 60th, all under Colonel Williams of the 60th Rifles, forming the advance. The division took a circuitous route towards the river and, according to a preconcerted plan, halted on the ground which had been pointed out to them, there to await the arrival of the several divisions and corps at the points assigned to each previous to the great attack.

The storming parties approached the breaches in silence. No sooner had they descended into the fosse than the foremost were blown to atoms by the explosion of shells and powder-barrels; many others were drowned by falling into the inundated part of the ditch; but the survivors pressed on, boiling with ardour, over the mangled bodies of their comrades, and, though assailed on every side by a plunging cross-fire, forced their way to the summit of the breach. But their way was barred by *chevaux-de-frise* formed of ponderous beams studded with sword-blades; their ranks were enfiladed by grape and musketry within pistol-shot range; and after two hours' hideous carnage they were withdrawn from the walls, 2000 having fallen.

Picton however had been more fortunate. The first attempt to scale the castle wall had been unsuccessful; many had been thrown from the ladders, and miserably transfixed on the bayonets of their comrades below; but the attack was renewed in a more accessible quarter, and Ridge of the 5th regiment having succeeded in mounting the walls, the castle at last was won.

The San Vincente bastion had also been carried, and the troops pouring into the town took the breaches in reverse. The victors were now in possession of Badajos; and Philippon, who had taken refuge in Fort Christoval, surrendered the next morning with 3,800 prisoners, 170 heavy guns, and immense stores.

But the English loss was 5,000 killed and wounded, of which 3,500 were struck down at the assault. The loss of the 5th 60th being, from 18th to 22nd of March, three riflemen killed and three wounded; between 23rd and 26th, one rifleman wounded; from March 31st to April 2nd, one killed and four wounded and at the assault on 6th and 7th of April, Lieutenant Sterne and four riflemen killed, and Lieutenant-Colonels Williams and Fitzgerald, Lieutenant de Gilse, Adjutant Broetz, two sergeants, and twenty-four riflemen wounded.

Lord Wellington's despatch, dated Badajos, April 7, 1812, gives many names of gallant men; and among them prominently appear Picton's, who led the 3rd division, and Colville's, who had some of the 5th 60th attached to him in the 4th division.[3] He says:

> The duties in the trenches were conducted successively by Major-General the Hon. G. Colville, Major-General Bowes, and Major-General Kempt, under the superintendence of Lieutenant-General Picton. I have had occasion to mention all these officers during the course of the operations; and they all distinguished themselves, and were all wounded in the assault.

3. See *Wellington Despatches* and Gleig's *Life of Wellington.*

I am particularly obliged to Lieutenant-General Picton for the manner in which he arranged the attack of the castle; for that in which he supported the attack, and established his troops in that important post.

And again later:

The officers and troops in the 3rd division have distinguished themselves as usual in these operations. Lieutenant-General Picton has reported to me particularly the conduct of Lieutenant-Colonel Williams of the 60th, Lieutenant-Colonel Ridge of the 5th, who was unfortunately killed in the assault of the castle, and Lieutenant-Colonel Fitzgerald of the 60th. . . .

During all this time Soult had been culpably negligent to the south of the Tagus; and it was not until April 8, when Philippon's messengers arrived at his camp and told him that the defence of Badajos could be no longer maintained,that he began to move. He set out the same day with 24,000 men, expecting to meet Marmont with 30,000, but in this he was disappointed, and his mortification was increased by learning that, only two days previously, Badajos had fallen. Ballasteros threatened Seville and the communications with his rear; he expected Wellington would advance into Andalusia, and he fell back hastily and took position at the debouches of the Sierra Morena.

Wellington would willingly have pursued and struck a decisive blow at the Marshal, but was again hampered by the inertness of the Spanish and Portuguese governments, whom he had failed to induce to put Almeida and Ciudad Rodrigo in a proper state of defence. Marmont too had advanced from Salamanca into the unprotected province of Beira, which he ravaged with much cruelty, and his advance endangered the two fortresses. Wellington therefore returned rapidly to his old position on the Agueda (April 35), while Marmont withdrew to his former cantonments about Salamanca, and both armies occupied the same ground which they had held at the commencement of the year.

Napoleon, whilst he censured his generals severely for the loss of the frontier fortresses, withdrew the Imperial Guards and other troops to the number of 40,000 from Spain, where they still however mustered not loss than 380,000 men, while Wellington had only 80,000 under his orders, of which 37,000 were Portuguese, and one-fourth of the whole were constantly non-effective from sickness.[4]

When however he had succeeded in repairing and victualling the two Spanish fortresses, as well as Almeida and Elvas, he prepared to assume the offensive in Spain.

But before commencing operations he resolved to attack the French fortifications which covered the bridge of boats over the Tagus at Almarez (all the permanent bridges having been destroyed); and Hill, with a column of 6,000 men, was entrusted with this difficult service. The attention of the French was diverted by a demonstration towards Andalusia, and Hill, by a rapid movement from Jaraicejo across the mountains, passed the castle of Mirabete, and assaulted the forts early on the morning of the 19th of May. After a brief but fierce conflict Fort Napoleon on the left bank was scaled and carried; Fort Ragusa on the opposite shore was abandoned by its defenders, and the bridge with all its defences was destroyed; and Hill retired unmolested to Merida, where he confronted Drouet in Estremadura, whom Soult had reinforced up to the number of 21,000 men.

Lord Wellington, in his despatch from Fuente Guinaldo, 28th of May, 1812, calls Lord Liverpool's attention to this 'brilliant exploit' of Hill's, whom be praises in the highest terms; and adds:

I have nothing to add to Lieutenant-General Sir R. Hill's

---

4. See *Epitome of Alison's History*.

report of the conduct of the officers and troops under his command, excepting to express my concurrence in all he says in their praise. Too much cannot be said of the brave officers and troops who took by storm, without the assistance of cannon, such works as the enemy's forts on both banks of the Tagus, fully garrisoned, and in good order, and defended by eighteen pieces of artillery.

Sir Rowland Hill, in his report from Truxillo, 21st of May, speaks highly of Wilson's brigade on the 16th, and General Howard's on the evening of the 18th, to each of which he had attached companies of the 60th at Arroyo Molinos; but they were not apparently in the final assault, as Sir R. Hill explains that the 92nd and part of the 71st had not been able to advance.

But the share which they had in the operations, and the zeal which they displayed, entitle them to my warmest commendation; and I cannot avoid to mention the steadiness and good discipline of the 6th Portuguese Infantry, and two companies of the 60th Regiment under Colonel Ashworth, which formed the reserve to this attack.

And now we approach the battle of 'Salamanca,' the victory not only the most important in its results, but the crowning point of a long series of the most brilliant manoeuvres, and Wellington's favourite battle. One reads and re-reads the description of these operations untired, whoever may be the narrator, and one would fain transcribe all the pages of Napier and Alison, Cust and Gleig, and then feel that the subject was not exhausted; but in this sketch, the object being only to connect the 60th with each of the Peninsular victories, we must be as succinct as we can; and in this place, as often has been done already, we must epitomise the *Epitome of Alison,* to give in a few pages the operations of thirty-five days.

On the 13th of June, then, Wellington, having completed his preparations, crossed the Agueda, and four days later appeared before Salamanca. Marmont retired as he advanced, after throwing garrisons into the forts of the town and the castle of Alba de Tormes, which commands the passage of the river.

In these operations on San Vincente, St. Cayetano, and La Merced, the 5th battalion 60th lost one rifleman killed and two wounded. But success did not always attend them. On June 23rd there was an attempt to storm the forts; but after a short cannonade it was repulsed, and General Bowes, who led the assault, was killed.

A general battle was now expected; but Marmont, after lying for several days in front of the English at San Christoval, withdrew (on learning that the forts had been taken on the 26th) the garrison of Alba de Tormes, and retired behind the Douro.

On July 7th Bonnet effected his junction with Marmont, raising his army to 45,000 men. Caffarelli was approaching with 12,000 more, and King Joseph was in motion with the army of the centre to fall on the right.

Wellington's situation became precarious; and Marmont making a skilful feint towards Toro countermarched rapidly to Tordesillas, and crossing the Douro there re-opened communications with Joseph.

This able manoeuvre left Wellington no alternative but a retreat; but in the commencement of this movement, on July 18, the British right (composed of the 4th and light divisions under Sir Stapleton Cotton) was for a time exposed to the attack of the greater part of the French force. The firmness of the troops however extricated them from the danger, and for ten miles the two hostile bodies marched together across the plains, in such close proximity that the officers saluted each other by lowering their swords!

In this affair, near Castrejon, the 5th 60th lost one rifleman wounded and two missing.

At Castrillo however the French cavalry sustained a severe repulse from Alten's German dragoons in an attempt to push past the English left; and on the 20th Wellington took up a position on the high land of Vallesa and there offered battle. Marmont however marched past, while Wellington followed in a parallel line on the other side of the Guarena; but towards evening it became clear that he was outflanked, and abandoning the parallel march he fell back towards Salamanca.

On the 21st he had established his whole army on the heights of San Christoval. The forces of the two armies were nearly equal. Neither general would attack without seeing that his opponent gave him an advantage; but none was given on either side. Marmont should, by waiting for his reinforcements and leaving the road open to the English to retire on Rodrigo, have, as Wellington wrote to Graham three days after the battle, 'given me a *pont d'or,* and he would have made a handsome operation of it.' Wellington knew of the proximity of the reinforcements, and waited but a day longer to see if the opportunity were given—and the 'star of England was in the ascendant'—and it was given.

The night of the 21st-22nd[5] was very stormy, torrents of rain had swollen the fords, and, as the men emerged dripping from the water, deafening thunder pealed, and the flashing lightning played vividly on the tops of the soldiers' bayonets, and about the scabbards of the marching cavalry. Some men were killed, and the horses frightened broke from their pickets after the bivouac was formed, and caused great confusion.

As the morning broke the French were on the march from their bivouac. Marmont, aware that the arrival of Joseph or of Jourdan (the senior Marshal in Spain) would supersede him in command, was ambitious of gaining a victory before they came up. He commenced operations by skirmishing with the allies till about ten o'clock, and seizing on the higher of the

---

5. See Alison's *Epitome* and Sir E. Cust's *Annals.*

two hills which stood up from the plain on the British right, called Los Hermanitos or Dos Arapiles, from the village below them. They were about half a cannon-shot apart. Both sides rushed impulsively to seize them; but though the French gained the higher the English got possession of the lower. This rendered a change of position on Wellington's part necessary; and as the British divisions defiled past the French Arapiles, the left of the enemy was pushed forward to menace the road to Ciudad Rodrigo.[6]

In pursuance of this plan the Duke of Ragusa resolved on seizing a height near Miranda, half a league from his left flank, and thus occupy the road to Tamames. The division Thomière, with the light cavalry and fifty guns, were directed, about two in the afternoon, to effect this object; and as they were put in motion a heavy cannonade was opened on the British, and Maucune's division, 10,000 strong, assumed a threatening attitude.

General Leith sent to the commander-in-chief, who came at once, and having satisfied himself that no operation of consequence was here intended ordered the 5th division to lie down, and repaired to the English Hermanito to see what was doing on his right flank. Arrived there, he observed through his glass the movement of the division Thomière, which by the extension of the French left wing to Miranda caused an interval of nearly two leagues unoccupied between their left and their centre; and he hit the blot.

---

6. This point at Dos Arapiles was of so much importance that Wellington threw into the village a light battalion of Guards under Lieutenant-Colonel Woodford, supported by two companies of the Seventh Fusiliers under Captain Crowder, to hold it against all comers; which they did for the whole day. The gallant Crowder was promoted to a well-merited majority, but both probably were better pleased with the recognition of their great service by their chief than by any other reward. In the *Salamanca* despatch Wellington wrote, 'I must also mention Lieutenant-Colonel Woodford, commanding the light battalion of the brigade of Guards; who, supported by two companies of the Fusiliers, under the command of Captain Crowder, maintained the village of Arapiles against all the efforts of the enemy, previous to the attack upon their position by our troops.'

A few brief orders passed his lips, and turning round to General Alava, he exclaimed, '*Mon cher Alava, Marmont est perdu!*'

Picton was still ill, and in his absence the command of his division had devolved on Pakenham, Wellington's brother-in-law; and whilst the different orders were being carried out by the several divisions, Wellington sat down on the grass with the 3rd division, that celebrated body known throughout the army as 'the fighting division,' and took a hasty repast.

After their simple and soldier-like meal the commander-in-chief gave his orders, somewhat in these words:—'Do you see those fellows on the hill, Pakenham? Throw your division into columns of battalions, at them directly, and drive them—to the devil.'

And Pakenham, as he mounted his horse, said, 'I will; but first give me a grasp of that conquering right hand!'[7]

Grand was the conduct of all during that 'forty minutes, in which,' said Wellington afterwards, 'I gave 40,000 French the finest beating they ever had.' But the 5th 60th are more connected with the 3rd division than any others, and therefore we note from Napier that it was five o'clock when Pakenham fell on Thomière; and while that general expected to see the English in full retreat pursued by Marmont, he found his troops suddenly taken in flank by two batteries of artillery, and Pakenham's massive columns supported by cavalry in his front; he and all felt that they were lost. Pakenham at once commenced the battle; and in spite of gallant resistance, bearing onwards through the skirmishers with the might of a giant, he broke the half-formed lines into fragments, and sent the whole in confusion upon the advancing supports. Some squadrons of cavalry fell on the right of the 3rd division, but the 5th Regiment repulsed them, and the division under Pakenham held on its tempestuous course against the division Thomière, and the scattered left wing of the French was ut-

---

7. See Sir E Cust's *Annals* and Napier's *History of Peninsular War.*

terly routed with the loss of 3,000 prisoners and its General Thomière killed, while Marmont, hurrying in person to the scene of danger, had his arm shattered by a shell.

Clausel's division at the same time was crushed by a brilliant charge of cavalry under Lord Edward Somerset and General le Marchant, the latter of whom fell in the moment of triumph; 2,000 prisoners and five guns were taken, and the French left was annihilated.

Pack's Portuguese in the centre had been signally foiled in an attack on the French Arapiles, and the 4th division was at the same time thrown into disorder, but Beresford brought up a brigade of the 5th division to restore what was lost.

The crisis of the battle had now arrived; victory was for the general who had the strongest reserves in hand; and Wellington, seen that day at every point where and when his presence was most required, brought up the 6th division and turned the scale. But the struggle was no slight one, and Hulse's brigade, to which a portion of the 5th 60th was attached, won their way desperately, and went down by hundreds.

Clausel however, who had succeeded to the command, though himself wounded, gallantly bore up against the torrent; and the divisions Foy and Maucune taking post on the ridge of Ariba, endeavoured to cover their retreat; but the steep ascent was surmounted by Clinton and Pakenham, and the latter, as day was declining, still bore onward with conquering fury, still out-flanking the enemy's left.

The French moved off with firmness and some degree of order under cover of darkness; Foy commanding their rearguard. Wellington pursued them hotly, fatigued as he was, with the 1st and light division; and riding with the latter in rear of the 43rd Regiment was struck on the thigh by a ball which, somewhat spent, had passed through his holster. Nevertheless he pushed on towards Huerta, believing that to be the only road left open; but once more was chagrin to come from the Spanish, who, in charge of the fort at Alba de Tormes, had evacuated it without even reporting that they had done so; and he found that his beaten enemy had slipped by him at Alba, or the whole must have fallen into his hands.

Even as it was the loss to the French was about 14,000, of whom half were prisoners, with two eagles and eleven guns; and the number of stragglers was so great that Clausel, three weeks later, could only muster 22,000 out of 44,000 who had fought at Salamanca.

The allies lost 5,200 killed and wounded; 3,176 British, 2,013 Portuguese, and eight Spaniards.

The loss of the 5th battalion 60th was Lieutenant-Colonel Williams wounded, Major Galiffe and Ensign Luck (both severely), six riflemen killed, one sergeant and twenty-three riflemen wounded, and three missing.

And here we must take leave of Colonel William Williams, who had proved a worthy successor to Davy. Wounded five times, at Busaco, Fuentes d'Onor, Badajos, and Salamanca, he had now exchanged into the 13th with Lieutenant-Colonel John (afterwards Lord) Keane, and left the Peninsula; but only to transfer his services to another sphere. He served in America under Sir George Prevost with great distinction.

On July 23rd the pursuit was continued, and Clausel's rear was overtaken, and three squares formed on the side of a hill were broken by an irresistible charge of Bock's Hanoverian dragoons, with a loss of 1200 prisoners.

Wellington pursued till the French reached Valladolid on the 29th, when, finding them totally disabled for a time, he left them to the care of the Galicians and Clinton's division. He himself turned against King Joseph and the army of the centre; but Joseph on the news of 'Salamanca' had retired again on Madrid.

The British force arrived at the Escurial on August the 10th, and their outposts were pushed the same evening to the neighbourhood of Madrid. On the 11th, Joseph with his whole court, and a motley multitude of 20,000 persons implicated in his fortunes, abandoned the capital and took the road to Aranjuez. On August the 12th the allies entered Madrid in triumph.

Lord Wellington had written to Lord Liverpool from Salamanca, June 18th, 1812:

> It is impossible to describe the joy of the people of the town upon our entrance. They have now been suffering for more than three years; during which time the French, among other acts of violence and oppression, have destroyed thirteen of twenty-five convents, and twenty-two of twenty-five colleges, which existed in this celebrated seat of learning.[8]

And now, on entering the capital, the people, who were wrought up to the highest pitch of enthusiastic joy, received him with rapturous plaudits, and he wrote to Earl Bathurst:

> Madrid
> August 13th, 1812
> It is impossible to describe the joy manifested by the inhabitants of Madrid on our arrival.

The French garrison left in the Retiro surrendered next day at discretion, and the new constitution was proclaimed amidst the acclamations of crowds.

The power of the French in Spain however was loosened, not destroyed. In some measure their loss of territory was of advantage to them by compelling concentration.

Soult, under repeated positive orders, evacuated Andalusia and Estremadura and marched on Murcia. This released Hill, who advanced to cover Madrid from the south.

Wellington however perceived that the vital point lay in the north, where Clausel was again strengthening himself; and on September the 1st he set out with four divisions for Valladolid.

---

8. See Sir A. Alison and the *Wellington Despatches*.

Clausel retired at his approach, first to Burgos (September 17th) and then to Briviesca, where a junction with Souham raised his force to 30,000 men; whilst the British laid siege to the castle of Burgos, which, besides commanding the great road from Bayonne to Madrid, contained all the stores and reserve artillery of the army of Portugal.

The siege presented unexpected difficulties, not so much from the strength of the defences as from the want of heavy artillery, which compelled the assailants to depend chiefly on the effect of mines.

The enterprise was persevered in for thirty days, and repeated but fruitless attempts were made to storm the works, but on the failure of a final assault (October 18th) Wellington determined to raise the siege.

The British force had lost 3000 men, of which the 5th battalion 60th had lost during the operations— at, the assault and capture of Fort St. Michael, on the 19th September, one sergeant and two riflemen killed, and Lieutenant O'Hehir (severely) and seven riflemen wounded, and one missing; and at the siege of the Castle of Burgos, from September 27th to 3rd of October, one sergeant killed, one rifleman wounded; 4th and 5th October, one killed and two wounded; 6th to 10th October, two riflemen killed; 11th to 17th October, two killed and one wounded; and from the 18th to the 21st October, two riflemen were wounded.

Clausel,[9] now joined by the army of the north, had 44,000 men; while Soult and Drouet had on the 29th of September effected their junction with Joseph in the south, and were advancing on Madrid with 60,000 men.

As usual Ballasteros and the Spaniards gave no assistance, and the whole weight fell upon the English. It was obviously necessary to abandon Madrid, and concentrate the army in Leon.

On the night of October 21st the British army defiled from

9. See Sir A. Alison and *Annual Register.*

before Burgos; while Hill, evacuating the capital, marched for the Guadarama pass (November 2nd), a few hours before Joseph made his entry. Great were the difficulties of the retreat. The French cavalry were active in pursuit; and our soldiers, plundering the caves where the wine of the vintage was stored, became mutinous and disorderly.

On October 25th a severe action took place on the passage of the Carrion, but the French were repulsed; and on October 29th the army crossed the Douro without molestation, destroying the bridges.

On November 6th the retreat was resumed, and on the 8th a junction with Hill was effected; and the united force of 52,000 British and Portuguese and 14,000 Spaniards were in their old position of the Arapiles.

The French, whose two armies had also joined, were 95,000 strong, including 12,000 horse and 120 pieces of cannon. Jourdan wished to attack, but Soult overruled his wish, and by extending his left and threatening the communications with Ciudad Rodrigo again forced Wellington (November 15th) to retreat. The march was only three days, but was a scene of distress and disorder. The weather was most inclement; the guns could hardly be dragged through the mire, and the regiments were in a state of universal intoxication.

But Soult's troops were equally distressed, and he did not continue the pursuit beyond the Huebra. On the 18th of November the British army arrived at Ciudad Rodrigo, and its ample magazines supplied all its wants.

Before breaking up from St. Christoval Hill had been ordered to occupy the town and castle of Alba, posting troops on the Tormes to support them; and on November 10th the enemy attacked the troops in Alba with a considerable force and twenty pieces of cannon, but finding they made no impression they withdrew at night; and when Wellington moved to the Portuguese frontier and established his headquarters again at Freynada, Hill withdrew southwards to Coria in Estremadura.

Of the 5th battalion 60th there were eight riflemen wounded on the 10th and 11th of November at Alba de Tormes; but no loss was sustained by the other portions of the battalion in the movements from 22nd to 29th October, or in the operations from 15th to 19th of November.[10]

---

10. On October 25th, 1812, the 5th battalion 60th had 729 men fit for duty, and 111 men sick. It was 170 short of its establishment, and there were 1010 at the Depôt at Lymington.

CHAPTER 9

Vittoria: 1813

Though we are rapidly approaching in time to April 1814
and the close of the Peninsular War, the extent of the operations and the number of the battles and combats are so
great that the compression of them into a sketch of the fifteen
months' work is a hard task, and rendered the more so by the
scattering of the Rifle companies to so many brigades, and
the change in the names of the brigadiers. It will be necessary
therefore to give the last distribution of which we are in possession for the army of 1813.

With the 1st division under Sir Thomas Graham, one
company of the 60th was attached to the Brigade of Guards
(Stopford's). With the 2nd division under Sir Rowland Hill,
one company was with Walker's brigade of the 50th, 71st, and
92nd, and one company with Byng's brigade of the 3rd, 57th,
and provisional battalion (31st and 66th); another company
was attached to the brigade composed of the 28th, 34th, and
39th. With the 3rd division were the head-quarters of the
battalion and three companies. With the 4th division under
Lieutenant-General Hon. G. L. Cole was one company attached to Anson's brigade, composed of the 27th, 40th, 48th,
and provisional battalion (2nd and 53rd). With the 6th division under General Clinton was one company attached to
Pack's brigade of the 42nd, 79th, and 91st.

The services of the 2nd and 3rd divisions under Hill and

Picton are those which most frequently arrest our attention, and we must pick up our other companies as we may be enabled to do by the mention of the brigades of Guards, Anson, and Pack.

The whole of the winter of 1812-13 was spent by Wellington in re-organisation. In December he went to Cadiz, where he was received with enthusiasm, and made *Generalissimo* of the Spanish armies; and, though meeting with constant disappointments, he managed to bring 20,000 or 30,000 of them into line with the British and Portuguese in the following spring.

In January, 1813, he was back at Freynada. The home government sent him out supplies, tents (of which he had previously had none, and now only three to each company), which were a source of comfort and health to his soldiers, lighter cooking-pots, a pontoon train, and strong reinforcements, especially of cavalry; and he himself prepared on the Coa a great number of light carts and an organised train of mules, which were most serviceable.

By these exertions he had by the spring nearly 200,000 allied troops ready in the Peninsula, though not more than half of these were British, Portuguese, and Germans. The strength of the Anglo-Portuguese army on the Coa was at the beginning of the year about 75,000, of which 44,000 were British, with 9,000 horse and ninety guns.

Soult was recalled into Germany, and Clausel took his place.

The intrusive King Joseph fixed himself at Valladolid. Marshal Jourdan was at his right hand, though not always attended to; the disposition the King made of the French troops was scattered and bad, and he did little more than send out moveable columns against the insurgents who intercepted the French communications. Of Wellington's plans he had no conception. To Wellington himself more than one plan of operations was open; and even when after deep consideration he decided on the line he would take, he contrived successfully, by clever manoeuvring and spreading false information, to keep the intruder in utter ignorance of movements not only intended, but being ably and rapidly carried out by his lieutenants and himself.

Of the two plans open to him, namely, of moving by Salamanca, passing the Upper Tormes, seizing Madrid and turning the enemy's left, or to turn their right by crossing through Tras-os-Montes, he eventually preferred the latter; and after being delayed by rains till the middle of May, he, on the 15th of that month, commenced to move in two principal columns. The left under Graham, about 40,000 of all arms, passed the Douro between Lamega and the mouth of the Agueda, and pushed through Tras-os-Montes towards the Esla.

Wellington waited till the 22nd, and then accompanied the right column, about 28,000 strong, advancing in the direction of Alba and Salamanca upon the Tonnes. So great was his confidence in the success of his plans that he is said, as he crossed the little stream which bounds the frontier of Spain, to have risen in his stirrups, and, waving his hand, to have cried out, 'Farewell, Portugal!'

The fort of Santa Martha and the bridge at Miranda were simultaneously carried after a trifling resistance; the division of General Valette being quite surprised, and that general's carriage, among other prizes, falling into the hands of the cavalry.

On May 30th Graham was at Carvajales, where Wellington joined him. On the 31st Zamora was occupied, and the junction of the two columns on the Douro was secure; and on June the 3rd the whole British army was concentrated on the north of the Douro between Toro and the Esla, after a march of 200 miles in ten days.

The French now hastily retreated to the Upper Ebro, whilst the British, rapidly pursuing, occupied Valladolid on the 4th, and passed the Carion on the 7th and 8th of June.

On the 14th the castle of Burgos, the unlucky ending-place of the last campaign, was blown up. The French had placed above 1000 shells in the mine made for the purpose;

but the explosion was premature, and the shower of iron, timber, and stone fragments as it fell destroyed 300 men who were working at its demolition. The noise was heard for fifty miles; and Wellington and his generals coming on the ground satisfied themselves with their glasses that Burgos Castle was utterly destroyed.

The King-intruder fell back to the higher ridges of Pancorbo, intending to make a stand on the Orea Mountains. Clausel and Foy reached the ground on the 15th, and Reille crossed the Ebro at Miranda on the 16th to keep open the road and protect the immense convoy of valuables which they hoped to carry into France. But Wellington, keeping firm to his tactics of moving always by his left, no sooner convinced himself of Joseph's intentions than he ordered his whole army to march by one flank-march to his left; and on the 15th the head of the column passed the Ebro by the Puente de Arenas, and at once moved down upon Frias.

The route was regarded as impracticable. The operation was bold and successful. Ever pushing on his left, and sweeping round the French right, he had cut off their communications with the coast, and established a new base of operations for himself with the English fleet at Santander; and there was consternation and discussion on the 17th at Miranda between Joseph and his generals when they found the English already in rear of their right threatening the communications by Vittoria into the Pyrenees.

The whole of the French troops and authorities had evacuated Madrid in a panic; and the road from the capital to Bayonne was crowded with innumerable vehicles bearing away the spoils of the usurped kingdom, amassed by the unceasing rapine of five years.

On the 18th Reille arriving at Osma found himself in the presence of the 1st, 3rd, and 5th divisions of the British under Sir Thomas Graham, which were debouching from the mountain passes, and already held the road to Orduna.

The 1st and 3rd divisions had with them half of the 5th 60th; and a sharp skirmish occurred in which Reille was a good deal ill-treated by the light division, which was part of Graham's force, and he retreated behind Salinas de Ana-ma with the loss of 400 men and a quantity of baggage and sumpter animals.

The forces were unequally matched. Wellington had 90,000 men and more than 100 pieces of artillery in hand; 12,000 of these were cavalry; 70,000 were British and Portuguese; and this mass of regulars was aided by all the Partidas: whilst the French, though they could collect 9,000 or 10,000 horse-men and 100 guns, had only (exclusive of Leval) about half as many infantry as Wellington, to whom therefore victory was open, and he 'marched on with conquering violence.'

There was another point in which the inequality was great-er. The generals with Joseph were good, and did all that such men as Jourdan, Reille, and Foy could do; but Joseph, unfit to contend with Wellington at any time, made the least, and not the most, of the troops he had, and poured the encumbrances of the armies into the basin of Vittoria, which (though one large convoy had marched on the 19th, thus diminishing the number of fighting men in front) was still covered with artil-lery parks and equipages when the intrusive King, infirm of purpose, took up his position.

The basin was eight miles broad by ten long— Vittoria being towards the right rear of the French position, the left resting upon the heights which end at La Puebla de Argan-zon, and the line extending thence across the valley of the Zadora in front of the village of Arinez, which was about their centre.

On the 20th[1] Wellington halted to allow all his columns to close up, and carefully examined the French position, doubt-ing whether they would fight; but finding them resolved to do so, he organised three columns of attack, which fought on the next day, as it were, three separate battles. On his left Graham, moving by the Bilbao road, was with 20,000 men, supported by Giron's Gallicians, to force a passage against Reille on the French right.

With Graham were the 1st and 5th British infantry divisions, with Pack's and Bradford's brigades of infantry, and Bock's and Anson's cavalry. Graham had to make a wide detour to his left and cross the Zadora at Vittoria to attack the French right and cut off their retreat to Bayonne.

Hill on the right with his own, the and division (with companies of 60th Rifles attached to both Walker's and Byng's brigades), and having Morillo's Spaniards, Sylveira's Portuguese, with cavalry and guns, in all about 20,000 men, was to force the passage of the Zadora river beyond the Puebla defile, and assail Maransin with his right, whilst his left, threading the pass to enter the basin on that side, menaced and turned the French left.

In the centre battle were the 3rd and 4th divisions of Picton and Cole under Wellington himself, with both of which divisions were portions of the 60th Rifles, then on the left again of these were the 7th and light divisions under Lord Dalhousie, the great mass of artillery, in all about 30,000 men. The 6th division was not up, being left at Medina Pomar.

The centre force was encamped along the Bayas, and had only to march over the ridge bounding the basin of Vittoria on that side to their respective points, the bridges over the Zadora; but the country was so rugged that exact concert could not be maintained, and each general of division was in some degree master of his movements.

At daybreak on the 21st the troops of the centre crossed the ridge and slowly approached the Zadora, while Hill commenced the passage of that river beyond the defile of Puebla. Hill attacked first with Morillo's troops and gained the heights; but the enemy, seeing their importance, reinforced

---

1. See Sir William Napier and *Wellington Despatches*.

their own troops to such an extent that Hill had to detach the 71st Regiment, the Rifles, and light infantry of Walker's brigade to maintain his possession, which he did by sending successively troops to this point The Hon. Colonel Cadogan, who commanded the first reinforcements, was here mortally wounded, but had himself so placed that he could watch the operations while life lasted.

The ground was rugged, the communications difficult, and Wellington waited for the development of his flank attacks before he engaged his centre.

The left centre column (3rd and 7th divisions) did not reach the Zadora until nearly one o'clock; the 4th and light divisions crossed it immediately after Hill gained possession of Subijana de Alava. The right brigade of the 3rd division followed the 7th division under Lord Dalhousie, the other brigades of the 3rd division fording higher up the river.

The 7th division and centre brigade of the 3rd division attacked the French right centre in front of the villages of Margarita and Hermandad.

The Marquis of Wellington, seeing the hill in front of the village of Arinez (about the centre of the French position) only weakly occupied, ordered the right brigade of the 3rd division under Picton in close column of battalions at a run diagonally across the front of both armies to that central point.[2]

Wellington led them in person, and the hill was immediately carried. The French withdrew under cover of a cannonade from fifty guns and a crowd of skirmishers to their reserves on the second range of heights. They still held Arinez on the great road leading to Vittoria, and the brigade advanced

---

2. The account given, in Robinson's *Life of Picton*, of what was here done by the 3rd division differs ranch from that given by Napier, and it is graphic and worth reading; but I cannot here abandon our great Peninsular historian, because he himself has placed a footnote, which runs thus: 'The conception and execution of this movement has been repeatedly given to Picton. Erroneously so. My authority is the Duke of Wellington.' Napier's *Battles and Sieges in the Peninsula*, p. 297.

to attack it. Three companies of the 74th under Captain Mc-Queen, and the companies of the 60th Rifles immediately dashed forward, charged through it, captured three guns, and drove out the enemy; they then halted till the remainder came up, and the French, who were again advancing, were driven back in confusion.

By the capture of Arinez the great road was gained, and the extreme left of the French was turned, and Hill was hard pressing his successful attack. They retreated on Vittoria, and for six miles the action became a running fight. Here they tried to make a stand, but the 3rd division opposed them, bearing the brunt of their fire until the 4th division carried a hill on their left, and they abandoned the position.

Meanwhile Sir Thomas Graham's attack on the French right had been successfully carried on, Gamarra and Abechucho were in his possession, and the enemy's retreat by the high road to France was intercepted. They were then obliged to turn to the road towards Pampeluna, but unable to hold any position, they were forced to leave guns, equipages, and all their spoil behind them, only carrying with them one gun and one howitzer.

Joseph's equipage was seized; he had barely time to escape on horseback; and the Field Marshal's baton of Marshal Jourdan was amongst the spoil, together with the colours of the 4th battalion 100th regiment and 151 pieces of artillery. In the day's fighting, of the 5th battalion 60th the losses were three riflemen killed, Captain Franchini, Lieutenant Joyce, four serjeants, and forty-three riflemen wounded.

The ground at Vittoria was not favourable to cavalry, but they followed close in support of the infantry divisions, and after the battle thundered in pursuit.

On the 22nd Giron and Longa pursued the convoy, which had moved under Maucune on the morning of the battle. Pakenham, with the 6th division, came up. Wellington pursued Joseph, who had been flying up the Borundia and Araquil valleys all night. Reille covered the retreat, and reached Huerta, thirty miles from the field, on the 22nd. Gazan's and D'Erlon's corps marched on Pampeluna. Hill pursued the main body in that direction, whilst Graham was sent after Foy and Maucune to overtake the French rear in Guipuscoa; on the 24th he came up with Foy at Villafranca, and finding him strongly posted in the mountains, dislodged him by flank movements, and drove him, with a loss of 400 men, from Tolosa. In this pursuit the last French gun was captured. The only howitzer was also abandoned in the retreat, but Foy conducted that retreat with so much address as to protect considerable property, and the whole of the intrusive King's court and *camarilla*; and then, throwing a garrison into San Sebastian, he crossed the Bidassoa.

It now became necessary for Wellington to get both Pampeluna and St. Sebastian; without doing so he could no more advance into France than he could invade Spain before he had possession of Rodrigo and Badajos; but as the 5th battalion 60th had no share in the capture of the two fortresses, we shall merely make such mention of it as is necessary to the understanding of the campaign.

And first of Pampeluna, the ancient Pompeiopolis, founded by the great Pompey. On the 6th July Wellington with Sir Richard Fletcher made a careful reconnaissance of the place. The works were found perfect; the garrison was 4,000 strong. The situation is in a perfectly level plain. On one side the river Arga shields it, on the other it is covered by a strong citadel, having the parapets of its walls so low above the plain as to render the breaching of it impossible. Lord Dalhousie therefore was ordered to blockade it with the 6th and 7th divisions; nine redoubts, armed with captured guns from Vittoria, were constructed 1,200 yards from the *enceinte*, and every expedient which art could suggest to Major Goldfinch to render the blockade effectual was devised by that officer; and for four months it remained so, until at the end of October the resolute garrison, reduced to the last extremity and placed on scanty rations of horse-flesh, surrendered at discretion.

The blockade of Pampeluna is a solitary example of the investment of a considerable fortress, close to the enemy's frontier, having been so successfully maintained that the garrison was absolutely precluded from any communication with their friends across the border.

The first siege of St. Sebastian as it is called, though the second, and intermediate blockade, may all be looked upon as one operation, commenced on June 27th by the appearance of a Spanish force before San Bartolomeo and a fight of small arms; but on July 3rd the British navy blockaded the fortress, and on the 9th Sir Thomas Graham invested the town. The attack was vigorous, the defence resolute; on the night of the 24th Graham ordered the assault, but met with a bloody repulse; and Soult having given revived activity to the French army, Wellington hastily converted the siege into a blockade, so as to avail himself of part of the besieging force to defend his position in the Pyrenees. When that danger had been averted, and after a delay in the arrival of siege stores (which at length were brought up on the 19th August), the siege was renewed. On the 26th, sixty-three breaching guns and mortars opened on the devoted place. But the siege of St. Sebastian is more remarkable for the defence than the attack, and it was not until seventy-three days from the first commencement, during which nine assaults had been attempted, six of them upon the body of the place, that on the 9th of September, Graham having received the submission of the Governor from Colonel Songeon, hostilities ceased, and the garrison marched out the same day with the honours of war, and deposited their arms on the ground.

But before this took place, the battle of the Pyrenees, a contest of nine days, had been fiercely fought.

Soult had been brought from Spain to Germany. But on

the news of Vittoria, and the rout of his army that followed, Napoleon superseded his brother and Jourdan, ordered the Marshal at once from Dresden to take command of the army of the Pyrenees, and according to his instructions (which forbade him even twenty-four hours' rest in Paris) he arrived at Bayonne on the 13th of July.

He found the French army extended in a scattered mountain position, from St. Jean Pied de Port to the sea; and though he would gladly have spent some little time in organisation, he at once, in obedience to orders, prepared to assume the offensive with an army of 80,000 to 90,000 men, of whom about 7,000 were cavalry, and 86 pieces of cannon well horsed and equipped, freshly drawn from the depots of Bayonne.

The allied army was posted in the passes of the mountains, with a view to cover the blockade of Pampeluna and siege of St. Sebastian. Byng's brigade (with which were some of the 5th 60th) and General Morillo's division of Spanish infantry were on the right in the pass of Roncesvalles. Lieutenant-General Sir L. Cole at Viscarret supported them; and Picton with the 3rd division was at Olague in reserve. Hill, with remainder of the and division, occupied the valley of Baztan, having also a Portuguese division, and detaching Campbell's Portuguese brigade to Les Aldudes in French territory. The light and 7th divisions occupied the heights of Santa Barbara and the town of Vera and the Puerto de Echalar, and kept the communication with Hill and the valley of Baztan. The 6th division was in reserve at San Estevan.

The defect of the position was that the communications between the several divisions were tedious and difficult, while those of the enemy in front of the passes were easy and short,

On the 24th of July Marshal Soult collected the right and left wings of his army, with one division of the centre and two divisions of cavalry, at St. Jean Pied de Port; and on the 25th he attacked Byng's post at Roncesvalles with 30,000 to 40,000 men. Cole moved up to Byng's support, and the post was maintained throughout the day; but the enemy turned it in the afternoon, and Cole withdrew in the night to the neighbourhood of Zubiri.

Whilst Byng, supported by Cole, was attacked at Roncesvalles by Soult with some 35,000 men, Drouet D'Erlon, with about 20,000, attacked Hill's position in the Puerto de Maya, and at first forced him to give way; but being reinforced, Hill recovered his lost ground, and could have maintained it, but as Sir L. Cole had fallen back, it was expedient for him also to retire.

Soult's object was to overwhelm the British right and relieve Pampeluna, then turn to his own right and relieve St. Sebastian.

On the 26th Soult put his left wing on Cole's track, but ordered Reille to follow the crest of the mountains and seize the passes from the Baztan in Hill's rear, while D'Erlon pressed him in front. Fighting continued the whole day, in the two combats of Linzoain and Maya, with great loss on both sides. At the end of the day Picton, who commanded all the troops on the right, thought the position at Zubiri not sufficiently secure, retreated before dawn on the 27th without hope of covering Pampeluna; and Soult was almost successful in his object, when Picton, feeling the importance of the crisis, suddenly turned on some steep ridges which stretched across the mouths of the Zubiri and Lanz valleys, and screened that important blockade.

Picton posted the 3rd division on the right, and directed Cole to occupy some heights a little in advance. Cole however, noting a salient hill about a mile further on and commanding the great road, directed his course there. Two Spanish regiments of the blockading troops were posted on it; and as Soult sent a detachment in full career to seize it, the Spaniards (seeing the British so close) charged them.

This was the stroke of fate for Soult, whose columns emerging exultant from the narrow valley stopped at the sight of 10,000 men crowning the height in opposition, and Picton, two miles further back, with a greater number, as Abispal had now taken post on Morillo's left.

And now Wellington appeared on the scene. He had been to see Graham at St. Sebastian, and the news of Soult's rapid attack only reached him on the night of the 25-26th, on his return to Lasaca. He got out of bed, sent orders to Graham to disarm the batteries, and, without raising the blockade, to send as large a portion of his force to him as was available. He wished to concentrate his forces on his right, and instructed the left and centre columns accordingly, specifying the valley of the Lanz as the line to follow. Then mounting his horse at two o'clock in the morning he made his way through lateral glens towards the alignments of the 3rd and 4th divisions; and on the 27th he pushed on, attended by a single, staff officer, Lord Fitzroy Somerset, to Saroren.

Wellington had been well pleased at the action of his lieutenants; and on arriving at the 3rd division, after leaving Hill at St. Estevan, had said loudly to Picton, 'You have taken up a position, Sir Thomas, of which any man might feel proud.'

Now, as he rode through Saroren, he saw Clausel's division in full march along the brow of the hill from Zabaldica, and seeing that the valley of the Lanz was no longer a safe line of communication for his troops, he dismounted at the bridge, threw his bridle to Lord Fitzroy, and under a heavy fire wrote with a pencil the necessary orders for the divisions then in motion; sending him off he remounted and rode alone, and crossed the valley to the opposite ridge. As he approached he was recognised by a Portuguese regiment, which raised a cry of satisfaction—which was taken up at once by the 3rd and 4th divisions; and Soult hearing the tumult and shouting, and understanding what it meant, halted his troops.

The delay was all that Wellington wanted; his orders by Lord Fitzroy simply changed the line of march of the 6th division, which made a detour instead of pushing up the valley of the Lanz, and filled the interval between Hill and the right of the army.

On the 28th Soult attacked, although D'Erlon was not up as he had expected, and the fighting was what Wellington described as 'bludgeon-work;' but the allies, admirably posted, met and repelled every attack of the French, though they were greatly superior in numbers. Wellington said:

> In the course of this contest the gallant 4th division, which had been so frequently distinguished in this army, surpassed their former good conduct. Every regiment charged with the bayonet, and the 40th, 7th, 20th, and 23rd four different times.

Hill and Dalhousie had been directed upon Lizaso, to be nearer to Picton and Cole, and they both arrived there on the 28th, and the 7th division came to Marcalain.

The French who had been in front of Hill followed his march and arrived at Ostiz on the 29th. Soult (occupying a strong mountain position little liable to attack) determined to try and turn the left of the allies by an attack on Hill's corps, and for that purpose drew in the troops from his left, thus connecting their right with the divisions for the attack on Hill.

Wellington however determined to attack the French positions on the 30th, and ordered Lord Dalhousie to possess himself of the top of the mountain on his front by which the enemy's right would be turned, and Picton to cross the heights on which the enemy's left had stood, so as to turn their left by the road to Roncesvalles. Arrangements were made for an attack on the whole front as soon as these movements on their flanks began to appear, and by these operations the enemy were obliged to abandon a position at once the strongest and most difficult of access, and to retreat with great loss.

Whilst Wellington attacked and dislodged the enemy a counter attack was being made upon Hill, who was reinforced and maintained himself; and Wellington, continuing the pursuit after the retreat of the enemy from the mountain to Olague, was at, sunset immediately in the rear of their attack on Hill; on which they withdrew from his front during the night, and on the 31st of July took up a strong position, with two divisions to cover their rear, on the pass of Dona Maria. Hill and Lord Dalhousie attacked and carried the pass; Byng's brigade and Cole's (the 4th) division turned the position there at the same time; Byng took a large convoy going to the enemy, and made many prisoners.

On August 1st the pursuit was continued in the valley of the Bidassoa, and many prisoners and much baggage was taken. Byng possessed himself of the valley of Baztan and the position of the Puerto de Maya; and on the night of August 1st the allies occupied nearly the same position as on the 25th July, and the battle of the Pyrenees, which had been eight days in fighting, was at an end.

Soult was nearly hemmed in, and would have been so entirely had not some marauders disclosed his danger; and he evacuated Spain with a loss of some 15,000 men and 4,000 prisoners, but at a cost of 7,000 to the allies.

The whole army was fighting, but it fell a good deal on those portions where the 60th Rifles were. Picton's, Cole's, and Hill's divisions were in daily contest with the enemy. Byng's brigade began and ended the fighting. Walker's brigade with Pringle's bore the brunt of the action on the 25th, when Hill's position in the Puerto de Maya was attacked; and in his report on the 31st to Lord Wellington of the part taken by his troops on the days previous, Sir Rowland said:

> Major-General Pringle, with Major-General Walker's brigade under Lieutenant-Colonel Fitzgerald of the 60th Regiment, supported by the 34th and (Portuguese) Regiments, opposed the ascent of the enemy to the ridge on the left of the position in a most gallant style.

On that day (July 25th) Lieutenant Van Dahlman was killed,

and also Joyce, who had been wounded a month before at Vittoria. On July 26th Ensign Martin was severely wounded. From July 30th to August 1st there were one rifleman killed, Kent (the adjutant), three sergeants and eleven riflemen wounded, and Lieutenant-Colonel Fitzgerald was amongst those reported missing on the 31st.

After a short delay the siege of St. Sebastian was resumed, and, as has been already stated, surrendered on September 9th. But it did not fall without one last effort on the part of Soult to save it. On the 29th and 30th August he collected about 25,000 men on his right, opposite to the heights of San Marcial; while 20,000 under Clausel gathered before the pass of Vera. Wellington had occupied the heights with 6,000 Spaniards, supported on either flank by a British division; and while he blocked the Vera pass with one brigade of the 7th division, he directed Hill to show the heads of his columns as if they were on the march towards St. Jean Pied-de-Port. These arrangements were entirely successful. Reille attacked the Spaniards in a loose and not very determined manner, and was repulsed.

Clausel drove out the brigade from Vera, but stopped short when he saw a stronger force in front of San Martial, and (Hill moving, as it were, round his left towards Bayonne) after a good deal of firing and some loss on both sides the French retreated; and though Wellington did not at this moment invade France, the combat of San Martial was the last that took place on Spanish ground, and the safety of the Peninsula was no longer his care. Though Marshal Suchet still occupied a portion of Catalonia with detached and insufficient garrisons and could not be altogether ignored, and Pampeluna had not yet fallen, still Wellington began to contemplate an invasion of the south of France, and to study the difficulties he had to overcome. These were very great.[3]

---

3. See *Wellington Despatches*.

The people of England (as impatient in success as they are in times of reverses) and the Government, calculating on the effect which operations in the south might have upon the war still going on in the north of Europe, urged their own field-marshal to attack the Duke of Dalmatia at once: 'indeed,' as Wellington said, 'if he had done all that was expected of him, he would have been before that period in the moon.' He wanted pontoons; he wanted to supply many deficiencies caused by the constant battles his troops had lately fought; and, above all, those troops wanted some repose.

The repose of the soldier was not shared in by their general. He had now before him a harder problem to solve than any he had had before. Soult had taken up a strong position, and for a month he was incessantly at work strengthening it: in rear of this again he had his fortified camp at Bayonne, and before these lines could be attacked the 'Bidassoa' must be passed.

Soult's position north of the Bidassoa[4] was the base of a triangle of which Bayonne was the apex, and the great roads thence, to Irun on the coast and St. Jean Pied-de-Port in the interior, formed the sides. This space was filled with a mass of rugged mountains, on the last ridge of which, overlooking the Bidassoa, the French army was stationed; while all the hill roads were commanded by works, and the summit of the Grand Rhune mountain, the highest part of the ridge, was crowned by a complete redoubt.

Soult thought he had repeated Torres Vedras, but he did not think that his old victor could cross the river in his front. He had already forgotten the lesson taught him at the Douro. It was quite beyond his conception that a general should try and pass his army over a river by fording it when the tides were known to rise sixteen feet; the lesson was therefore repeated. Wellington having learnt from some Spanish fishermen that the river was fordable for a short time at the lowest ebb, made

4. See Sir A. Alison.

careful preparations for an operation which depended altogether on the nicest calculations of time.

He directed Sir Thomas Graham, with the 1st and 5th divisions and Wilson's Portuguese brigade, to cross in three columns below the site of the bridge, and in one above that spot. The Spanish army under *Don* M. Freyre was to cross in three columns at fords above those used by the allied British and Portuguese troops. The former were destined to carry the entrenchments about and above Andaye, the latter those on the Montagne Verte and on the height of Mandale, by which they were to turn the enemy's left.

At three o'clock in the morning of the 7th October[5] the British army was in march to carry out these operations; a thunderstorm helped to conceal the movements of the pontoon trains of the artillery, which was placed in secret positions under the heights of San Marcial. Not a shot was fired until Graham had passed the low-water channel, when a signal was given from the steeple of Fuente-Arabia.

Then the artillery opened from San Marcial, from whose crest seven columns were seen descending at the same moment, along an extent of five miles; and the French, taken completely by surprise, found at daybreak 24,000 men directed against the lower Bidassoa, and 20,000 (chiefly Spaniards) against the Rhune and its ridges. The lines were carried, the first heights were cleared of the enemy without much difficulty, but obstinate fighting took place at the Mont Louis XIV and the Croix de Bouquets, and the position was eventually stormed by the 9th Regiment, while Giron with the Andalusians was equally successful at La Grand Rhune and a vast projecting rocky ridge called the Boar's Back. Soult happened to be absent in Espalette, and before he could reach the point of danger all his redoubts were carried.

The 1st and 5th divisions were the earliest engaged on the

---

5. See Sir A. Alison and *Wellington Despatches.*

left, then the 4th and the light divisions, then the 6th division. The 2nd and 7th divisions were not at first brought into line, but towards the close of the day the 2nd got into action and was carried by the impetuosity of the men a little too far.

The enemy remained for the night in possession of the 'Hermitage,'[6] and on a rock on the same range of mountain with the right of the Spanish troops. On the 8th, when the fog had sufficiently cleared to enable Wellington to reconnoitre, he found the point least inaccessible was on the right, and might be connected with an attack on the works in front of Sarre. He then ordered a concentration of his reserves to his right, and, attacking with the Spaniards and part of the 7th division sent on by Lord Dalhousie for the purpose, carried the entrenchment; the enemy withdrew from their post at the Hermitage and from the camp at Sarre during the night, and thus the whole of the almost impregnable positions, which the French had been fortifying for a month previously, fell into the hands of the allies, and the English standards entered France.

In the operations of these two days the 5th battalion 60th had only one rifleman wounded, and two reported missing.

Wellington now waited for the fall of Pampeluna, which took place October 31st.

Soult endeavoured to get Marshal Suchet, Duke de Albufera, to co-operate with him, but failed; he however turned the respite from attack to good account. He had constructed a triple line of defences of great strength and solidity on the Nivelle, stretching from the sea and St. Jean de Luz to Mont Daren, and defended by 70,000 men; he having received an accession of 16,000 recruits.

On reconnoitring this formidable position[7] Wellington determined to direct his principal attack against the centre, between the Petite Rhune (which was still held as an outwork to the main line) and the bridge of Amotz over the Ni-

---

6. See Sir A. Alison.

7. See *Wellington Despatches*.

velle. This duty was assigned to the 3rd, 4th, and 7th divisions under Beresford, supported by Giron's Spaniards; while Hill was to assail their left, and Sir John Hope, who had succeeded Graham in the command of the left wing, was to make a feint against the hills by St. Jean de Luz. Hill, it must be recollected, had been disengaged from covering the blockade of Pampeluna, and had been moved on the 6th and 7th November into the valley of the Baztan, with the intention of the attack taking place on the 8th, but the state of the roads in consequence of bad weather caused a delay.

On the morning of the 10th the attack was made. Hill had command of all the troops on the right, consisting of the 2nd and 6th British divisions under Stewart and Clinton, a Portuguese and a Spanish division, Grant's brigade, and Tulloh's (Portuguese) brigade of cavalry, with three mountain guns. Beresford directed the movements of the right centre, having under him the 3rd division under Colville, the 7th division, and 4th (Sir L. Cole's) division, which last attacked the redoubts in front of Sarre, that village, and the heights behind it, supported by Giron's Spaniards, who attacked to the right of Sarre the slopes of La Petite Rhune, and the heights behind the village on the left of the 4th division.

General Alton, with the light division and Longa's Spaniards, attacked and carried the positions of La Petite Rhune; and then co-operated with the right centre in the attack of the heights behind Sarre.

Cole obliged the enemy to evacuate the redoubt in the right front of Sarre; on the approach of the 7th division the one to the left was abandoned, and Cole attacked and possessed himself of the village, which was turned on its left by the 3rd division. The whole then attacked the position behind the village; the the 3rd and 7th divisions carried the redoubts on the enemy's left centre, the light division those on the right, while the 4th division with the Spanish reserve attacked the positions in the centre. By these attacks the enemy were forced from their strong positions, fortified with so much care and labour, and a whole battalion left in the principal redoubt was captured.

While these operations were going on in the centre, the 6th division, under Sir H. Clinton, crossed the Nivelle, driving in the enemy's picquets on both banks, covered the passage of Hamilton's Portuguese division, and then, by a 'most handsome attack' on the position behind Ainhoué and on the right of the Nivelle, carried all the entrenchments and the redoubt on that flank; and then the British and Portuguese together attacked and immediately carried the second redoubt.

Pringle's brigade of the 2nd division drove in the picquets on the Nivelle and in front of Ainhoué; and Byng's brigade of the 2nd division carried the entrenchments and a redoubt further to the enemy's left in an attack styled 'most distinguished' in the despatch, and for which Byng received special thanks from Wellington.

By these operations under Hill the enemy were forced to retire towards the bridge of Cambo on the Nive, except that part which were pushed by two divisions towards Baygorry.

The heights on both banks of the Nivelle being carried, the 3rd and 7th divisions were sent by the left of that river towards St. Pé; the 6th division were directed on the same place by the right bank, while the 4th and light divisions held the heights above Ascain, covering the movement on that side, and Hill covered it on the other. Wellington was thus established in rear of the enemy's right; but the day was so far spent that he had to wait for the morrow.

The enemy however evacuated Ascain in the afternoon, and quitted all their works and positions in front of St. Jean de Luz during the night, retiring upon Bidart and destroying all the bridges on the Lower Nivelle. Sir J. Hope followed them with the left of the army as soon as he could cross the river, and Beresford moved the centre of the army as far as the state of the roads would allow; and on the night of the nth the enemy retired again into the entrenched camp in front of Bayonne, leaving all the intermediate country, with the port of St. Jean de Luz, to the allies, and having lost 4,300 men, including 1,400 prisoners, with fifty-one guns, and all his field magazines.

The loss on the side of the allies was severe, but not so much so as might have been expected from the nature of the position and the triple line of entrenchments attacked. That of the 5th battalion 60th was Lieutenant Eccles, three sergeants, and four riflemen killed; Captain Stopford, Lieutenant Passley, and Ensign Shewbridge, with three sergeants, one bugler, and fifty-four riflemen wounded, and two missing.

The inclemency of the weather prevented Wellington from proceeding further, and he had difficulties to deal with in the Spanish armies, which proved cruel marauders when their opportunity of revenge came. But, though he could not but feel the loss of troops with such a position to attack as the fortified camp at Bayonne, he sentenced to death British and Spanish alike when caught in the act; and disarmed and sent back Mina's mutinous battalions, ordered Giron's Andalusians into the valley of the Bastan, Freyre's Galicians to Ernani, and Longa's across the Ebro. Murillo's Spaniards, whose conduct had been better, he retained with the army in France.

The position however of the allied army was neither good nor convenient, and the nourishing of 9,000 cavalry and the equipages of 100 guns was a difficulty; it was therefore determined to widen the 'emplacement' of the army and to force the line of the Nive, so as to establish more productive quarters on the left bank of the Adour. The posts had already by degrees been advanced from Bidart, but not without contest and loss. After careful reconnaissance Soult's position appeared to be one impossible to attack, and that the best mode of obliging the enemy to abandon it, or at least to weaken his defence of it, was to pass the Nive and bring forward the right wing up to the Adour.

On the 9th of December Hill passed to the right bank of the Nive near Cambo, and Beresford at Ustaritz; Hope making a demonstration with 24,000 men and twelve guns along the whole front of the entrenched camp. D'Armagnac fell back before Hill, and Foy had to change ground in consequence. Pringle with his brigade and the 6th division manoeuvred with a like result on Berlier. The cavalry captured and secured a valuable convoy. The 14th Light Dragoons established outposts and pickets at Hasparren for the night, and followed Paris through St. Palais next morning.

Soult arrived on the ground from Bayonne about one o'clock, but found Wellington in possession of the entire field of operation to the left of the French army.

But by this success the British army fell into the same fault that attached to Soult's position on the Nivelle. Their wings were divided by the Nive, and the army was extended over at least three leagues of ground. Soult resolved at once to fall on the part of the British army on the left bank of the Nive; and, confident of success, wrote to the Duke de Feltre, French Minister of War, saying, 'I hope that I shall have a victory to announce to you.'

There was heavy rain on the night of the 9th;[8] but the morning broke fair on the 10th of December, when Soult filed four divisions through Bayonne and over a boat-bridge across the Nive to the attack of Hope's corps. This force was placed at the number of 60,000 men with forty guns.

The British force opposed to him was greatly inferior, and at first suffered severely in the bloody conflict that was kept up during the whole day; but, about two o'clock, when Soult was renewing the attack, Wellington, who had been away on the right bank of the Nive, ordered up the 3rd, 4th, 6th, and 7th divisions, and restored the battle. Both armies rested on their arms on the field that night, and two German regiments came over to the allies.

---

8. See Sir E. Cust's *Annals of the Wars.*

On the morning of the 11th all was quiet, and the British were cutting wood and cooking their rations when there was a cry of 'Stand to arms;'[9] and under cover of a fog the French made an attack, and their divisions, with cries of '*En avant, en avant,*' into the coppice, which was filled with men of all nations intermingled in a perilous manner; but the 9th Regiment reformed, and with the 85th drove the French out.

About 10 o'clock on the morning of the 12th (when General Howard came to take the duties at Barrouillet) another fight arose, but chiefly an artillery affair. An English battery having opened fire, Reille brought up a number of guns to reply to it, and a fire was kept up for several hours without, any object, but there were casualties to the amount of about 400 on each side.

'Soult's plans,' as Wellington said, 'were always good, but he never knew the proper moment for striking his blow.' He found now that he had shot his bolt on the left bank, and resolved to change the direction of his attack to the right bank of the Nive, and, leaving two divisions in the entrenched camp, he marched through Bayonne on the night of the 12-13th with 35,000 men and twenty-two guns to attack Hill at St. Pierre, whose force he had discovered to be only 13,000 men and fourteen guns; and under cover of a mist he formed his order of battle on the 13th at eight o'clock in the morning.

Hill was strongly posted on a wooded and broken ridge,[10] and the first onset of the Abbé division in the centre was repulsed with loss. The number of the assailants at length prevailed, and the crest of the ridge was won; when Hill, pushing forward two brigades of Portuguese infantry, regained his vantage-ground. It was now about midday, when the 6th division came marching up in order of battle to St. Pierre. Wellington too was at their head, and riding up he took Sir Rowland's hand in a frank and manly way, and said affectionately, 'My dear Hill, the day is your own!'

10. See Sir E. Cust and Sir A. Alison.

The crisis was past; Hill's day of glory was already complete, but the 3rd and 4th divisions followed in rapid succession, some brigades of the 7th were also coming up; Byng with his brigade attacked a hillock where two guns had been playing without ceasing, and captured them; and at two o'clock, Wellington ordering an advance of the whole line, Soult retreated fighting to his entrenched camp, leaving the country between the rivers in possession of the British. The fight was considered on both sides as the French described it, '*sans contredit une des plus sanglantes batailles.*' Their casualties were about 6,000. The total loss of the British between the 9th and 13th was 5,061 killed and wounded, of which the loss of the 5th battalion 60th was, on December 9, one lieutenant (Dickson), one sergeant, and twelve riflemen wounded; and on the 13th, one ensign, two sergeants, and sixteen riflemen wounded.

Thus ended the campaign of 1813. The rigour of the season forced both combatants into cantonments. The French withdrew into the entrenched camp, Foy's division on the right bank guarding the passage of the Adour; and the allies were established in winter-quarters in the towns on the coast, drawing ample supplies from the rich fields of Bearn and the harbour of St. Jean de Luz.

CHAPTER 10

Orthes & Toulouse: 1814

From the end of December, 1813, up to the middle of February, 1814, operations were confined to occasional affairs of outposts. The French would from time to time drive in an English picquet, or push a reconnaissance along the front of the British line, which would get under arms here and there, repel the attack, and return to its cantonments.

The army lay in a semicircle of nine miles in extent, with its left upon the sea at Biarritz, its centre at Ustaritz and Villa Franca, and its right on the space between the Nive and the Upper Adour. Head-quarters were at St. Jean de Luz, and the bulk of the cavalry was kept, for the sake of forage, along both banks of the Ebro beyond the Pyrenees. The total strength may be taken at 90,000 men, of which 10,000 were cavalry, and there were 100 field-pieces. This includes 30,000 Spaniards.

Soult's force had been reduced by further withdrawals of troops to the army of the Seine, and he had placed 6,000 men in garrison at Bayonne; he could not bring into line more than 35,000 to 40,000 men. But he had great advantages of position; whilst, move which way he would, Wellington had deep rivers to cross, swampy ground to pass over, and many villages, crowning steep heights, to carry. One road alone, the one leading from Irun to Bayonne, was a fair one; the rest were lanes, running often between steep banks, and in wet weather impassable for artillery and cavalry.

The government at home urged active operations, but the state of the weather and the country made this impossible. They suggested the transfer of the whole army to Northern Europe, but against this policy Wellington produced unanswerable reasons; but, whilst he allowed his troops some necessary and enforced repose, he meditated one of the boldest strokes of his military career, and quietly prepared for its execution. He had received reinforcements and supplies, and, what he chiefly wanted, money; and finding the people of the south of France, relying on his protection, very willing to trade, but unwilling to take any but French money, he sought out die-sinkers and men who had been coiners from the ranks and struck new French coin, carefully preserving their just fineness and weight.

But there was another stroke for which he was preparing. Bayonne was the support of Soult's right, and Wellington could make no further inroad on French territory, while leaving it with all its accumulated strength in his rear; it was necessary to drive the French from the Adour, and cross the deep and rapid river, wide at its mouth and defended by the action of dangerous tides and a flotilla of gun-boats.

Wellington collected *chasse-marées*, cordage, and all the material for his wondrous bridge, everything being numbered and ready, at Passages. Admiral Penrose with his naval officers made minute examinations and took soundings, whilst military draughtsmen made observations of the shores; and when all things were ready, he took his principal step, of concealing his design from his enemy by advancing his right boldly and threatening Soult's left.

The cavalry were called up, and on the 14th of February the army took the field and commenced to manoeuvre towards the Upper Adour in the direction of Orthes. Hill began by driving Clausel's posts beyond the Joyeuse, turning the line there and cutting the direct communication with St. Jean Pied-de-Port; and that done, he, on the 15th, marched upon

Garris, pushing back Harispe's rear-guard. Soult believing that Wellington's object was to turn his left by Hill's corps and pass Hope's troops over the Adour above the fortress, keeping Bayonne in check with the Spaniards, felt quite secure on his right, and resolved to fight on the Bidouze and the two Gaves of Mauleon and Oleron in succession.

On the 15th the combat of Garris was fought; and on both days the 5th 60th suffered: on the 14th Captain Blassieres was severely wounded, and on the 15th Lieutenant Gottlieb Lerche (arm amputated) and Lieutenant Stepney St. George were also severely wounded. On the 16th Hill crossed the Bidouze, and the centre divisions passed the Joyeuse. On the 17th Hill advanced towards the Mauleon, and General Paris tried to destroy the bridge of Arriveriete. But Wellington was too quick, and secured the passage. Paris relinquished the Gave on the morning of the 18th and retired, and the Allies seized the main road on the left bank of the Gave d'Oleron.

Soult, thrown from the commencement on the defensive, was at a loss to discover his opponent's object, but decided to hold the Gaves as long as he could, and when they were forced, to concentrate at Orthes and attack the first column that approached.

Wellington having established his right, and anxious to throw his stupendous bridge below Bayonne in person, returned to St. Jean de Luz. Everything was ready, but the weather was boisterous; and fearful of letting Soult strengthen himself on the Gave d'Oleron, he decided on pressing the operations on that side himself, and on the 21st left the throwing of the bridge to Sir John Hope and Admiral Penrose.

The description of the bridge and the interesting account of its completion must be read in Napier's *History*, or other accounts of these operations, of which perhaps none is better than that of the late Chaplain-General (Gleig), who served in the 85th, and has given us that admirable volume *The Sub-*

altern; but the 60th Rifles took a part in the passage of the Adour, which must be recorded.

On the night of February 12nd Hope cautiously filed his 1st division, with six 18-pounders and a rocket battery (used for the first time in the Peninsula), towards the Adour. The gun-boats and *chasse-marées* should have reached the mouth of the river, but the wind was contrary, and they were not there.

Hope resolved to try the passage with the army alone; and having passed sixty men of the Guards to the other side, he formed a raft of the pontoons, stretched a hawser across, and sent over Colonel Stopford with 600 men of the Guards and the 60th Rifles, and some rockets. The battery of 18-pounders engaged the attention of the enemy on the opposite shore by firing on a French corvette at anchor in the river. The 60th Rifles passed first, then the light infantry of the Guards, who beat up their ground, sent out picquets, and reported 'all well'; and then immediately followed five companies of Guards. At the next passage of the raft it was nearly lost, and the enemy were seen advancing about 2,000 strong. Scarcely 500 British troops were there to oppose them, with the sea on their rear and left, and the large river on their right—no assistance, no road of retreat.

The 60th Rifles and light infantry of the Guards began to fight; all were deliberate and cool. The other companies formed line, covering the raft, with a detachment of the rocket battery on either flank. Fifty men carrying four rockets each had crossed in a small boat in trips and formed up in two divisions.

It was getting dark when the enemy advanced with loud cheers; the 60th Rifles and light troops kept up a well-directed fire, the rockets seemed to set the firmament in a blaze, and the field-guns from the opposite bank plied the flank of the French with shrapnel. Luckily the rockets flew straight, and the French column pierced and amazed fled, leaving thirty men on the ground. Three different times had the light troops turned the head of the attack; and at last the enemy retired, having many casualties, whilst those on the side of the Guards and 60th Rifles were not more than half a-dozen wounded.

Hope, who watched them, anticipating another fate, was heard saying, 'Well done'—'Bravely done, Guards;' and the huzzas of comrades from the one bank cheered those who had crossed and occupied the other, and who were left unmolested till noon on the 24th, on which day the *chasse-marées* came sailing in, and the naval officers and engineers formed the bridge below Bayonne, and Hope was enabled to pass all his force over the Adour.

On the 24th Wellington effected the passage of the Gave d'Oleron with the centre and right of his army. On this Soult, leaving Bayonne to its own resources, drew back his whole force to the heights of Orthes, behind the Gave de Pau, and on this formidable position awaited the approach of Wellington, who advanced with 37,000 men, all Anglo-Portuguese veterans, including 4,000 cavalry and forty-eight guns.

The battle of Orthes was commenced at daybreak on the 27th by Beresford, who with the 4th (Cole's) division and the 7th under General Walker turned the enemy's right and gained the road to Dax beyond it; while Picton with the 3rd division, and the 6th division under command of Sir H. Clinton, was to move along the great road from Peyrehorade and attack the centre, and Hill to force the passage of the river on the left.

But Beresford was checked on the ridge beyond the village of St. Boes by the heavy concentric fire of Reille's artillery, and driven back in disorder. At the same time Soult saw Picton's attack was repulsed, and slapping his thigh, exclaimed exultingly, 'At last I have him!'

Fatuous Duke of Dalmatia! Wellington saw the crisis as well as yourself, and suddenly he changed his whole battle. Sending up Anson's brigade to support Ross, he ordered the 7th division and Barnard's brigade against the height, and threw the 3rd, 6th, and light divisions on the enemy's centre. Colborne with the 52nd crossing a swamp, in which the men sunk to their knees, rushed on with the bayonet as they touched firmer soil; Picton and Clinton renewed the attack upon Reille's left wing, and disorder soon extended along the whole French line.

These simultaneous attacks were decisive. Reille's victorious wing, now assailed on both flanks, were driven headlong from the heights, while the fall of Foy, severely wounded, threw his men into disorder; and Hill having at the same time forded the Gave and cut off the retreat by the great road to Pau, Soult ordered a general retreat.

The French retired in good order, making a stand at each favourable position, till on perceiving Hill preparing to anticipate them at the bridge of the Luy de Bearn, and being charged at the same time by Sir Stapleton Cotton and Lord Edward Somerset's dragoons, a great part of their troops fell into utter confusion, and many prisoners were taken before they could cross the river. Their loss of killed, wounded, and prisoners was about 4,000, besides 3,000 conscripts who deserted. The loss of the Allies was 2,000 killed and wounded, of which of the 5th 60th Captain Ignace Franchini and Lieutenant John Currie were among the wounded; and Wellington and Alava were both struck.

Soult retreated towards Tarbes, hoping to effect a junction with Suchet.

Wellington pursued, and on March 1st had his head-quarters at St. Sever. Uncertain of Soult's movements, he directed Beresford to march on Mont de Marsin, and Hill and Cotton on Aire. At the former place extensive magazines fell into Beresford's hands, and on March 2nd Hill came up with Clausel, who was prepared to defend those at Aire with the divisions Villatte and Harispe. Hill attacked at once with his old 2nd division and Da Costa's Portuguese; the 50th and 92nd supported the Portuguese, who seemed losing the ground they had won, and they soon restored the battle. The French bravely resisted until Byng's brigade came up, when they were forced out of Aire and across the Lees.

Soult continued his retreat up both banks of the Adour, but he was not followed by the Allies, new combinations having opened to the view of the English general.

A Royalist movement had now commenced at Bordeaux,[1] and on the 12th Beresford arrived at that place with 12,000 troops to watch the progress of the movement.

Both Soult and Wellington remained inactive, each thinking the other the strongest; for Wellington had 12,000 men before Bayonne and 12,000 at Bordeaux, thus reducing his force to about 28,000 men, which also was about the number with Soult.

Soult was astounded by the proclamation of Louis XVIII at Bordeaux, and issued a counter proclamation. There was great excitement among his veterans, and he was anxious to take advantage of it. On March 12th, therefore, having determined to resume the offensive, he moved forward.

Wellington ordered up the Spanish divisions of Freyre and Giron, raising his force to 36,000 men.

Soult fell rapidly back again towards Toulouse, and having had a sharp conflict on the 20th before Tarbes, reached that place on the 25th of March, and Wellington came up in his front on the 27th.

Between the 28th of March and the 4th of April a good deal of manoeuvring occurred. It was executed under great difficulties, for heavy rain continued to fall, and all except the great paved roads became mud-tracks.

On the 4th a pontoon-bridge was laid upon the Garonne, and Marshal Beresford, with the 4th and 6th divisions of infantry, two brigades of cavalry and some guns, crossed. More troops were to have crossed, but a heavy fresh came down and the pontoons had to be moved to avoid destruction. For three

---

1. See Gleig's *Life of Wellington* and Sir A. Alison.

days of terrible suspense Beresford's force remained exposed to the attack of the whole French army, but Soult remained immovable in his position, which he had fortified with great care during the interval thus afforded.

On the 8th the bridge was again laid down, and the remainder of the army passed, Hill staying on the left bank to menace St. Cyprien.

Soult meanwhile, whose troops were refreshed and invigorated by seventeen days of rest, awaited the approach of the enemy, with his main body posted on the north-east of the city on an elevated platform called the Calvinet, on the summit of Mont Rave, about two miles long, and strengthened with field-works; while the canal, with its fortified bridge, formed a second line of defence, and the walls of the city a third.

The allied army was 53,000 strong, including 7,000 horse and sixty-four guns, but 12,000 of these were Spaniards. The French force amounted to about 40,000, with eighty heavy guns, and the advantage of a strong central position, which could only be attacked by the Allies on detached points of the circumference. Wellington's plan of attack was, that Hill on the left of the Garonne should menace the suburb of St. Cyprien, while the third and light divisions should menace the northern front and drive the enemy's outposts within the canal, and Beresford, with the 4th and 6th divisions, should cross the Ers and carry the heights beyond the hill of Pugade, which was to be attacked by the Spaniards.

Portions of the 5th battalion 60th Rifles were therefore with each of the three attacks in this the last great battle of the Peninsula.

And now the storm for which Soult was watching was to burst. At 6 o'clock on the morning of the 10th of April the different columns advanced according to orders. The 3rd division under Picton drove the enemy's outposts for above three miles, as far as the bridge of Jumeaux on the canal; but the bridge was defended by a strong palisade *tête-de-pont*, approachable only on the flat, and too high to be forced without ladders and without artillery, and commanded by the enemy's guns from the opposite side of the canal[2].

Picton, whose attack was intended to be a feint, made it a real one. The French occupied the work in force, and he was unable to dispossess them, and a great and unnecessary loss was the result.

Clinton and Cole had crossed the Ers and advanced against the French right, skirting the level ground at the foot of Mont Rave under a tremendous flank fire from the summit in the right centre. Meanwhile Freyre's Spaniards, about 9000 strong, advanced in good order to assault the redoubts on the Calvinet; but the grape from the heavy guns on the ridge, sweeping down a level slope, produced such a frightful carnage that, in spite of the gallantry of their officers, they were driven back with the loss of 1500 men. Past Wellington they came, sweeping by in confusion, but all that he said to his staff was, laughing good-humouredly, 'Well, I never before saw 10,000 men run a race.'

---

2. Robinson, in his *Life of Picton*, makes Picton's attack take place after the retreat of the Spaniards. He says that Picton 'had seen the retreat of the Spaniards, and justly concluded that the left wing would have a frightful struggle against an immense superiority of force. This at once decided him in making a diversion in their favour, which has since been canvassed with some degree of severity by military men.'
'The right brigade, under the command of Major-General Brisbane, was immediately ordered to leave the plantation in which they had been bid, and attempt to force a passage over the canal, by means of a bridge situated near its junction with the river Garonne. The bridge was covered by an extremely strong redoubt in front, and a formidable range of artillery on each flank. Sir Thomas Picton personally directed this attack, which was made by the 45th, 7th, and 88th Regiments, with three companies of the 5th battalion of the 60th, in the usual style of "the fighting division," moving to the assault with that impetuous courage which nothing could daunt. The artillery attached to Sir Rowland Hill's corps, perceiving the intention of Sir Thomas Picton, opened a heavy fire across the river; but unfortunately they struck down some houses which had served to protect the light troops of the division, and this left them exposed to the incessant shower of grape which was kept up by the enemy.'

Soult, having the advantage on the two attacks of Picton and Freyre, prepared to pour down with 15,000 infantry and 1,200 horse on Beresford and the British left; he had been unable to drag his guns through the marshy ground on the bank of the Ers, but halting and deploying into line, the British troops received and repelled the shock, and following up their advantage with Pack's brigade in front, carried in the confusion the redoubts of Sypiere.

The French defences were now threatened in flank, and Soult instantly threw back his defeated right wing at an angle, presenting a fresh front; but the battle was not resumed till about 3 p.m., when Beresford's guns having been at last got up, the attack was resumed on the redoubts in the centre of the Calvinet.

By this time too Freyre's Spaniards were reformed and could be led to the attack, and as soon as this was effected the Marshal continued his movement and carried with Pack's brigade of the 6th division the two principal redoubts and fortified houses the French centre. The enemy made a desperate effort from the canal to regain them, but were repulsed with considerable loss; and the 6th division continuing its movement along the ridge of the height, and the Spanish troops pursuing a corresponding movement upon the front, the French were driven from the two redoubts and entrenchments on the left, and the whole range of heights were gained by the British. Their guns now commanded the suburb of St. Etienne as far as the old walls of the city, and Soult withdrawing his troops from the remaining works on the Calvinet, ranged them behind the canal which formed the second line of defence.

The loss of the French was about 3,000, that of the Allies 4,500, 2,000 of whom were Spaniards.

The loss of the 5th battalion 60th was two sergeants and nine riflemen killed; Captain Purdon, Ensign Shewbridge and Ensign Bruce, with four sergeants, and forty-four riflemen wounded, and one reported missing.

This was the fourteenth and last of the great battles and victories fought in the Peninsula, in each of which the 60th Rifles had had their share, and their loss also was heavier than in any other engagement.

On April 11th both armies remained on the same ground. Wellington required ammunition, and was making fresh dispositions which Soult observed would cut off his retreat to Carcassone. Without betraying his purpose he began sending off his baggage, and on the night of the 11th he decamped, and when Wellington was prepared to renew the battle on the 12th he found even the sentinels had been withdrawn, and no troops were left save 1,600 wounded, including the gallant Harispe and two other generals, who wore entrusted to British humanity.

On the 13th April then Wellington entered Toulouse in triumph, and was received with the same enthusiasm by the French as he had met with at Madrid when hailed as a 'deliverer.' At the same time arrived from Paris Colonel Cooke and Colonel St. Simon, with information from the Provisional Government of the downfall of Napoleon, and a cessation of hostilities was at once proposed to Soult. He evaded a formal agreement until the 18th, being anxious to communicate with Suchet and to ascertain the real sentiments of the army.

It has been thought by some that Soult knew of the altered state of things before the 12th of April, and fought and sacrificed needlessly at Toulouse thousands of lives, but on this being said in after years in the House of Lords, the Duke stood up in his place and affirmed that 'Marshal Soult did not know, and could not know, what had taken place in Paris when he fought the battle of April 10th, 1814.' But this cannot be said of General Thouvenot who commanded at Bayonne, and a lamentable and needless bloodshed must be recorded for which he must ever be held responsible.

It will be recollected that on the departure of the main army to the Upper Garonne, Sir John Hope was left in charge of the siege of Bayonne, and he had conducted the investment with the utmost zeal and diligence; he had heard rumours of what had occurred in Paris by April 7th, and had communicated it to the French outposts.

About 1 o'clock in the morning of the 14th, a deserter came to General Hay and told him that a sortie was projected. Hay not understanding French sent him to General Hinuber, who put his own troops under arms and transmitted the intelligence to Hope. Hay unfortunately did nothing except to order that in case of alarm his brigade should form at the village of Boueant.

At about 3 o'clock in the morning the French poured out of the citadel, in number about 3,000, and fell upon the picquets on the left and centre of the British line. These fell back surprised on St. Etienne, and whilst giving directions for the defence of the church of that village Hay was shot dead. The enemy were for a time successful in spite of a brave opposition, until the second brigade of Guards under Stopford, who with his detachment of 60th Rifles had performed the exploit of the passage of the Adour, charged the assailants and re-established the British post in the centre.

On the right the attack was also disastrous; the picquets were driven in, and all was tumult and disorder. The guns of the citadel opened, guided only in the darkness by the flashes of musketry, and some gunboats dropping down the river sent random shot and shell booming through the lines of fight, so that before day 100 guns were in full play and had set fire to the fascine depot, casting a horrid glare over the scene. Hope ordered up supporting columns, but had his horse shot under him, and it fell on him; his staff tried to release him, but some of them were wounded, and with him became prisoners in the confusion. But when day dawned General Howard brought up the reserve brigades of Guards in compact order, and these with a shout of defiance drove the French into their own works with great slaughter.

The French lost 900, the British close on 1,000 of killed, wounded, and missing, including officers. And thus in a blaze of useless bloodshed died out the Peninsular war, and the 60th Rifles, who with the 95th had opened the war in 1808 at Obidos, saw it fairly (or rather unfairly) completed at Bayonne, for with their General (Stopford) there were wounded on this luckless night Lieutenant Hamilton (severely), one lieutenant-colonel, and four riflemen, and four others were reported missing.

The war is over. No paragraph of panegyric could be written long enough and strong enough to express the admiration one feels for Wellington and his army. He, now created a Duke, proceeded to Paris, where, crowned with the fruits of his six years' labours, he was admitted the equal, and more than equal, among the kings and princes of Europe; and the troops, who had earned for themselves, and those that should come after, the right of blazoning on their appointments the fourteen great victories which commence with Roleia and end with Toulouse, were separated from their long comradeship and dispersed in different directions.

The cavalry marched through France and embarked at Calais for England.

The infantry were sent to Bordeaux and its neighbourhood, and from thence went, some to America, where hostilities were still being carried on, and some to England. Among the latter was the 5th battalion 60th. At the beginning of July, 1814, H.M.S. *Clarence* was ready for them at the mouth of the Gironde. Marching down from Bordeaux to Pauliac below Modoc, large river vessels put them on board the ship, and embarking on July 5th, they were disembarked at Cove of Cork on July 25th, 1814, from which place they had sailed with Sir Arthur Wellesley and his expedition under Davy's command in July, 1808.

What a changed battalion landed at Cork! They had sailed in the three transports, *Malabar, Juliana,* and *Atlas,* with thirty-five officers and 909 non-commissioned officers and men; one ship sufficed to bring back eighteen officers and 232 non-commissioned officers and men. Instead of Davy and Woodgate, Galiffe and Schoëdde were the two senior officers in charge; and besides them, one officer only of the eighteen (Lieutenant Muller) had gone out with the battalion.

To complete the establishment at that time, there were wanting 613 non-commissioned officers and men; and five officers and 178 non-commissioned officers and men were prisoners of war not yet returned to the ranks.

CHAPTER 11

Endings: 1814–1818

The 5th battalion 60th having landed at Cork, marched soon afterwards to Buttevant, but of how they employed themselves no record has been preserved; probably in much the same way as other regiments did.

If it be asked, 'how was that?' the writer of this sketch can answer, that when a subaltern in the 1st battalion 60th in 1850 he was for two or three monsoon months in Bombay, and the hospitable officers of the 78th Highlanders gave him the privileges of honorary membership of their mess. Whilst there the excellent Major Taylor died, and was buried beyond the Colabah Lighthouse. He had seen service in Spain when young, and had kept a most interesting diary from about the time of the battle of Vittoria till the return of the army to England from Bordeaux. In the last pages of this diary he told how his regiment on its return was quartered at Kilkenny, and received large arrears of pay. So much money had they that it was thought best to give the whole battalion several days' leave to spend their time and money how they would; and they showed their idiosyncrasies accordingly.

One favourite amusement was for parties, as large as could crowd themselves upon a coach, to hire one and drive about the country with four horses, horns, and hampers.

One who loved solitude and 'the gentle river's side' got a large tub, which he provisioned and launched below the bridge, and gently floated down the stream in a state of 'real enjoyment.' But though his condition may be said to have been 'good all round,' there was neither helm nor prow for mirth and pleasure to take their seats at, and the solitary crew found the ship impossible to guide. Quietly floating and gyrating he pursued his spiral course till he came to the weir, a mile or so below the bridge, when his short but happy voyage was ended by his passing over the fall, and tub and stores went various ways towards the sea, whilst he, the yachting man, scrambled out as best he could.

Madidaque fluens in veste Menœtes
Summa petit scopuli, siccaque in rupe resedit.[1]

Such possibly may have been the general line of action of our 60th Riflemen, with money to spend, and having certainly earned a relaxation by their laborious campaigns.

There was of course much to do in completing the battalion and refitting generally, the responsibilities of which must have fallen on Galiffe and Schoëdde, who had brought the battalion home, and who were the two senior officers on its embarkation for Gibraltar the following year.

It may be well here to explain that Lieutenant-Colonel Fitzgerald, whose name has occurred several times in the Peninsular War, became virtually commander of the battalion after Colonel Williams left.

Colonel Williams exchanged in 1812 with Colonel John Keane of the 13th Regiment, but Keane does not appear to have commanded the 5th battalion 60th. Keane began his service by being appointed to a company in the 124th foot on the 12th of November, 1794; was on half-pay from 1795 till November 1799, when he was appointed to a company in the 44th Foot.

He joined at Gibraltar, and served on the staff in Egypt, and in the actions of the 13th and 21st of March, 1801. In

---

1. Æneid, v. 179, 180

May 1802 he obtained a majority in the 60th, and remained in the Mediterranean on the staff till March 1803, when he returned to England and was appointed lieutenant-colonel of the 13th Regiment in August 1803, and joined that corps at Gibraltar 1804. He served in the campaign of Martinique, and was present at the siege of Fort Desaix. On January 1, 1812, he was appointed 'colonel in the army,' and in June the same year he came back to the 60th *vice*. Williams; but from his seniority he was employed as colonel on the staff in command of a brigade, and became, on June 4th, 1814, a major general, and eventually Lord Keane of Ghuznee and Cappoquin.

Colonel Keane then being always detached, the command fell on Major and Brevet, Lieutenant-Colonel Fitzgerald. As there were three Majors Fitzgerald, it is necessary to distinguish them. There were Majors Henry Fitzgerald and Edward Fitzgerald. The latter was a near relative of Lord Edward Fitzgerald, and served in the Peninsula, winning the good esteem of the Duke of Wellington. The third, but senior, was Major and Brevet Lieutenant-Colonel John Forster Fitzgerald. He was the son of Edward Fitzgerald, Esq., M.P., of Carrigoran, and was born in 1786. In 1793, when only seven years old, he obtained a commission as ensign. In 1794 he was promoted to a lieutenancy, and on the 9th of May in the same year to a captaincy in the old 79th regiment (not 79th Highlanders). On October 31, 1800, at the age of fifteen, and having been a *titular* captain for seven years, he was brought on full pay in the 46th Regiment; he was placed on half-pay in 1802, restored to full pay in July 1803, and on September 25 in the same year became brevet-major when only seventeen years old!

In November 1809 he was appointed major in the 60th Rifles, and became brevet lieutenant-colonel on July 25, 1810.

Having joined in the Peninsula he behaved with considerable distinction at the siege of Badajos, where he was wounded, and at Salamanca. After Colonel Williams exchanged with

Keane he was the senior officer present with the 5th 60th, and commanded the light infantry battalion, of which the head-quarters and three companies formed the nucleus, in the 3rd division. He served at Vittoria, and in the battles of the Pyrenees; and at one time commanded a brigade and was taken prisoner, but subsequently exchanged. He received the Gold Cross for his services, was made a Companion of the Bath, and became a full colonel in 1819, but continued in his rank of regimental major until 1824, when he was appointed lieutenant-colonel of the 20th Regiment. He became major-general in 1830; commanded a division in the Bombay Presidency; lieutenant-general in 1841; and in 1854 he became full general. In 1862 he was created a G.C.B., and on May 29, 1875, he was appointed Field Marshal. Two years later, at the age of ninety-one (for eighty-four years of which he had been a commissioned officer), he died at Tours in France, when, by order of the Minister of War, the military honours paid to French officers of his rank were rendered to his remains, and the whole garrison escorted the body to the grave.

In April, 1815, H. R. H. the Prince Regent was pleased, in the name and on behalf of his Majesty, to approve of the 60th (with other regiments) bearing on their appointments the 'word "Peninsula" in addition to any other badges and devices that may heretofore have been granted in commemoration of its services during the late war in Portugal, Spain, and France under the command of Marshal the Duke of Wellington.'

The 5th battalion 60th was not in the Netherlands, and, though the regiment was represented by two or three officers on the staff, they cannot talk of 'Waterloo' as being in any way connected with it. They have not the less pride and satisfaction in contemplating the acts of those who had followed such great men as Beckwith and Barnard during the long years they had fought for the freedom of Spain and of Europe, and who now were allowed to put the coping-stone on their pile of honours by helping to win the greatest victory of modern or ancient days, after which 'the land had rest for forty years.'

In February, 1816, the 5th battalion 60th moved from Buttevant to the Isle of Wight, where it was completed to its establishment by a large draft of recruits from the depot at Harwich; and in May they were once again embarked for foreign service in the Mediterranean, at Cowes, in the transports *Minerva*, *Duncombe*, and *Isabella*.

The detail was as follows:

Embarked at West Cowes on the 4th of May, 1816, on board the *Minerva* for Gibraltar, Brevet Lieutenant-Colonel John Galiffe commanding—11 Officers, 21 Women, 316 N. C. O.'s and men, 13 Children. On board the *Duncombe*, Captain McKenzie commanding—14 Officers, 19 Women, 279 N. C. O.'s and men, 16 Children. On board the *Isabella* Brevet-Major Schoëdde commanding—4 Officers, 16 Women, 175 N. C. O.'s and men, 13 Children. Making a total of: Officers—29; N. C. O.'s and men—770; Women—56 and Children—43[2]

The battalion sailed from Spithead on May 16; and on its arrival at Gibraltar the 8th battalion 60th was disbanded, and all its effective non-commissioned officers and men were turned over to the 5th 60th; and the staff and a number of the officers were sent home to England to be placed on half-pay.

On September 26 a draft for the 5th battalion 60th was sent out from the Isle of Wight in the *Mary* transport; but there is nothing further to record beyond the fact that the old blue pantaloons had been exchanged for green ones, and that at this time the battalion dress was a green double-breasted jacket with skirts, red facings, and gold wings, and a cap of the then regulation pattern. It would not be an easy task to enumerate all the changes that have taken place in the sixty years since then.

The years 1816 and 1817 pass quietly on. We are fast approaching 1818, when the 5th battalion was disembodied; and

---

2. For full details of embarkations, see Appendix.

we cannot find a better place than this for telling how their Peninsular reputation clung to them as years went by.

It was about 1835 or 1836 when a battalion of the 60th was again in the Mediterranean and quartered at Malta, when Marshal Marmont visited the island; and the Governor, Sir F. Ponsonby, attached Captain Freeman Murray (now General Murray and colonel-commandant of 2nd battalion 60th) as a staff officer and interpreter to the person of the old Duke of Ragusa, Wellington's opponent at Salamanca. General Murray told the writer—

> Amongst other things the troops were turned out, and Marmont expressed his great satisfaction at having the opportunity of seeing English troops in detail. "For," said he, "I know what they can do in the field of battle, for they taught me that at Salamanca; but I never saw them *en detail*, and I am the more interested in doing so, as I am writing a work on all the armies of Europe." As the manoeuvres proceeded I explained the reason and manner of performing each of them. He declared himself *emerveillé*. "You have," said he, "*l'immobilite des statues, et la rapidité de l'eclaire.*" What astonished him equally was the perfect stillness and silence in the ranks.
>
> "For," said he, "I have discovered that you are well acquainted with the French army, and you, therefore, are aware of the impossibility we have in obtaining silence; the hubbub increasing in proportion to the importance of the occasion." He said, "Now that I have seen these manoeuvres, I can state that I have seen the top and bottom of the ladder. Today I have seen the top (for this is the first infantry in the world), and I have just come from Constantinople, where the Turks are trying to form an army according to the modern system; as yet they are at the bottom."

I must add that his admiration of the 60th was very

gratifying. The troops on the ground were the 7th Fusiliers, 53rd Regiment, 60th Rifles, 92nd Highlanders, and Maltese Fencibles (the latter quite equal to the occasion). Marmont also gave me an account of the manner he was interfered with and thwarted in the defence of Paris, which explained what appeared to be unpardonable and unaccountable blunders on the part of an experienced soldier.

With this interesting little anecdote and conversation between Marmont and General Murray we must close this sketch.

In 1818 large reductions were made in the army, and arrangements were made to reduce the establishment of the 60th Regiment to two battalions. In carrying out this plan all the battalions were disintegrated except the 2nd and 3rd, which, being amalgamated with the 5th and other battalions, became eventually the present 1st and 2nd battalions. In May, 1816, the 8th battalion sent drafts to the 5th battalion, and the remainder were disbanded at Portsmouth. In 1817 the 7th battalion was drafted into the 2nd and 3rd battalions. In February, 1818, the 6th battalion was disbanded, and the men sent to the 3rd battalion at Halifax, Nova Scotia; and in May of the same year the 5th battalion was relieved by the 64th Regiment at Gibraltar, and left there May 10th in the transports *Borodino*, *Ocean*, and *Kennersley Castle*, under the command of Brevet Lieut.-Colonel John Forster Fitzgerald.

The battalion arrived at Portsmouth on June 4th, and went on to Cowes and were disembarked on the 18th. The detail was as follows: From the *Kennersley Castle,* Lieutenant-Colonel Fitzgerald commanding—7 Officers, 36 Women, 263 N. C. O.'s and men, 37 Children. From the *Ocean*, Major Galiffe commanding—11 Officers, 28 Women, 236 N. C. O.'s and men, 32 Children.[3]

Of the numbers on board the *Borodino* no return could

---

3. For further details, see Appendix.

be furnished by the Horse Guards, but, very kindly, a list was given of the officers who must have sailed in her, thereby completing the list of those who belonged to the battalion at the close of its career, to place in an Appendix with the list of those who belonged to it when embarking for Portugal.

On landing at Cowes they marched into 'Albany' barracks, and were there disbanded on the 25th of July. The foreigners of the battalion were sent to Calais, Ostend, and Cuxhaven in the transport *Crown*, and the British were drafted into the 2nd battalion at Quebec. They sailed from Cowes to join it on August 2nd, 1818, in the transport *Sarah and Ann*, and the 5th battalion no longer had a place, except in history; and the latest letter connected with it does not recognise its number or existence:

> Sir Henry Torrents to the Duke of Richmond
> Horse Guards
> Sept. 26th, 1818
> *My Lord Duke,*
> I have had the honour to receive and lay before the commander-in-chief your Grace's letter of 30th July last, and to acquaint you in reply that 400 men sailed on 2nd *ult.* to join 2nd battalion 60th Regiment.
> I have the honour, &c.
> (Signed) *H. Torrens*

The 5th battalion 60th was merged in the 2nd (Rifle) battalion, and portions of other battalions were drafted into it and the 3rd battalion, and these two became, after a short interval, the 1st and 2nd battalions of 60th, or King's Royal Rifles. For sixty years the 60th has been employed in all parts of the world, and, like Henry Lawrence, 'has tried to do its duty.' In the attempt it has been stimulated by its old traditions, and the necessity of maintaining the high reputation which it inherited from its predecessors, and it is partly with a view of recording the past that these pages have been compiled; but partly also in the hope of animating a future generation to emulate their deeds, we will finish with a *resumé,* of the services of six Sires of the 60th.

Lieutenant-General Francis Baron de Rottenburg

In our opening chapter some account was given of the earlier services of this officer and his connection with Count Hompesch. He came of an Austrian family of rank, and so high was the opinion which the Duke of York formed of him that he appointed and promoted him in the British service.

He was made major in Hompesch's Hussars in 1795, lieutenant-colonel in 1796, and was appointed lieutenant-colonel in the 60th in 1797, when the 5th battalion was raised. He formed it and served with it in Ireland in the rebellion of 1798. It was the first Rifle regiment which England ever possessed. He wrote the book of drill for riflemen and for outpost duties, for light infantry and their conduct in the field, which was so highly approved of by the Duke of York that H.R.H. as Commander-in-Chief made it general for the army in a complimentary order, and it was embodied in the book of *Field Exercises and Evolutions of the Army.*

He went out with the battalion and served at the taking of Surinam in 1799, and in 1805 received tin-rank of colonel. In 1808 he received the appointment of brigadier-general, and four battalions of light infantry were placed under him for instruction at the Curragh under Sir David Baird. In the same year he was transferred to the English staff, and employed on the same duty at Ashford in Kent.

In a letter which he wrote from Ashford to Major Davy in the Peninsula, he says:

> The Duke with his usual kindness towards me permitted my postponing to proceed to Canada until the spring of next year, and soon after appointed me to serve on the staff in Kent for the purpose of superintending the

68th and 85th Regiments, to be transformed *sub alarum mearum (sic)* into light bobs; they are quartered at Brabourn Lees barracks, and my old bones undergo a trott *(sic)* of ten miles *per diem.*

The 71st and 52nd also were instructed by him, and other regiments, and in fact he introduced the light infantry system into our army which, with modifications, still exists.

In 1809 he served throughout the Walcheren expedition and the siege of Flushing in command of a light brigade, and was the first to land and the last to leave, and then returned to the staff in Kent.

In May 1810 he was placed on the staff in Canada, and in command of the garrison at Quebec. He was promoted major-general the same year, and in 1812, on the breaking out of the American War, he took command at Montreal.

In 1813 he commanded the whole of the troops in the Upper Province, and was sworn in President of Upper Canada. In 1814-15 he commanded the left division of the army in Canada, and in September of the latter year he returned to England—of course to receive due reward for such varied services?

Yes—in 1816 he was nominated a K.C.H., and was knighted by the Prince Regent. 'But surely,' someone will say, 'he met with more substantial reward than that?' Well, in 1813 he had been made colonel-commandant of the regiment '*de Roll*,' but in 1816 it was disbanded, and he lost about £1,200 a year. As a foreigner he was ineligible in time of peace to be colonel of a regiment, or to hold a government or command a fortress. So they put him on half-pay at the rate of 9s. 6d. a day! On memorial to the Prince Regent this was increased to the daily sum of 16s.! His friend the Duke of York died. No further pension was found for him. He became a lieutenant-general in 1819, and in 1832, thus neglected, he died on the 24th of April at Portsmouth.

Sir William was major with de Rottenburg, and took over the command of the 5th battalion 60th from him In 1808, was the eldest son of Major Davy, H. E. I. C S., the Persian Secretary to Warren Hastings. He was educated at Eton, and got his first commission in 1797 in the 61st Regiment.

He served in the earlier part of his career at the Cape of Good Hope and in Canada, and on the 1st of January, 1802, he became captain in the 60th, and major on the 5th of February, 1807.

In 1808 he proceeded to Portugal, and his acts are detailed in the foregoing pages. Having commanded at Roleia, Vimeira, and Talavera, he was promoted lieutenant-colonel and honoured with the Gold Medal for his services; but being ordered home he did not again return to active service in Spain, and with the peace which was concluded in 1815 he settled down at Tracy Park, near Bath.

He became a colonel in the army on the 12th of August, 1819; major-general on the 22nd of July, 1830; lieutenant-general on the 23rd of November, 1841; and general on the 20th of June, 1854.

In November, 1842, the Duke of Wellington made him colonel-commandant of the 1st batt. 60th Royal Rifles, the one which represented that which he had done so much to form, and had commanded in the Peninsula. His interest in his battalion and his kindly assistance to some of the old Germans who applied to him in later years only ceased with his death, in the 76th year of his age, at his seat, Tracy Park, near Bath, which took place on the 25th of January, 1856.

Colonel William Woodgate

A friend and fellow-worker of Davy, has also been freely mentioned in these pages, and his letters to his old comrade and colonel have been given. He was appointed lieutenant in the 6th Foot November 19, 1800; and captain in the 60th April 6, 1803. In the early years he saw a good deal of service in Canada and the West Indies. He was promoted major on the 13th of August, 1807, and went to Portugal in 1808, and served at Roleia, Vimeira, Talavera, Busaco, Fuentes d'Onor, Badajos, and Salamanca. He several times had command of half the battalion, and commanded it when Davy went home on promotion until the arrival of Colonel Williams; and when that officer was badly wounded on the first days' fighting at Fuentes d'Onor, Woodgate succeeded to the command of the head-quarters of the battalion and the light infantry of the 3rd division. He was wounded in the battle, mentioned in Wellington's despatch, was given the Gold Medal, made brevet lieutenant-colonel for his services on the 30th of May, 1811, and lieutenant-colonel of a battalion on the 16th of June, 1814, till the reduction in 1817. He became Companion of the Bath and was promoted colonel in the army in 1821; but he had retired from active service, and lived on for forty years, dying in Paris at the age of eighty on the 12th of January, 1861.

Sir William Williams

Commenced his service in the 40th Regiment in June, 1794; was lieutenant in April, 1795; captain in September, 1799; major in the army in June, 1802; and major in the 81st Foot 26th of October, 1804. He had served with great credit in the expedition and battle of Corunna, and, on Colonel Davy's promotion, was appointed lieutenant-colonel of the 5th battalion 60th Rifles on November 15, 1809. He joined them in time to command them and the light infantry of Picton's division at Busaco, where he was twice wounded; on the retreat to Torres Vedras; at, the battle of Fuentes d'Onor, again very badly wounded; sieges of Ciudad Rodrigo and Badajos, again wounded; the pursuit of Massena and battle of Salamanca, where he was wounded once more. He is frequently mentioned in the Wellington despatches, and had the honour of receiving the Gold Cross and one Clasp for the events in which he took part; and on March 11, 1813, he was licensed to accept and wear the Portuguese order of 'Knight of the Tower and Sword,' but without the privilege of a Knight Bachelor of prefixing the 'Sir' before his name. After Salamanca, having exchanged with Colonel John Keane of the 13th regiment, he proceeded to take command of it, and in 1814 was employed in America.

He commanded at St. John's at the posts in advance on the Richelieu river; and after the attack thereon by the American General Wilkinson, Sir George Prevost, Commander of the Forces, expressed in general orders:

> . . . . his most entire approbation of the judgement, zeal, and unwearied assiduity displayed by Lieutenant-Colonel Williams in his arrangement for the defence of the important posts placed under his immediate command.

On the enlargement of the Order of the Bath in 1815 he was made a Knight Commander; became full colonel in 1819, major-general in 1830; and on June 17, 1832, he died at his house in Marlborough Buildings, Bath.

COLONEL GALIFFE

Brought the battalion home from Bordeaux in 1814 to Cork (whence he had embarked with it in 1808), had a very varied service in the beginning of his career. From 1785 to 1792 he was in the French service; he then entered the Dutch service in the hussar regiment of Timorman, in which he made part of the campaigns of 1793 and the whole of 1794. At the time the French took possession of Holland he came over to England, and was appointed lieutenant in the 6th West India regiment; he joined in the West Indies in 1796, and was made captain in the York Rangers in October of that year. On the York Rangers being disbanded he was appointed to the 5th battalion 60th on the 30th of December, 1797 (just as it was raised), and, as has been already observed, proceeded with it to Portugal in 1808.

He was wounded at Talavera, and received the Gold Cross for Nivelle, Orthes, and Toulouse; and having been promoted brevet lieutenant-colonel for his services on March 3, 1814, he came home in command of the battalion. Colonel Galiffe remained in the 60th with regimental rank of major till he was promoted lieutenant-colonel in 1825, and then left the regiment, being succeeded as lieutenant-colonel in the 2nd battalion by Major Henry Fitzgerald. There is no record of what became of him after that date, but he lived on till 1847-48.

Lieutenant-General Sir James Holmes Schoëdde

The 'child of the regiment,' and perhaps its most deserving son. He was born in the regiment, his father, Lieutenant-Colonel C. Lewis Theodore Schoëdde, having entered the 60th in the year 1780, and left it as lieutenant-colonel in 1805. James Holmes Schoëdde was born in 1786, and obtained an ensigncy in Lowenstein's Levy in May 1800, when only in his fifteenth year. He served the campaign in Egypt in 1801, and for his services received the Gold Medal from the Grand Seignior. In April, 1803, he was appointed to the 60th, and became captain in 1805, when nineteen years old, and did not obtain another step in regimental rank for twenty years. His name has occurred several times in the foregoing pages, and in Major Woodgate's, Galiffe's, and Andrews' letters; and it has been noted that he embarked as a captain with Major Davy in the *Malabar* transport at Cork, and returned there in 1814 with Major Galiffe, having been in every one of Wellington's battles and sieges (besides innumerable minor affairs), with the exception of Albuera, and there he could not be as he was at the time with that portion of the 60th Rifles which fought at Fuentes d'Onor. He, as well as Galiffe, was given the Gold Medal for Nivelle, and he was promoted brevet-major for Vittoria. In addition to his own duties he was for a time acting-paymaster in Portugal and Spain, and he said that, 'when he handed over his accounts, there was only one half-penny for which he could not account.'

He served in Gibraltar from 1816 to 1818, in Canada from 1818 to 1824, and then, having returned home, and having been promoted major in January 1825, he went with the 1st battalion 60th Royal Rifles to revisit some of the scenes of his former services in Portugal, with the force known as 'Canning's expedition.' They remained in Portugal 1826 and 1827. Schoëdde returned home in the latter year, and served with the 60th until March 1829, when he was promoted to an unattached lieutenant-colonelcy. In June 1830 he became lieutenant-colonel of the 48th regiment, and in March 1833 went to command the 55th regiment, of which he continued in command for twelve years; eventually going on half-pay in 1845, having been forty-five years on active service and being sixty years of age.

The greater part of his time in the 48th and 55th was actively employed, for from October 30 to November 6, 1841, he was in the East Indies, and from November 7, 1841, to February, 1844, in China. In 1841-42 there was war in China, and Schoëdde (who had become colonel in the army in November, 1841) commanded the left column at the affair of Chapoo; and as major-general in 1843 under Lieutenant-General Sir Hugh Gough he commanded the 2nd brigade at the escalade and storming of Tching-Kiang-Foo.

Sir Hugh Gough thanked him in his despatch dated Chapoo, 20th of May, 1841. And again, in his despatch dated Tching-Kiang-Foo, July 25, 1842, he used the following words:

SCHOËDDE

I cannot too strongly express my approval of the spirited and judicious way in which Major-General Schoëdde fulfilled my orders.

His name was included in the vote of thanks from both Houses of Parliament for the 'energy, ability, and gallantry with which the various services had been performed;' and having been made A D.C. to the Queen on November 25, 1841, and colonel in the army, he was, on the 23rd of December 1842, made major-general in India, Knight Commander of the Bath, and received the medal for the China campaign.

In November, 1845, Colonel Sir James Holmes Schoëdde exchanged to half-pay. He became a major general 20th of June 1854, and colonel-commandant of his old corps (the 55th Regiment) 28th of May, 1857.

What an amount of adventure the old general had to tell! But he never told it; nor did he leave any papers or diaries. He spent his last years at Lyndhurst; and when the writer of these lines wrote to the clergyman there to see if any information could be gleaned relative to the 60th, the reply was that 'the good old general was most reticent, never speaking of the part he had played in the world in his long and active career.' So too when his old friend Sir H. C. Daubeney was enquired of, he could give but little—little that is of anecdote or early life, he kindly sent an accurate copy of the *Regimental Records of Service,* and confirmed the clergyman's statement that Sir James Schoëdde 'never talked of himself or his own doings.' Strange it is, but had he ever talked with anyone it would have been with Sir H. Daubeney, who was his regimental adjutant, on his staff as brigade-major in China, and succeeded him both as lieutenant-colonel and colonel-commandant of the 55th regiment. But he says this in a letter to the writer:

I am able to say of my own knowledge that by the mere force of his own example, and without resort to any penal measures whatever, he effected a complete revolution in the tone of his regiment after he joined it, and left his mark so indelibly stamped on the corps that it has not, yet at all events, lost the high moral character and amenability to discipline which so highly distinguished it under his command.

'His works do follow him;' and may the contemplation of his good example help generations of 'riflemen' to 'go and do likewise.'

At Lyndhurst, in the New Forest, he died, and was buried; and in the church there his old friend and whilom adjutant, General Daubeney, placed a large and handsome brass plate to the memory of 'Lieutenant-General Sir James Holmes Schoëdde, K.C.B., aged seventy-five years.'

One word more and we have done. We have tried to trace the action of the 5th battalion 60th throughout the Peninsular War, and have shown how it won honour on each battlefield in turn. Many were the gallant men who fought at one or several of these actions; but to Schoëdde alone it was allotted to help at all; and yet he had no medal for all these 'well-stricken fields,' till he had retired after five-and-forty years' hard work. Then, in 1847, the Queen gave the war medal and clasps. Schoëdde had had gold and silver medals and crosses; he had the Star of Knighthood of the Bath; but he had at last, in the thirteen clasps attached to his silver war medal, an acknowledgement that he had individually taken part in every one of those events, the bearing the names of which on their appointments constitutes the pride and creates the *esprit* which exists in each officer and rifleman belonging to the 'Sixtieth.' He had clasps for:

Roleia	Vimeira	Talavera
Busaco	Fuentes d'Onor	Ciudad Rodrigo
Badajos	Salamanca	Vittoria
Nivelle	Nive	Orthes
Toulouse		

Returns of Killed, Wounded and Missing

Totals

Obidos and Lorinda, Aug. 15th, 1808

One rifleman killed; five wounded; seventeen missing   23

Roleia, Aug. 17th, 1808

Three officers wounded, Lieutenants Steitz, Darcy, and Adjutant de Gilse. Eight riflemen killed; five sergeants and thirty-four men wounded; sixteen missing   66

Vimeira, Aug. 21st, 1808

Two officers, Lieutenants Koch and Ritter, wounded. Fourteen riflemen killed; one sergeant and twenty-one men wounded; ten riflemen missing   48

Talavera, July 27th, 1809

One officer, Captain Wolf, wounded. Four riflemen wounded; one bugler and eighteen men missing   24

July 28th

Five officers, Brevet-Major Galiffe, Captain Andrews, Lieutenants Zuhleke, Ritter, Mitchell, and Ensign Altenstein, wounded. One bugler and six riflemen killed; one sergeant and twenty-four men wounded; two sergeants and ten men missing   49

Busaco, Sept. 21st, 1810

Five officers wounded, Lieutenant-Colonel Williams, Captain Andrews, Lieutenants Joyce, Eberstein, and Franchini. Three riflemen killed; sixteen riflemen wounded; five missing — 29

1811. Pursuit of Massena

14th March, Lieutenant Wynne wounded. 15th March, Lieutenant Sawatsky killed. 3rd April, two riflemen killed; one sergeant and one rifleman wounded — 6

Fuentes d'Onor, 3rd May, 1811

Two officers wounded, Lieutenant-Colonel Williams and Lieutenant Duchatelet. Three riflemen killed; nine riflemen wounded; eight riflemen missing — 22

5th May, 1811

Two officers, Major Woodgate and Lieutenant Wynne, wounded. One sergeant and eleven riflemen wounded; one rifleman missing — 15

Albuera, May 16th, 1811

One officer, Lieutenant Ingersleben, wounded. One sergeant and one rifleman killed; two sergeants and sixteen riflemen wounded — 21

Before Badajos, 1811

In the trenches on May 5th, one rifleman wounded. May 10th, repulse of sortie, one captain and seven riflemen wounded — 9

Aldea del Ponte, Sept. 27th

One officer, Captain Prevost, wounded — 1

Cuidad Rodrigo, Jan. 18th

Two riflemen wounded. Jan 19th (assault), one officer wounded. One sergeant killed; three riflemen wounded — 7

Badajos, March and April, 1812

From March 18th to 22nd, three riflemen killed; three riflemen wounded. 23rd to 26th, one rifleman wounded. 31st to April 2nd, one rifleman killed; four riflemen wounded. 6th and 7th April (assault), Lieutenant Sterne and four riflemen killed; four officers, Lieutenant-Colonel Williams, Lieutenant-Colonel Fitzgerald, Lieutenant de Gilse, and Adjutant Broetz, wounded. Two sergeants and twenty-four riflemen wounded   47

Salamanca and operations

Siege of Fort St. Vincente, 18th to 24th June, 1812, one rifleman killed; two riflemen wounded. On 18th July, one rifleman killed; two riflemen missing. July 22nd, battle of Salamanca, three officers, Lieutenant-Colonel Williams, Major Galiffe, and Ensign Luck, wounded. Six riflemen killed; twenty-three riflemen wounded; three riflemen missing   41

Fort St. Michael, Sept. 19th

One officer wounded, Lieutenant O'Hehir. One sergeant and two riflemen killed; seven riflemen wounded; one rifleman missing   12

Burgos, 27th Sept. to 3rd Oct

One sergeant killed; one rifleman wounded. 4th and 5th Oct., one rifleman killed; two riflemen wounded. 6th to l0th, two riflemen killed, 11th to 17th, two riflemen killed; one rifleman wounded. 18th to 21st, two riflemen wounded   12

Alba de Tormes, Nov. 10th and 11th

Eight riflemen wounded   8

Vittoria and Pyrenees, 1813

Two officers wounded, Captain Franchini, Lieutenant Joyce. Three riflemen killed; four sergeants and forty-three riflemen wounded. 4th and 5th July, one sergeant and five riflemen wounded. 25th, Lieutenants Van Dahlman and Joyce killed. 26th, Ensign Martin wounded. 30th July to 1st Aug., one rifleman killed; Adjutant Kent wounded; three sergeants and eleven riflemen wounded. 31st July, Major Fitzgerald missing   78

Bidassoa, 7th and 8th Oct

One rifleman wounded; two men missing   3

Nivelle, Nov. 10th

One officer, Lieutenant Eccles, killed; three sergeants and four riflemen killed   8

Three officers wounded, Captain Stopford, Lieutenant Passley, and Ensign Shewbridge. Three sergeants, one bugler, and fifty-four riflemen wounded; two riflemen missing   63

Nive, Dec. 9th

One officer, Lieutenant Dickson, wounded. One sergeant and twelve riflemen wounded. Dec. 13th, one officer, Ensign ————, wounded; two sergeants and sixteen riflemen wounded   33

1814. Feb. 14th

Captain F. P. Blassiere wounded, 15th, Lieutenant Got Lerche, and Lieutenant Stepney St. George, of 2nd battalion 60th, wounded   3

Orthes, Feb. 27th

Two officers wounded, Captain Franchini and Lieutenant Currie. Numbers not given as to regiments, only grand total returns of the losses of the whole army   2

Toulouse, April 10th

Three officers wounded, Captain Purdon, Ensigns Shewbridge and Bruce. Four sergeants and forty-four riflemen
wounded; one rifleman missing   52

Sortie from Bayonne, April 14th

Two officers wounded, Lieutenant-Colonel ———— and
Lieutenant Hamilton. Four riflemen wounded; one sergeant and four riflemen missing   11

Total of killed, wounded, and missing   693

At the close of the war, there remained as prisoners in the
hands of the French, five officers and 178 non-commissioned officers and men   183

Outgoings & Returns

**Strength of 5th battalion 60th (Rifles)
on embarkation at Cork, June 1808
in the *Malabar*, *Juliana*, and *Atlas* transports**

Field Officers	2
Captains	7
Lieutenants	11
Ensigns	7
Staff Officers	6
Total officers	33
Serjeants	52
Corporals	50
Buglers	21
Riflemen	886
Total	1009

Wanted to complete non-commissioned officers and men 69
Total establishment non-commissioned officers and men 1078
Embarked women, 60   Embarked children, 50

Nominal roll of the thirty-three officers who embarked

Field Officers

Major Wm. Gabriel Davy
Major William Woodgate

Captains

John Galiffe
Alexander Andrews
Thomas Hames
Michael Wend (de Wendt)
James Holmes Schoëdde
Peter Blassiere
John Antony Wolff

Lieutenants

C. W. H. Koch
George Henry Zulke
Alexander McKenzie
Francis Holmes
Lewis Ritter
Frederick Steitz
Charles Sawatsky
M. M. du Chatelet
Henry Muller
William Linstow
Francis Baron Eberstein

Ensigns

John Sprecher
Isaac Robateau d'Arcy
William Wynne
John Joyce
Julius van Boek
John Louis Barbaz
Charles de Bree

Paymaster

George Gilbert

Adjutant

Frederick de Gilse

Quartermaster

J. Adolphus Kemmeter

Surgeon

Michael Edward Parker

Assistant-Surgeons

J. A. du Moulin
Charles Wehsarg

Absent

Lieutenant-Colonel de Rottenburg (Staff of America)
Captain de Salaberry, his brigade major
Captain McMahon, on leave from Commander-in-Chief
Captain Prevost, A. D. C. to Sir G. Provost
Lieutenant Schruine, duty with 6th battalion, West Indies
Lieutenant Hoffman, recruiting in Germany
Lieutenant du Chesnay, absent without leave
Ensign William Morgenthal, D. A. Q. M. G. with Sir John Moore

Embarkation of 5th battalion 60th Regiment in H.M. S. *Clarence* at Pauliac, 5th July, 1814

Disembarked at Cove, 25th July, 1814. eighteen officers, 232 non-commissioned officers rank and file

Major Galiffe	Lieut. C. Forneret
Brevet-Major Schoëdde	Lieut.J. Moore
Capt. F. Franchini	Lieut.J. Stewart
Capt. W. Wilkinson	Ensign H. Shewbridge
Lieut. F. Muller	Ensign J. Bruce
Lieut.A. F. Evans	Paymaster Biggs
Lieut.S. O'Hehir	Adjutant Kent
Lieut.P. N. de Kruger	Quartermaster Recknoy
Lieut.T. Came	Assist.-Surg. W. Stevenson
Officers Absent	

Lieutenants W. Linstow and E. Franciosi, on duty with Portuguese army

Captain C. Kinsinger and Lieutenant Erdberg, recruiting service, Heligoland

N.B. The regiment wanted 613 non-commissioned officers and men to complete its establishment at that time, and had five officers and 178 non-commissioned officers and men prisoners of war

Embarkation of 5th battalion 60th at West Cowes, Isle of Wight, 4th May, 1816 in the *Minerva*, for Gibraltar

Officers[1]

Major John Galiffe	Ensign K. Supple
Capt. J. Franchini	Ensign T. Keal
Lieut. F. Muller	Ensign J. Robinson
Lieut. J. Currie	Paymaster H. Biggs
Lieut. J. Shewbridge	Adjutant J. Kent
	Assist.-Surg. W. Stevenson
316 N. C. O. and men	21 women
	13 children

---

1. Captain Purdon was included in Return, but did not embark, having obtained leave.

Embarkation of 5th battalion 60th at West Cowes, Isle of Wight, 4th May, 1816 in the *Duncombe*, for Gibraltar

Officers

Capt. C. McKenzie	Lieut. A. F. Evans
Capt. R. Kelly	Lieut. E. T. Bruce
Capt. W. Wilkinson	Ensign W. Bernard
Lieut. S. O'Hehir	Ensign H. Colclough
Lieut. S. Serjeant	Ensign D. Dickson
Lieut. Van Dyke	Quartermaster C. Recknoy
Lieut. J. Cochrane	

279 N. C. O. and men   19 women
16 children

Embarkation of 5th battalion 60th at Isle of Wight, 14th May, 1816 in the *Isabella*, for Gibraltar

Officers

Brevet-Major Schoëdde	175 N. C. O. and men
Capt. Stepney	16 women
Lieut. Picht	13 children
Lieut. Harkwill	

Disembarkation of 5th battalion 60th from the *Kennersley Castle*, at Cowes, 18th June, 1818 from Gibraltar

Officers

Major Fitzgerald (Lt.-Col.)	Ensign Dickson
Capt. Kelly	Paymaster Biggs
Capt. Bowers	Quartermaster Recknoy
Lieut. Eason	

263 N. C. O. and men   36 women
37 children

Disembarkation of 5th battalion 60th from the *Ocean*, at Cowes, 18th June, 1818 from Gibraltar

Officers

Major Galiffe	Lieut. Stewart
Brevet-Major Schoëdde	Lieut. Goldicut
Capt. Franchini	Ensign McKay
Lieut. Evans	Adjutant Adams
Lieut. Kent	Assist.-Surg. W. Stevenson
Lieut. Muller	

236 N. C. O. and men	28 women
	32 children

There is no disembarkation Return of the *Borodino*, but judging from the Return of officers of the 5th battalion 60th present at Gibraltar just before the departure of the regiment, the following officers must have coe home in her:

Capt. C. McKenzie	Lieut. C. Ross
Capt. C. Campbell	Lieut. S. Ridd
Capt. Stepney	Lieut. B. Clare
Lieut. H. B. Altenstein	Ensign R. Newman
Lieut. S. O'Hehir	Ensign C. H. Couper
Lieut. G. Cochrane	

The following officers were 'absent with leave' from Gibraltar: Captain Hewitt, student Royal Military College; Lieutenant J. Moore and Ensign F. Moore, at Army Depôt; Captain Purdon, Lieutenants Currie, Forneret, Tressider, Pictet, J. Cochrane, and R. Hall, Ensigns Heal, J. Robinson, and H. Colclough.

The following were 'absent without leave' from Gibraltar: Lieut.-Colonel J. Stopford, Captain W. Wilkinson, Lieutenant H. Shewbridge, and Surgeon M. Cathcart.

A Rifleman's Song

This song of the bivouac was a favourite in Spain, and has never (I believe) been printed. It was given to me by an old idolater of the 'Great Duke,' who was born in the last century, and cherishes the memory of many Peninsular friends. He told me that he had it from Colonel Parry-Yale, known in Spain as 'fighting Parry' of the 48th. As a young officer at Albuera when Colonel Duckworth was killed, and most of the officers killed and wounded, as was the case in the 57th and 29th Regiments, Parry commanded the 48th, and received the Gold Medal, which was only given to 'commanding officers.'

A Bivouac in Spain

The chilly dawn, the waning flame,
The bat-mule's savage cry,
The sullen bugle-blasts proclaim
The enemy is nigh!
Stand, stand to arms!

But thick the mist is rolling—
Look out along the hill,
And send some men patrolling
To yonder ruin'd mill.
Stand, stand to arms!

Now all the camp is stirring;
The day begins to clear;
Hard, hard the staff are spurring—
The enemy is near!
Stand, stand to arms!

I see his horsemen sweeping
Just where the picquet stood;
I see the grey coats creeping
Along that copse of wood.
Stand, stand to arms!

Bright are the bayonets gleaming,
Loud is the trumpet-call;
A Marshal's star is beaming
Beside yon cottage wall!
Stand, stand to arms!

Ay! now a single musket rings,
Swift comes the hissing lead;
I see the silver eagle's wings
Above the colours spread.
Stand, stand to arms!

Note.—Parry took the name of 'Yale' with a property in Wales. He was undecided whether or not to live on the estate, but on going to look at it, 'I found,' he said, 'the steep hills near the residence were just like Busaco, so I was reconciled to leaving the service.' He did so, and went to live where he was constantly reminded of that great victory.

SPAIN AND PORTUGAL

Scale of Miles

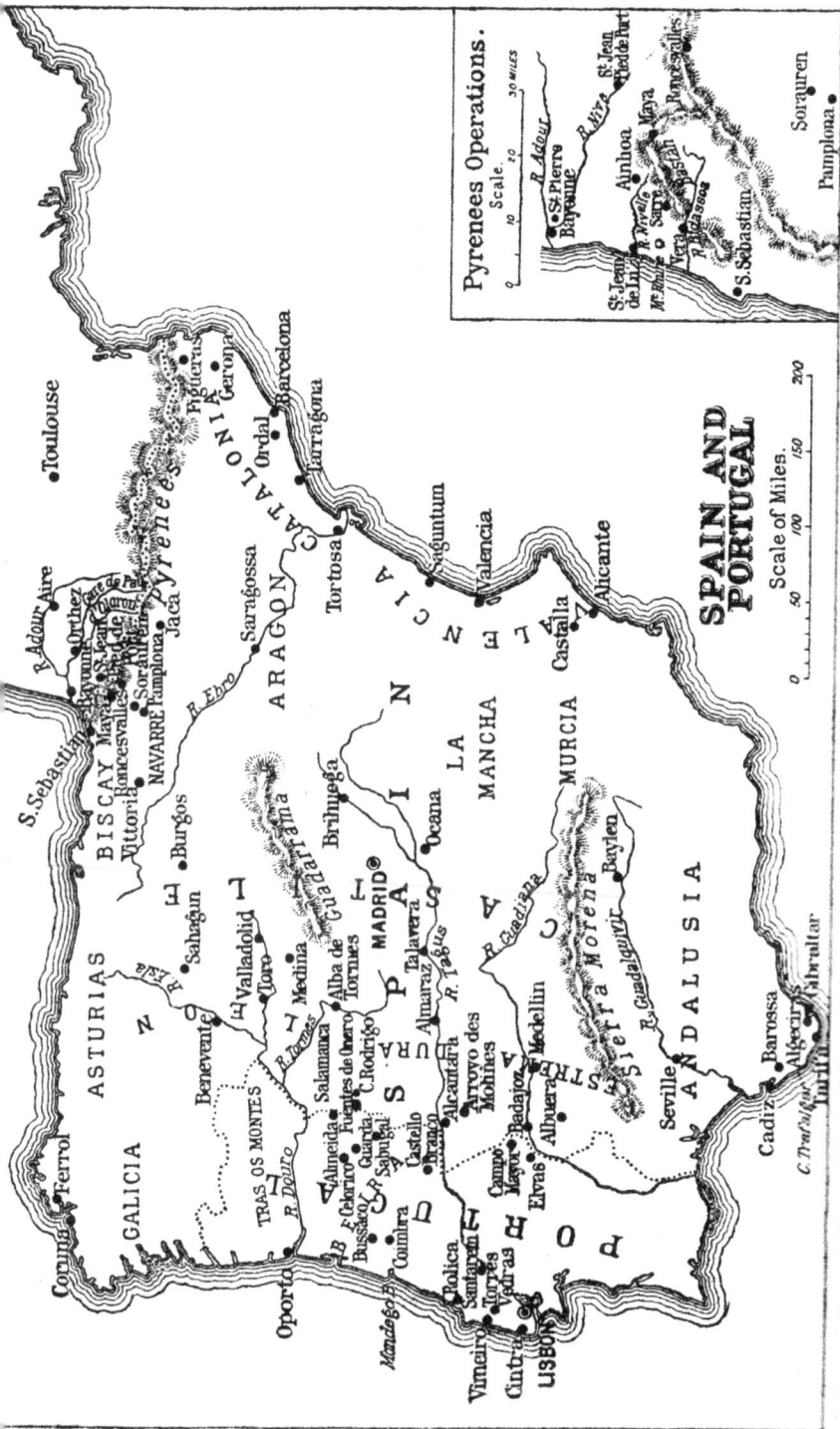

Pyrenees Operations.

LEONAUR

ALSO FROM LEONAUR
AVAILABLE IN SOFTCOVER OR HARDCOVER WITH DUST JACKET

THE JENA CAMPAIGN: 1806 *by F. N. Maude*—The Twin Battles of Jena & Auerstadt Between Napoleon's French and the Prussian Army.

PRIVATE O'NEIL *by Charles O'Neil*—The recollections of an Irish Rogue of H. M. 28th Regt.—The Slashers— during the Peninsula & Waterloo campaigns of the Napoleonic wars.

ROYAL HIGHLANDER *by James Anton*—A soldier of H.M 42nd (Royal) Highlanders during the Peninsular, South of France & Waterloo Campaigns of the Napoleonic Wars.

CAPTAIN BLAZE *by Elzéar Blaze*—Elzéar Blaze recounts his life and experiences in Napoleon's army in a well written, articulate and companionable style.

LEJEUNE VOLUME 1 *by Louis-François Lejeune*—The Napoleonic Wars through the Experiences of an Officer on Berthier's Staff.

LEJEUNE VOLUME 2 *by Louis-François Lejeune*—The Napoleonic Wars through the Experiences of an Officer on Berthier's Staff.

FUSILIER COOPER *by John S. Cooper*—Experiences in the 7th (Royal) Fusiliers During the Peninsular Campaign of the Napoleonic Wars and the American Campaign to New Orleans.

CAPTAIN COIGNET *by Jean-Roch Coignet*—A Soldier of Napoleon's Imperial Guard from the Italian Campaign to Russia and Waterloo.

FIGHTING NAPOLEON'S EMPIRE *by Joseph Anderson*—The Campaigns of a British Infantryman in Italy, Egypt, the Peninsular & the West Indies During the Napoleonic Wars.

CHASSEUR BARRES *by Jean-Baptiste Barres*—The experiences of a French Infantryman of the Imperial Guard at Austerlitz, Jena, Eylau, Friedland, in the Peninsular, Lutzen, Bautzen, Zinnwald and Hanau during the Napoleonic Wars.

MARINES TO 95TH (RIFLES) *by Thomas Fernyhough*—The military experiences of Robert Fernyhough during the Napoleonic Wars.

HUSSAR ROCCA *by Albert Jean Michel de Rocca*—A French cavalry officer's experiences of the Napoleonic Wars and his views on the Peninsular Campaigns against the Spanish, British And Guerilla Armies.

SERGEANT BOURGOGNE *by Adrien Bourgogne*—With Napoleon's Imperial Guard in the Russian Campaign and on the Retreat from Moscow 1812 - 13.

LEONAUR

ALSO FROM LEONAUR

WELLINGTON AND THE PYRENEES CAMPAIGN VOLUME I: FROM VI-TORIA TO THE BIDASSOA by *F. C. Beatson*—The final phase of the campaign in the Iberian Peninsula.

WELLINGTON AND THE INVASION OF FRANCE VOLUME II: THE BIDAS-SOA TO THE BATTLE OF THE NIVELLE by *F. C. Beatson*—The second of Beatson's series on the fall of Revolutionary France published by Leonaur, the reader is once again taken into the centre of Wellington's strategic and tactical genius.

WELLINGTON AND THE FALL OF FRANCE VOLUME III: THE GAVES AND THE BATTLE OF ORTHEZ by *F. C. Beatson*—This final chapter of F. C. Beatson's brilliant trilogy shows the 'captain of the age' at his most inspired and makes all three books essential additions to any Peninsular War library.

NAVAL BATTLES OF THE NAPOLEONIC WARS by *W. H. Fitchett*—Cape St.Vincent, the Nile, Cadiz, Copenhagen, Trafalgar & Others

SERGEANT GUILLEMARD: THE MAN WHO SHOT NELSON? by *Robert Guillemard*—A Soldier of the Infantry of the French Army of Napoleon on Campaign Throughout Europe

WITH THE GUARDS ACROSS THE PYRENEES by *Robert Batty*—The Experiences of a British Officer of Wellington's Army During the Battles for the Fall of Napoleonic France, 1813.

A STAFF OFFICER IN THE PENINSULA by *E. W. Buckham*—An Officer of the British Staff Corps Cavalry During the Peninsula Campaign of the Napoleonic Wars

THE LEIPZIG CAMPAIGN: 1813—NAPOLEON AND THE "BATTLE OF THE NATIONS" by *F. N. Maude*—Colonel Maude's analysis of Napoleon's campaign of 1813.

BUGEAUD: A PACK WITH A BATON by *Thomas Robert Bugeaud*—The Early Campaigns of a Soldier of Napoleon's Army Who Would Become a Marshal of France.

TWO LEONAUR ORIGINALS

SERGEANT NICOL by *Daniel Nicol*—The Experiences of a Gordon Highlander During the Napoleonic Wars in Egypt, the Peninsula and France.

WATERLOO RECOLLECTIONS by *Frederick Llewellyn*—Rare First Hand Accounts, Letters, Reports and Retellings from the Campaign of 1815.

LEONAUR

ALSO FROM LEONAUR
AVAILABLE IN SOFTCOVER OR HARDCOVER WITH DUST JACKET

WAR BEYOND THE DRAGON PAGODA by *J. J. Snodgrass*—A Personal Narrative of the First Anglo-Burmese War 1824 - 1826.

ALL FOR A SHILLING A DAY by *Donald F. Featherstone*—The story of H.M. 16th, the Queen's Lancers During the first Sikh War 1845-1846.

AT THEM WITH THE BAYONET by *Donald F. Featherstone*—The first Anglo-Sikh War 1845-1846.

A LEONAUR ORIGINAL

THE HERO OF ALIWAL by *James Humphries*—The days when young Harry Smith wore the green jacket of the 95th-Wellington's famous riflemen-campaigning in Spain against Napoleon's French with his beautiful young bride Juana have long gone. Now, Sir Harry Smith is in his fifties approaching the end of a long career. His position in the Cape colony ends with an appointment as Deputy Adjutant-General to the army in India. There he joins the staff of Sir Hugh Gough to experience an Indian battlefield in the Gwalior War of 1843 as the power of the Marathas is finally crushed. Smith has little time for his superior's 'bull at a gate' style of battlefield tactics, but independent command is denied him. Little does he realise that the greatest opportunity of his military life is close at hand.

THE GURKHA WAR by *H. T. Prinsep*—The Anglo-Nepalese Conflict in North East India 1814-1816.

SOUND ADVANCE! by *Joseph Anderson*—Experiences of an officer of HM 50th regiment in Australia, Burma & the Gwalior war.

THE CAMPAIGN OF THE INDUS by *Thomas Holdsworth*—Experiences of a British Officer of the 2nd (Queen's Royal) Regiment in the Campaign to Place Shah Shuja on the Throne of Afghanistan 1838 - 1840.

WITH THE MADRAS EUROPEAN REGIMENT IN BURMA by *John Butler*—The Experiences of an Officer of the Honourable East India Company's Army During the First Anglo-Burmese War 1824 - 1826.

BESIEGED IN LUCKNOW by *Martin Richard Gubbins*—The Experiences of the Defender of 'Gubbins Post' before & during the sige of the residency at Lucknow, Indian Mutiny, 1857.

THE STORY OF THE GUIDES by *G.J. Younghusband*—The Exploits of the famous Indian Army Regiment from the northwest frontier 1847 - 1900.

www.ingramcontent.com/pod-product-compliance
Lightning Source LLC
Chambersburg PA
CBHW030357100426
42812CB00028B/2750/J